THE GOLDEN HOUR

ALSO BY MATTHEW SPECKTOR

That Summertime Sound
American Dream Machine
Always Crashing in the Same Car

THE GOLDEN HOUR

A STORY OF FAMILY
AND POWER
IN HOLLYWOOD

MATTHEW SPECKTOR

An Imprint of *HarperCollins*Publishers

"Epigram," by Tomas Tranströmer is from *New Collected Poems*,
translated by Robin Fulton (Bloodaxe Books, 2007), and is reproduced
with permission of Bloodaxe Books.

The photo at the opening of Chapter 8 is courtesy of Stefan Kraszewski/
Alamy Stock Photo. All other photos are courtesy of the author.

HarperCollins books may be purchased for educational, business, or
sales promotional use. For information, please email the Special Markets
Department at SPsales@harpercollins.com.

Ecco® and HarperCollins® are trademarks of
HarperCollins Publishers.

FIRST EDITION

Library of Congress Cataloging-in-Publication Data has
been applied for.

ISBN 978-0-06-300833-5

25 26 27 28 29 LBC 5 4 3 2 1

for Allison Devereux

The 20th Century is on film. It's the filmed Century.

—DON DeLILLO, *The Names*

CONTENTS

THE GOLDEN HOUR

PROLOGUE

—THE MAN COMES OUT of the crowd and stands next to me.

"Congratulations," he says.

"For what?"

I am twelve years old. Around us, the hot Hollywood action of a party somewhere in the hills: men and women in Sunday denim, cigarettes and Soave Bolla, faces glowing yellow in the late-afternoon sun. My parents are somewhere, afloat on the room's tide of wine and dope, but I don't see them. It is 1979.

"For being born lucky."

"Oh?"

Perhaps I am already too used to this, to being tossed on those tides myself. The people here, they are mostly artists—writers, directors, actors, and actresses—and so the mood is riotous, a little unhinged. But not this man, who seems an avatar from another world.

"What makes you say that?" I ask. He is clumsy, oddly ill-at-ease, with a golly-gee demeanor that feels beamed in from another decade, which may be why he's stopped to talk to a child who's otherwise not attracting much notice here. "Why am I lucky?"

He is clean-cut, clean-shaven; in a roomful of beards and bushy Jewish curls he is milk-fed, Midwestern, with a dry brown pompadour and the pillowy features of an old-fashioned matinee idol. His white shirt is buttoned to the neck, and he wears pink slacks with one regular leg and the other cropped short, cut-off well above the knee.

"You're Freddy's boy, aren't you?"

"I am."

"You gonna be an agent like your dad?"

I study him a moment, this man who is, after all, just making party chatter with a young person who stands between him and a platter of warming camembert. The truth is, I don't know, but this question has lately come to occupy my thoughts. Art or money? I see my mother, whose creative ambitions have recently asserted themselves seemingly out of nowhere, waking up to write for an hour or two in the detached cabana behind our house before she has to head off to work. Likewise, my father, whose paychecks have increased and whose manners have taken on a kind of scaliness, a rough edge of aggression. He has recently changed companies, though not jobs, and in this I can detect him striving for something new, some bigger, grander place in the world.

"I dunno." I stare down at the man's bare leg, which is pale and hairless, and at the long, tailored sleeve of the other, the color of a strawberry malt. "I haven't decided. What do you think?"

The man studies me. The truth is, I will engage this question sooner than one might expect—two summers from now I will go to work in the mailroom of my father's office, an insurgent company called Creative Artists Agency, and I will begin my own ambivalent passage through the motion picture business—but at this moment I am captivated by this man's strangeness.

"I doubt it," he says. "Personally, I think you're an artist."

"You do?"

In a minute, my father will emerge from the crowd and greet the man, with whom he will talk a little shop, but right now I am pinned within his modest yet oddly piercing gaze.

"I do," he says. "But I suppose that's just my guess."

Mine, too. But what do I know, even of my own nature, at this age?

"Hiya, David."

"Hello, Freddy. Good-looking boy you have here."

"Thanks. You know my wife, Katherine?"

Later, as we leave, my father will tell me this man's name ("David Lynch. He directed an interesting little movie called *Eraserhead*."), but as I stand there he's just a hypnotic stranger. The future—not just my family's but that of the entire film industry, the relationship between talent agents, businesspeople, and the makers of the films themselves—rests on a knife's edge, although of course nobody here knows it. The movies will boom, and then they will bust, and in the course of a few short decades will drift away from their place at the center of American cultural life, thus ceasing to exist as I have already come to know them. But not yet.

"Come on," my mother claps her hand on my shoulder. "Let's find your sister."

"You don't know where she is?"

My sister and I, we are just bystanders, the industry's possible future casualties. But for us, too, it is early. This party remains in full swing. My mother and I walk out of the house and into the garden—we are up in the canyons above Malibu beach—to find her.

The man's prediction haunts me. I am going to need to occupy the minds of other people, to use an artist's privileges, to tell the story I'm about to tell. There's no other way to do it. And as to whether I've been lucky, I'll let you decide.

"Johanna? Johanna?!"

My mother's voice echoes, carrying just slightly over the party chatter, the smell of sinsemilla, the sound of Steely Dan's *Aja* as we tromp down a dirt path behind the house. She hands me her wineglass, so I can take a robust swallow. Sunlight pierces the canopy of trees overhead, its beams chalky and golden, and in this light, the light of both memory and intermittent invention, I might begin . . .

I

THE CITY

1. A GREEN DREAM

—

1956–1962

MY FATHER RIDES LOW in his seat, sinking into its velveteen embrace. Next to him, in the darkness of the Fine Arts Theater in Beverly Hills, a woman: she is twenty-three, as he is, her breathing shallow as she tilts her head upward to look at the screen.

"Well, Reverend, it looks like you've got yourself surrounded . . ."

John Wayne towers above them. My father is nothing like Wayne—skinny, Jewish, and coastal where Wayne is gentile, Midwestern, and broad—but he is rapt all the same. Wayne is not one of his favorite actors—those would be Kirk Douglas, Bill Holden, and Marlon Brando—but Wayne speaks to him the way he speaks to, and for, so many people in these days when America still believes in its own innocence.

"You think they mean to charge us, Uncle Ethan?"

So many, but hardly all. My father looks on, a little skeptically. He may be as pale as a trout in the room's ghostly light, but he isn't deaf to the movie's troubled politics, its blunt and unmistakable racism.

"That's all right, Captain. I don't need any formal invitation to kill a Comanch."

Unmistakable, and yet the movie is also kicking against it. And my father is thinking of other things: the soft throat of the girl sitting next to him, as naked and sweet as a lily; the placement of her arm on the seat between them. They are right in the middle of that period of suppressed sexual fervor, the dryness of the Eisenhower years, that will break wide open in another decade or so. For now, a young man's erotic drives are still furtive, a world of discreetly purchased condoms and magazines sold in plain brown wrappers.

"What d'you think?"

My father, bless him, would genuinely like to know. He is more thoughtful than many, as he leans over to whisper in her ear. If the movies are where America's erotic energy tends to collect, he is plenty able to sublimate it. Which is to say he possesses the roots of a genuine sensibility, even if he is not yet sure what to do with it.

"Not bad," the girl whispers. "John Wayne's not really my thing. Did you see *Lola Montès*?"

Alas, no. But he likes women whose intellect might outpace his, who are, as this one seems, more cultured, better educated. He settles back into his seat and turns his attention once more to *The Searchers*. His is a gentle face, heavy-eyed and soulful, with an aquiline nose and warm brown eyes that make up for a weak chin. People trust him, as perhaps they should. He has, within the cauldron of his still developing character, an advanced sense of decency. Watching the movie, he identifies more with Jeffrey

Hunter's Martin Pawley—delicate-tempered, impetuous, protective of his missing sister—than he does with Wayne's surly Ethan Edwards. My grandfather, Ruby, would like to see him become a lawyer or an accountant, those steady professions so often idealized in these days by immigrants—rough men, like Ruby, who are without education—but he happens to lack the one thing that would allow him to convert his potential into ordinary American prosperity: patience. The additional years of college it would require for him to become one of those things are beyond him. He has in his possession a diploma from UCLA—whether he has fully earned it or if he remains, indeed, a few credits short is a fact he will remain cagey about for the rest of his life—but what he will do with it remains an open question. For years to come he will remain haunted by the thought of what might have been. When he sees Gregory Peck play Atticus Finch in the film adaptation of *To Kill a Mockingbird*, he will feel a pang of regret. Should he have gone to law school? He will not imagine—he certainly cannot now—that he will one day know Mr. Peck: that the star of *Spellbound* and *Roman Holiday* will phone his home and his office regularly, that they will share meals, confidences, jokes, and cigars. But today, he is simply impatient. Today he is eager for his life to begin.

★ ★ ★

"SO, WHAT NOW?"

Outside, they stand upstream of the theater's blazing marquee on Wilshire Boulevard, next to a pair of skinny, tilting palms.

"Gonna have to do better than to take me to the movies if you'd like to see me again," the woman says. "I'm no cheap date."

"Oh? What'd you have in mind?"

"Dinner."

"Sure thing." He smiles. "Where d'you wanna go?"

Ah. The rub. My father has everything: a college degree; charisma; an advanced, if not yet expensive, sense of style. His soft white collar hangs open just so beneath the tailored lapels of his navy jacket, his hair, a wavy black quiff, is smartly cut. He has everything, as he digs into his jacket pocket for a cigarette, everything except—

"I went with a guy to Perino's the other night," she says. "We could go there."

"Could we?" Everything except—y'know. Perino's is a place for high rollers. They could go if he sold his beat-up car. "You sure you wanna go all the way across town?"

His hair shimmers in the yellow light of the marquee, the dotted electrical glow of Los Angeles. He flicks his lighter a few times and then stabs it back into his pocket, rocking on the balls of his feet.

"Perino's is a little out of my league," he says, deciding to play this one straight. "I'll take you to Nate'n Al's if you want."

"Nate'n Al's?" She laughs. "What am I, your mother? I think I'll go out with the boy who took me to Perino's. He said he can get a table at Chasen's."

"Oh yeah?" Another strength, one that will serve him better than he knows: he rebounds quickly from rejection. "What does he do, your fancy friend? Is he a bank teller, or does he—"

"He's an agent."

"An agent." He tugs on his cigarette, his gaze blank. "Of what?" Insurance? Travel? For a moment he has no idea what she means. "Real estate?" Houses would do it. "Does he work for the CIA?"

She laughs. Not all is lost! She likes him, and he has his wits, his charm to go with a boyish vulnerability, the latter being one of his best qualities, along with a certain tenacity.

"He's a talent agent."

"What's that?"

"You know. Actors, writers. Like that movie we just saw, somebody had to put Natalie Wood into it. It didn't just happen by itself."

"Right." He deadpans. "Kind of like a pimp."

"No!" Her eyes widen. She exaggerates her indignation, knowing he is also kidding. "He works for MCA."

MCA. This name rings a distant chime—he's heard it somewhere, or maybe it just sounds as if he has, like NBC or RCA or IBM, one of those initialisms that denote a sturdy corporate concern—but he doesn't quite know what this is.

"He makes a good living," she says. "Drives a nice car."

"I'm sure," my father says. "If he's taking you to Perino's!"

Decision time, for both of them. For the girl, who is beautiful, and looks a bit like Natalie Wood herself, and for my father, also, in ways that have nothing to do with her. He's pinned inside that stark crucible where he doesn't have a clue what he hopes to become. Twelve years of schooling plus four of college interrupted by a year and a half in the army—he was a reservist, stationed at Fort Ord—all of this has brought him all the way around back here, to a street just a few blocks away from the home in which he grew up, where his parents and younger twin sisters still live, and from which he remains desperate to get away.

"C'mon," he says. Life isn't supposed to go round and round in circles. You're supposed to go somewhere and become somebody, but where, and who? "I'll buy you a drink."

"A drink?" She squints like someone inspecting a dubious piece of produce at the supermarket. "That's it?"

No Perino's tonight. And so, no luck. When I ask my father years later who this woman was, he won't even remember her name. He turns his palms up, balancing them like the pans of a scale. *Comme-ci, comme-ça.* Easy come, easy go. Around them, there is the warm darkness, the faint jasmine-and-eucalyptus sweetness of a spring night on the coast. Down the Wilshire corridor, pale, broadly spaced Streamline and Art Deco high-rises are like obelisks lit from below. Where other cities sparkle from their heights, this one seems to breathe its pockets of light from the ground. From where he stands he can read red blurts of neon signage—SILVERWOODS, MULLEN BLUETT—as the boulevard snakes off toward downtown. He may dream of escape, but he is never leaving Los Angeles. Who in their right mind would? Long-finned sedans rush past, toothpaste-blue and butter-yellow, their radios blaring Nelson Riddle and Patti Page from their blood-dark interiors, their engines' warm rumble fading to a soft, tidal hiss. He is still locked inside the movie, its immaculate final shot that turns Edwards out into the desolate light of the frontier, the door of the homestead closing upon him as he walks away across the burning plain, alone again and forever. Who's in and who's out, my father wonders, as he is trying to find his way—too—through the doorway onto the wide-open space of his fortune.

"C'mon," he says. "Come on, I'll drive you home."

★ ★ ★

WHO'S IN, WHO'S out?

The movies—and the movie business—will ask this question over and over across the years, but just then Fred Specktor is out. He doesn't know anybody in the film industry. His own father is what they call a "jobber," a man who buys small businesses that have drifted into default and turns them around with the sweat of his brow. A dry-goods store in Arizona; a little grocery shop in Las Vegas: my grandfather has hopped from one post to another over the three and a half decades he's been in America. Not a prosperous man, but solidly middle class, Reuben Specktor lives on the southern edge of Beverly Hills just north of Olympic Boulevard, where the grandeur of the movie stars' homes has long since given way to dingbats and duplexes that are split into smaller units, rental properties whose bright green lawns and orderly facades belie their chintzy construction. Growing up, the family had briefly had a neighbor who was a camera operator at one of the studios. That is as close as my father has ever come to show business in any capacity other than as an audience member, but then—he remembers. He does know someone. A friend of his from UCLA—not really a friend, a fraternity brother, someone he at least knows well enough to call—has gone to work in the business, and for MCA no less. Small world. Or rather, large company. The Music Corporation of America has offices in New York, Chicago, Los Angeles, and elsewhere. If my father had ever stopped to read an exposé that had appeared in the *Saturday Evening Post* ten years earlier, he would have known that the company's unofficial nickname was and remains "the Octopus," because they have their long and sinuous arms dipped in every aspect of entertainment: music, of course, both recorded and performed; nightclubs from coast to coast; Broadway; cabaret shows; Vegas acts ranging from magicians to dancers to comedians. And the movies, naturally. MCA is very much into the movies. Everywhere there is a stage, a performer, an audience, and a camera, there stands MCA, ready to take its cut. My father still doesn't know how it works exactly, but he likes the respectable ring of those three letters, which make it seem (ironic, considering the air of bloodsucking sleaze that has hung around the profession of "talent agent" since its inception) the sort of job he could parade before his father, with whom he doesn't especially get along, and be proud. "Music Corporation of America." Like "International Business Machines," the name feels inarguable, an engine of prosperity that will last a thousand years. So he calls his friend, manages to get his foot in the door in the form of an interview with a man named Earl Zook.

"So, Mr. Specktor? What makes you want to be a talent agent?"

Earl Zook's office, now that my father has been summoned inside the building at 360 N. Crescent Drive—from the street, it is neatly classical, almost municipal-looking with its Greek Revival colonnade—seems more like a private room inside a Victorian men's club: leather chairs, hunting prints, walls paneled with cherry wainscoting. A pair of eighteenth-century breakfronts filled with leather-bound books, the kind with gilt spines and uncut pages, looms behind him. But my father doesn't have an answer to this question, and those books aren't going to tell him.

"It's an advocate's job, isn't it?" His eyes flick toward those breakfronts once again, their shelves as densely crowded as a law library's. "Your clients trust you. They look to you for advice. You fight for them. It's—admirable."

"Admirable." Earl Zook's nostrils flare with amusement. A face like a Neanderthal's: simian, heavy-browed, that Kissinger-esque ugliness of a certain kind of mid-century American male. He wears what my father recognizes immediately as a kind of uniform, the same as every other man in the building: white shirt; black suit; dark, monochrome tie. The crisp shell of an FBI man, the blandness of a forensic accountant. "Were you really a Boy Scout or are you just completely full of shit."

My father stares. There is just enough hardness in him, having been a Marine. He can stand up to inspection just fine. He's full of shit, but he's not only full of shit. "An agent's clients are artists, no? And artists need help?"

Zook studies him. He sees no special potential in my father— just another jug-eared Jewish boy from Beverly Hills, of which he's seen plenty—but he correctly perceives a resilience, and a stubborn streak.

"All right." He kneads the pouches under his eyes with his fingertips. He's already asked all the rudimentary questions: education, personal background, what-do-your-parents-do? But like any job, the proof will be in the doing. "Be here at eight a.m. on Monday."

★ ★ ★

MY FATHER IS to live the rest of his life in a kind of eternal present tense. He is not today, nor will he ever be, an introspective person. Which is not to say he lacks depth. Only that his mind

rides the crest of its present moment like a surfer's, neither looking too far ahead nor sulking upon its history. It's a quality that
will serve him well, but here in the summer of 1956, when he goes
to work for MCA, he remains fundamentally green. Do you need
talent to enter the motion picture business? Do you need to be
able to dance or sing or ride horses? No. Do you need to be over-
whelmingly good-looking? Not really. My father is a nice-looking
man, but he is handsome in a way that doesn't spur any double
takes on the street. Do you need to be ruthless? Depends on who
you ask. My father is not, but right now it doesn't matter because
he starts, like everyone else, at the bottom, pushing a mail cart
around the halls of 360 N. Crescent Drive, a building he learns
was designed twenty years ago by the great Los Angeles architect
Paul Revere Williams.

"Hey, kid. Take this over to Herman Citron's office, willya?"

Designed to what purpose, for what symbolic end besides to
serve as this talent agency's home, he does not yet know, but he is
beginning to understand already that he has entered a business of
presentation, and that the suave, civilized air of this place, which
is only a veneer—these offices are filled with men who shout on
the telephone, then race down the hall to puke blood in one of
the washroom toilets—exists to convey a message. But what message? As he trundles along with his cart, as he begins to learn more
about this labyrinth, and about the man, a kind of Minotaur, really,
who stands at the center of it, he only knows that the profession
of "talent agent" remains, to some small extent, disreputable, and
that all this cultivated, Anglophilic style exists to counteract the
public imagination. You think a talent agent is supposed to be
some hook-nosed hustler, a cigar-chewing Shylock in an off-the-rack
suit? You've come to the wrong place, Charlie. These guys are
Ivy Leaguers, or at least—my father's not the only guy here who's
barely set foot outside the city limits—they look like Ivy Leaguers,
which is more the point. How you dress, how you talk, how you

manage information, bluffing like a poker player at one moment but then turning cagey and coy the next: these things are at the heart of what it takes to become an agent. Just now, my father is only a schlepper. This means he drives, hauling packages over the hill to Universal's decrepit blot of land in Studio City, and to Paramount's pale yellow citadel on Melrose Avenue. He gets to know the lay of the land—Twentieth Century-Fox, too, mere blocks from where he grew up, with its ranchland greenery and golf course— and to understand something about the city in which he has lived most of his life, how it is organized by these mild-looking enclaves that hide their interiors but govern the public's dream life, which is to say its real life, absolutely.

He spends all day in his car, running envelopes from one place to another, pocket-sized ones that contain checks, fatter ones stuffed with screenplays or deal memos, driving up the serpentine corridor of Laurel Canyon or over the blazing hot Cahuenga Pass to Barham Boulevard (Warner Brothers, with its Spanish-looking bungalows and haciendas, looking almost resort-like in the sun), winding over to private homes up Benedict or Coldwater, places he knows belong to movie stars—the names on the envelopes tell him this, the opulent air of stillness and privacy that hangs around these massive but discreetly hidden houses as he rings the buzzer of an exterior gate and waits for a maid or secretary to appear— although he never actually sees one. He lives in his car, eats in his car—too many greasy burgers; too many turkey sandwiches from Nate'n Al's, which he scarfs down hunched over the wheel so as not to dribble Russian dressing on his trousers—and when he returns to the office it is merely to be handed another task. Does he have a name? Does he even need one? Other than his fellow functionaries, the baker's dozen office boys who work in the mailroom with him and a handful of secretaries (women, they are all women, just as the agents are all men) with whom he flirts unsuccessfully, no one seems to know it. Now and for the next few years, my father will remain invisible. He learns to dress like all the other men in the building—no colors or stripes on his shirt or his tie, just a black suit and a close shave—and he knows now this is part of a corporate culture so engrained that people at other places make fun of it, that the talent agents who work for MCA are known around Hollywood as "blackbirds." Later he will learn that Jack Warner, the legendary head of Warner Brothers studio, is the person who coined this term. Warner views these agents as pests, pecking at his contracted stars like crumbs of stale bread. For my father, the term is neutral. Blackbirds travel in pairs, they travel in small groups like *federales*, and they project a slick verbal confidence, a bluff chatter—note the hip ease with which they refer to "Rock," or to "Jimmy" or to "Marilyn," people they've perhaps never met but claim by association—which my father absorbs. He understands that this is a real place, and these are real people. No use getting sweaty over a movie star. In the summer of 1957, he sees a movie that explains something of the mood and the spiritual temperature of the world in which he now finds himself. *The Sweet Smell of Success* stars Tony Curtis and Burt Lancaster. In it, Curtis plays Sidney Falco, a sleazy press agent under the thumb of Lancaster's J. J. Hunsecker, an even sleazier gossip columnist. But it isn't the churning world of Manhattan media he recognizes. All that is a grind of a slightly different order. It is the fear, the relentless ethical terror that runs through the movie's every frame, the sign of Hunsecker's brutal reign. Where *The Searchers* was expansive, shot in Technicolor against the Western vistas of Monument Valley, *The Sweet Smell of Success* is black-and-white, claustrophobic and narrow, with its brassy Elmer Bernstein and Chico Hamilton score, its montage images of Times Square neon over prowling taxicabs and newspaper vans capturing the hectic energy of New York City. It is like a panic attack twisted into a poem, a movie that makes him want to run home and take not just one shower but three. Its sheer, skin-crawling discomfort, an atmosphere of dread worse than

any Universal Pictures creature feature, grows from our awareness that Hunsecker is going to wreak a kind of violence—the kind
from which there is no returning, a spiritual violence—upon every person he touches. This fear, my father recognizes because it
has infiltrated his days, because this movie, which he watches on
a Sunday afternoon, one of those few stolen hours that still belong
to him and not to his employer, depicts it better than anything:
a feeling that pulses through the corridors of the Music Corporation of America. Standing out on the sidewalk afterward he is
lightheaded, almost nauseous, because he knows tomorrow morning he will confront it again, the terror he has managed to conceal
from himself even though he knows. He has seen the senior blackbirds sprinting down the halls, staggering out of the men's room
like drunks, their faces flushed and their hands shaking as if they
have just gazed upon the face of the devil himself, tottering back
to their offices where they guzzle those bottles of antacid whose
medicine-blue outlines, the placid color of swimming pools, are
the only splashes of brightness to be seen in the room. The antiques, the eighteenth-century literature, the fox prints and line
drawings and Louis XIV breakfronts that scream of gentlemanly
conduct: these things are a fucking joke. This place is as bloody as
an abattoir.

My father's time at MCA will be brief. His education there is
like a coat of primer, a flat layer of paint on a personality that is
already a little opaque. But he knows one thing: the boss dog in
this place is not Tony Curtis (although he has seen Curtis, indeed,
walking through the halls, seemingly at home in a way that suggests
the place belongs to him and not vice versa) or Burt Lancaster or
J.J. Hunsecker, but rather the man who is its epicenter, the gen-
erator of all this real-world dread, one Lew R. Wasserman. As
my father learns the names of all the senior agents—Arthur Park,
Herman Citron, Jennings Lang—it is Wasserman's alone that creates alarm, that carries, even in the most passive context, a latent

voltage. *Run this down to Mr. Wasserman's office.* Wasserman is not the company's founder—that would be Dr. Jules Stein, the ophthalmologist from Chicago who learned at a young age that he could make more money booking jazz bands into nightclubs than he could practicing medicine, and who is now the chairman of MCA's board—but he is its core. He is the person everyone here strives to please, and certainly never to displease—God, no—because if you run afoul of Lew Wasserman . . .

What? What happens then? Lew Wasserman does not breathe fire. He cannot incinerate you on the spot, or smite you with lightning. He is tall, and lean as a snake, and his suit is just as Quaker-plain as everyone else's. His white shirt is so crisp it seems as if you could bounce a quarter off him the way you would off a military cot; his gold watch is luxurious but discreet, hidden under a cuff that is cut a quarter-inch wider to accommodate it; his emerald-green Bentley gleams outside in the building's driveway, crouched like a lion in the afternoon sun. But his presence is crisp. It is no-nonsense. He does not prowl the halls like an angry ship's captain, menacing his employees. If anything, he is silent and swift like a hospital orderly. He prefers not to attract attention, and if he is known, now, beyond the precincts of Hollywood—that five-part profile of MCA that ran in the *Saturday Evening Post* was largely a tribute to Wasserman's mysterious acumen—this is largely to spite the one piece of advice he's been known to offer gratis to his troops. "Stay out of the spotlight, it fades your suit." For Wasserman, a man of very few words indeed, believes agents should act like God or gravity: their workings must remain invisible, unnoticed even by those who are dominated by their laws. He carries no briefcase, nor so much as a fountain pen. There are no photographs or personal decorations in his office. His desk holds a telephone and a leather blotter. For a business as predicated upon paper as this one, this is unusual. But Wasserman keeps it all in his head. Once, and once only, as my father pushes his trolley down the hall, he will meet the man's gaze and realize—he will never understand how—that Wasserman knows who he is, that Fred Specktor's name and background down to his exact date of hire is all in there. There is no gesture of recognition, no exchange of words—my father remains among the smallest cogs of a company that has hundreds—but there is a cool sense of computation, an understanding that he is a known data point as Wasserman glances him over—the eyes are piercing, lively, and shrewd behind an oversized set of horn-rims—then moves on. My father swivels to watch him go, the man's lanky frame—as stark as a line drawing—moving down the hall, zagging almost like lightning touching down in a field. This is not the wide-hipped saunter of a John Wayne: even his walk is sleek and modern, his stride loping but swift, like the motion of a vehicle that keeps its power in reserve.

Wasserman. The name alone can raise the hairs on the back of his neck, commands a respect that not even the movie stars— Curtis is so small when you see him in person, like a dollhouse model of himself; Marilyn Monroe is mousy, barely recognizable behind a scarf and big sunglasses—who pass through these halls can manage. This is the wizard behind the curtain, the dragon who waits inside the cave. And if my father doesn't yet understand just what it is that makes this unprepossessing man so terrifying, he is going to learn. Sixty years later, when I ask him what his first employer was like, I watch his eyes as it all comes flooding back.

"Scary." It's like that fear has sprung to life right in front of him. "Lew Wasserman was fucking scary."

★ ★ ★

IS HE SCARY to everyone, this man? Is he scary as he stands at the bathroom mirror, scrutinizing his face—mask-like, impassive—as he shaves?

"Lew?" His wife's voice carries up to him from downstairs. "Hey, Lew?"

"What?" His voice is flat, a little nasal as he calls back. "I'm upstairs getting dressed."

Picture a set of matryoshka dolls. Picture my father nestled inside this man just as I am nestled somewhere inside my dad, inside a future that will not exist without the interventions of Lew R. Wasserman. I'm going to describe his life—which creates the conditions for my own—from the inside out, just for a moment, as he stands in front of his bathroom mirror in the house on Sierra Drive with a little slash of sunlight falling on the marble basin in front of him, tugging a safety razor across his cheek.

"Nancy would like to know if we can meet them tonight at eight instead of seven-thirty?"

Edie's voice floats up from the vestibule. He dabs a spot on his chin where he has nicked himself—see? He bleeds just like anybody else—and turns away, satisfied.

"That's fine," he murmurs. "OK."

This man, this austere Midwesterner who is, like all of us, largely invisible to himself, his inner motives unknown. I cannot tell you why he does the things he does, only that his influence is like the weather: within the climate of his personality, which is at once transparent and opaque, an entire generation will grow.

"Take the Bentley." He knots his Sulka tie, then strides out and down the stairs to the vestibule where Edie is waiting. "I'll have somebody drop me off tonight for dinner."

I won't dwell on the particulars of his marriage. I'll only note that he married, as powerful men often tend to, a person who is his equal, and whose symbolic value might offer some small key to his personality. He still sees in her what he saw long ago, when she was the extroverted rich girl from Cleveland Heights—short, pretty, her wavy hair dark like a doll's—and he was the young man with nothing to his name but ambition.

"I'll see you tonight," he says, leaning forward to kiss her cheek. "Bye bye."

As he sails out the door, some part of him remains who he'd been: the young boy from Woodland Avenue who'd worked as a theater usher after school, marching proudly up Short Vincent in his red uniform, its brass buttons gleaming like that of an organ grinder's monkey. He was twenty-two when he met Edie—like those buttons, she was a glittering prize, a lawyer's daughter— already the manager of a swanky nightclub called the Mayfair Casino. Now he is forty-four, and if he has already risen to become the most powerful person in the film colony, worth tens of millions of dollars at a time when this represents an unthinkable fortune, he has not yet reached his peak. Jules Stein had hired him as an office boy out of Chicago and he's done nothing but earn ever since. When Stein decided to make his push into Hollywood in 1939, Wasserman was the emissary he sent, and if the old doctor had seen in him enormous promise, he'd still had no idea how far his little office boy would go.

Sunlight mantles his shoulders, the flawless blue serge of his suit, as he walks down the green meridian of Beverly Gardens Park, passing beneath its narrow canopy of ficuses and figs. For a moment his mind is still: the furious gnawing on deal points that consumes him day and night—he is always looking out for his clients, even if the real beneficiary is himself—hasn't begun. His vices are candy, M&M's, and poker, not drugs or liquor or women. Of course, there are mistresses, as he's no saint, but he's no Quasimodo of the casting couch either. He is a disciplined man (does it bother him that Edie cheats, that her ongoing affair with the filmmaker Nicholas Ray is an open secret? Yes, but—not really. It keeps her occupied, and it keeps him free), but he is, famously, a cold one. And like most cold people, that coldness grows around a hot seed of vulnerability. His older brother, Max, an epileptic, was shipped off to a state asylum because their poverty-stricken parents couldn't afford his care. Himself a stutterer, with a speech impediment, Wasserman had been just another persecuted kid, drawn to numbers because they didn't require eloquence, and he liked things you could control. But as he walks now through the pockets of shadow that fall beneath the trees, ignored, unseen by the drivers who roar along Santa Monica Boulevard twenty feet away, he is exactly what he has always wanted to be: not just the star but the stage itself, invisible to the inattentive eye. Just another blackbird, lost among the kaleidoscopic patterns that make up the fugitive heart of Los Angeles.

★ ★ ★

"JIMMY, JIMMY, LISTEN to me—"

All day long, Wasserman deals with people he doesn't understand but admires, even loves in his own way. People think he's all business, and he is, but that business is not manufacturing, after all. Even as a small boy he'd been drawn to entertainment, the pop and glamor of the movies.

"—listen to me, why don't you do the western first? You can still do the other one, I'll talk to Harry and get him to push it back. But you do the western and then—exactly, yes." But it is not pop and glamor for him now, as he speaks on the phone. "Then you can do the next picture with Hitch."

Is he really so powerful if he spends his days pleading with these people—children, they are like: they spend all day playing make believe—to act in their own best interest? The world pretends he's some mastermind, but it's like herding cats. These actors are always at war with themselves.

"Lew?" A junior agent looms in the doorway of Wasserman's office after he hangs up. He won't come closer unless his employer commands. "We have a problem with that thing at Universal."

"What kind of problem?"

Wasserman's jaw tenses, but his voice remains even. He looks to the door with a serpentine coolness, gazing at the poor subordinate who stands with his hands behind his back like a prisoner awaiting execution.

"They don't want to meet Heston's fee." The junior agent quivers. "They're not comfortable with the budget where it sits. They think Welles is gonna run over."

They are still at that place, that delicate fulcrum of the century in which language remains publicly polite, even though the movie business remains a place where men and women have always sworn like sailors. When Marilyn Monroe signed her most recent, and lavish, contract with Twentieth Century-Fox, one that paid her a hundred thousand dollars per picture coupled with all sorts of outlandish perks, a deal Wasserman, of course, had negotiated, she'd told the press that the deal meant she'd "never have to suck another cock again." But there is still a fiction, a pretense of gentlemanly conduct that prevails.

"Fix it." Inside the movies, also, there is no swearing; the cigarette girl who is handed around like a party favor in *The Sweet Smell of Success* is understood to be a fallen woman. But all this decorum is still a dam waiting to burst. Today, Wasserman's famous temper—you don't kick a dog when they know it's coming—remains in check. "Tell them the fee is the fee. If you need me to call Milt Rackmil, I will."

The agent darts down the hall, hustling off to do his master's will. But all this polite fiction, the eighteenth-century antiques—the agent brushes by my father with his mail trolley, nearly knocking him over—the fox hunting prints, the uncut volumes of Thackeray, whom no man in this office, Wasserman very much included, has ever read, or could even identify: all of this is not Wasserman's dream but Dr. Stein's, the dream of a man born to European immigrant stock in South Bend, Indiana, just before the turn of the century. Stein is a crucial seventeen years older than Wasserman. In his heart, Stein had aspired to an old-world gentility, which is why he'd bothered to earn a medical degree before deciding that his little side hustle might prove the shrewder long-term play. But Wasserman's dream is different: it isn't a genteel aristocracy he admires, or those East Coast swells who'd knocked Dr. Stein and his wife around a little, until they decided to seek their respectability out here, but something more modern and metropolitan. Wasserman's parents are immigrants just like Stein's—refugees from Odessa, Orthodox Jews—but he dreams not of regattas and fox hunting parties, but of subtler operations of power.

"What else?" He gazes down at his calfskin blotter a moment, lost in thought. "What else do we need here?" But then his voice rises, his will projecting itself outward again as he shouts for his secretary. "Hey, Caroline? Caroline, who called?"

★ ★ ★

WHAT MIGHT THOSE subtler operations be? When Wasserman arrives that night at Chasen's, brushing past the valet and the maître d', he cuts the same figure he always does: a sallow man in a room full of radiant stars. This is the motion picture colony, and if this man—he slashes across the room like a pilot fish through an aquarium—is its ruler, you wouldn't know it from the way he heads silently for a table in the back, passing Frank Sinatra and then Cary Grant, who lifts a hand in greeting. If there are people who come here to bask in the world's attention, that's what the industry is all about, right? It's just pageantry, nothing important, and there are people even in Los Angeles who recognize all this for the trifle that it is. The room is crowded. The carmine-red booths are arranged back-to-back, a chaotic pattern like bumper cars in collision. Within each one, a couple or a foursome hunch forward in their own sphere of privacy. Elbows rest on checkerboard cloths; martinis glow dully, the opaque white of jellyfish in the intimate puddles of lamplight that fall across each table. This is just another funhouse, and those outside it who recognize

Wasserman's name might think of him as the prince of a Lichtenstein or a Monaco, a man whose influence is regional and unimportant.

"You made it." An actor looks up as Lew slides into the booth, one whose oatmeal plainness has recently made him a television star. His eyes are as dull and dark as raisins. "I was just saying to Edie here that it's easier to get hung up coming from half a mile away than it is from the Santa Monica Mountains."

"That's true," Wasserman says, looking back at the man with a taut, almost fatherly smile. "Star" is perhaps a misnomer; the actor is the host of a popular weekly show is all, thanks to the agent's interventions. Prior to that he'd been a failure on the big screen, a contract player at Warner Brothers. "Lucky traffic was light."

"Have a drink," the actor says. "I'm having an orange blossom special."

"I think I will," Wasserman says, opting for a rare indulgence. "Vodka rocks."

The man's wife is also in pictures, but let's focus for a moment on the actor. He is dark-haired and Germanic-looking, handsome but . . . vague, in a way that had made him castable but never memorable on the big screen. He is perfect for TV—perhaps he didn't have the talent to carry a motion picture either—but he had fought against the transition until Wasserman had fixed him up with so much money, he'd gone from fretting over alimony owed from his previous marriage to buying several acres of ranchland overnight. He's successful enough—he's president of the Screen Actors Guild as well as the host of this program, which is called *General Electric Theater*—but in a roomful of people of which more than half might be greater contributors to MCA's bottom line, he's small potatoes. So why are Lew and Edie Wasserman (the man's wife is no marquee player either, just the C-list star of pictures like *Donovan's Brain* and *Hellcats of the Navy*) having dinner with these two? Why not with Elizabeth Taylor over there?

"Sir? Madam?" The waiter arrives, bearing Wasserman's drink. "Have you ladies and gentlemen decided?"

Why indeed? Lew Wasserman isn't even this man's agent—technically, that would be Taft Schreiber, Wasserman's longtime rival at the company—but he's looked out for him again and again, winning him a deferment of service during the Second World War, driving his price up to a million dollars for a seven-year contract at Warner Brothers. Maybe it was just ordinary business, but I like to think he knew a shapable piece of clay when he saw it.

"—sand dabs. Excellent choice, madam." The waiter's eyes focus, training themselves upon the actor. "And what about you, sir? What will it be for you this evening, Mr. Reagan?"

★ ★ ★

THE FUTURE IS unwritten. Ten years hence, my father will sit in this room with his client, a Canadian actor named Arthur Hill, and smoke a celebratory cigar on the night of my birth at Cedars of Lebanon hospital across town. But right now all that matters is that Fred Specktor has entered a world of limitless potential, and that Hollywood—you can see its elemental tensions here in this collision between artist and representative, businessman and labor leader (a strange role for Ronald Reagan, of all people, to embrace, but like I say, the man is soft clay), between raw commerce and something that might be a little too blunt and utilitarian to call "art"—is much bigger than it seems.

"I'll have the chicken tetrazzini, Carlos, thanks."

"Mr. Wasserman?"

It doesn't matter what they eat, or what they say. What matters is the radical vacancy that shimmers between them, between these two figures without a compass besides their own respective self-interests, who face each other like convex mirrors. Reagan has recently helped the agent with MCA's push into television production, granting the company a waiver—for there is an obvious conflict that has hitherto prevented agents, who are sellers, from also acting as producers, or buyers—just as Wasserman had helped to install Reagan as SAG president a few years ago, confident that having a friend in this position would soon enough prove useful.

"So?" Quid pro quo. The art of the deal. These are the things that ensure that, instead of a forgotten man, consigned to the junkyard of Hollywood history, the actor is a household name, with all the future that implies. "Here's looking at you."

Wasserman smiles. He tips his glass and rattles the ice like dice in a tumbler. They are friends, these people, but neither of them seems to have much of a gift for intimacy. If "the best lack all conviction," as Yeats put it, well, these two aren't exactly filled with passionate intensity either. Wasserman is not a person of idiosyncratic taste, someone who can tell you from his kishkes just exactly what he thinks is good. He will not say that John Ford is a genius but he prefers Hitchcock (although he does prefer Hitchcock, simply because Hitch is his client), or that he's just nuts about Sam Fuller or John Huston. His likes are his clients' likes. He is nothing but a chameleon. And Reagan? The man may be a union leader and a loud anti-communist, but ten years ago he was both a Democrat and a scab. Wasserman had once needed to warn him against attending an anti-nuclear rally lest Jack Warner, Reagan's far-right employer, think he was a pinko. Some union man he is, and some anti-communist, this straw-stuffed figure whose positions are as fickle as the day is long.

What matters is the emptiness. What matters is the deal. What matters is this vagueness of character, something a little more slippery than pragmatism, that shapes the world around my father. Only one of the two men will go on to embed himself in global history, but Wasserman is the stronger, and by far. Like any good illusionist, and like anyone who wields real power, he knows that the strongest hand is the invisible hand, and this means creating a world that seems to fulfill your desires automatically, one that is no volition and all dream. He will amass more power than he has today, and how, but now he is Hollywood's premier broker of talent, its most gifted magician, a man who ensures that the rest of us, as F. Scott Fitzgerald put it, "cannot see the ventriloquist for the doll."

★ ★ ★

WHAT THE FUCK is the matter with you?!

When my father goes home at night, it is Wasserman's voice he hears, a voice that has by now saturated him to the bone. It is 1959, and my father has ascended, if "ascended" is the right word, to the position of the great man's factotum. He is Lew Wasserman's assistant, his driver, his shadow, his gofer: his own personal secondary self. My father fetches the big boss's lunch. He fetches coffee. He delivers gifts—on Wasserman's daughter's sixteenth birthday, he pulls a gleaming new cream-pink Ford Thunderbird convertible into the driveway at dawn—and he audits, sometimes, Wasserman's meetings. (He is there to remember, but never to take notes: the boss does not like anything written down.) He arrives at seven a.m. and stays until eight or nine at night, until sometimes it is just the two of them, alone in those offices that have slowly emptied themselves out around them. Does this create an opportunity for my father to get to know his employer? Alas, no. No more intimacy exists between the two of them than between a person and their own shadow. My father might wonder if Wasserman has forgotten his name—he has not, but it is of no more concern to the man than a sidewalk penny—as he has become little more than an extension of his boss's will, another soft tentacle flapping from the octopus's massive head. At night when he lies in bed in his studio apartment, the place on Norton Avenue in West Hollywood he will occupy for the next few years, his body all but vibrates at the memory of Wasserman's voice.

How can you be so incompetent?

Lying in bed, he replays the day's tantrum—or no, doesn't "replay" it, exactly. The strange thing about his master's rage is that it has penetrated, now, to become a part of him. It never recedes, just recirculates, coursing through his body like blood.

Do you know? Do you know what you did wrong?

Just this afternoon there was an episode, which kicked off, as such episodes always do, with a slight escalation, a tensing of the jaw you can see from across the room, my father pinned frozen in the man's attention like a dog caught crapping on a rug.

"Why the fuck is Gregory Peck still waiting on that script?"

My father is no dog. He knows Wasserman respects firmness, that it will go better for him if he doesn't flinch.

"I delivered it last night."

"You delivered it? He doesn't have it. Therefore, you didn't deliver it."

"I brought it to the house at—"

"I didn't ask if you brought it." Wasserman's voice rises, but it is still within the realm of the rational, the modestly miffed tone of a sarcastic professor. "I asked if he had it. I don't give a shit if you brought it to him because he doesn't have it."

My father grasps, immediately, his mistake: he'd arrived at nine-thirty, ringing the doorbell three times before it became obvious—the lights were off—the actor wasn't home. Short of breaking into the man's house it was impossible to deliver the package directly, so he'd left it on the stoop. Foolish, but what was he supposed to do?

"You didn't deliver it," Wasserman repeats. "Because if you'd delivered it, he'd have it." This kind of circular logic is common in the motion picture business. It is a sort of ontological perversion, an existential violence that asserts my father's non-being: you screwed up, therefore you are not. "You're a fucking idiot."

Wasserman's eyes narrow. Now my father feels seen, as they

face each other in the circles of sullen, wintry lamplight. It is January, late afternoon, and so it is the hour when this room most resembles a gentleman's club, a dim hutch against the encroachment of darkness outside. My father notices—all his life, he will notice such things, because he has been remolded to see such detail—a gray flake of cigarette ash clinging to the polished edge of the desk, although Wasserman is a nonsmoker; a crumb of rye toast on the leather blotter; a soup stain on the man's white shirt, like a tiny orange raindrop.

"Do you want to work here?"

"I—"

"Do you like working here?" (Noticing these things, which he will remember all his life: these trivialities we affix to in moments of terror.)

"Yes."

"Then do your fucking job." His voice rises. "Do your fucking job. Are you stupid? Are you a moron? Have I hired an imbecile? Do. Your. Fucking. Job!"

He lifts up out of his chair and his voice lifts with him. At top volume, it might be audible from the lobby, or from the street two stories below.

"Who hired you? Did I hire you? Who fucking hired you? You are without a doubt the stupidest person who's ever walked through these halls. Get your things. Go home. No wait," he says, before my father can even turn around. "Stay. I'm not finished. Not by a long shot."

On it goes. My father is a "cocksucker." He is a "little shit." He is a "stain." He is "fired"—he knows even as this word is spoken it is not true, that he will come back tomorrow and begin again for he is chained to the great man's desk like Prometheus to his rock—but just now he is "worthless," he is "nothing." Little flecks of saliva spray from Wasserman's mouth, the barest remainder of his childhood speech impediment, and by the time he is done, winding down with the command that my father should run a copy of the script over to Mr. Peck's house right now and wait until he is able to press it into the actor's hands, all night if need be, by the time he is done, his body aches as if Wasserman has beaten him physically; his palms are raw from where his own nails have dug into them, hard enough almost to draw blood . . .

Lying awake, these few hours later, he remembers. Light from a streetlamp paints him, pushing through the venetian blinds to draw lurid stripes upon the bare wooden floor. The apartment is so empty, as transient in its way as a motel. My father sits up, fumbles for a cigarette, strikes a wooden match against his thumbnail. Bathing in its speck of sulfurous radiance, he thinks of the war—the one he didn't fight in, in Korea—and of soldiers and foxholes. He shakes it out and lies back in the dark, smoking. He is not a fragile man, and yet he finds himself bathed in sweat, his heart still racing at the memory. He knows—well, he does not "know," but he can feel—he is being formed, that every hammer blow brings forth the shape of what he will become. He knows the movies aren't "real," that they are, of course, just an illusion of plastic and camphor and projected light, and that they are spiritually insubstantial, that it is the world beyond the movies, the one his father lives in for instance, that counts. But they happen to be the thing he wants. And once you let the movies into your system, you are like someone succumbing to a drug dependency: you are like an opium smoker going under, both unable and uninterested in parsing reality from the dream.

He smokes. The burning tobacco crackles faintly, a small animal rustling through the woods. In the darkness, there is the bed, a television, a skeleton set of dishes, the dishes of a person who neither cooks nor entertains, abandoned at different stations: a saucer with Tuesday's half-eaten toast atop the TV; a bowl with sad scraps of midnight spaghetti by his bed. Only the closet is organized, with his shirts and trousers beautifully pressed, his shoes glossed to perfection. There is a book, *Tevye's Daughters: Collected Stories of Sholom Aleichem*, on the night table next to his wristwatch, but my father has never opened it. That is my grandfather's book, the kind of thing Reuben Specktor is always pestering him to read, but he is not compelled by Jewish history, Jewish lore, or Jewish fables. That is my grandfather's book.

He has not been to the movies in weeks. The last one he saw was Budd Boetticher's *Ride Lonesome*, though he is expected to keep up (with what time? There are days when he struggles to find thirty seconds to pee) with everything, to know the stars, the bit players, and above all the numbers, the box office tallies he reads every week in *Daily Variety*, studying the finest details, how last weekend *Some Like It Hot* had performed well in Chicago but even better in St. Louis, not because anyone will ever ask him, but because Wasserman himself knows down to the decimal point. Tomorrow morning he will arrive and his boss will lay a light hand on his bicep—no more than that, for barely more than a second—as he passes and my father will know that they are back to zero, that the crisis with Peck (which, in fact, had resolved itself even before he left the office: the actor had called to say he'd found the script behind a planter on his porch) is forgotten.

He tugs on the cigarette. The air smells of detergent, tobacco, the staling scent of recently fresh paint. He is never here: the lipstick smudge on a bone-white coffee cup, a collar stay that has fallen on the floor, the dampness of a towel draped over the shower rod: these things testify to a life outside the office, whatever small part of him remains beyond the property of Lew Wasserman. Here I am, he thinks. Fred Specktor. Whatever that means, exactly, a set of syllables that sound hollow now even to himself. He drops the cigarette into a glass of water to douse it—it amazes him to find the days so draining he practically has to remind himself not just who he is but what; it really is like the army, the grinding of a human being into an instrument—and rolls over, closing his eyes in the dark.

★ ★ ★

IS WASSERMAN THE man my father would hope to become? A cold, conquering master of the universe? Does he dream one day of equaling his master's influence, the power of the talent agent he watches so closely every day? MCA does not have a formal training program—there are agencies that do, like the William Morris Agency across town—and so he can only observe and deduce from the evidence how to behave. If my father wants to become an agent, he must look to Lew Wasserman. Is this who he wants to become?

No. To his credit, no. My father does not aspire to the green Bentley. He does not want to be filthy rich. His governing motivation is not to accumulate the kind of money Wasserman and his forerunner Dr. Stein have amassed, the kind that buys entire companies with no more hesitation than if they were springing for a pack of gum at the pharmacy, nor does he really want power of the kind that breaks people. He has seen this in action, has seen his boss pick up the phone and, with one terse, elliptical conversation, end another human being's career, and the idea of doing this, of bullying some client who thinks to leave or some poor schlub executive who has slipped up on a deal, repels him. What he wants is self-determination, the freedom to live as he pleases. Does this involve money? Of course, but when it comes to the perks held by the chief officers of MCA—Stein's hilltop estate, Misty Mountain, with its tennis courts and servants' quarters; Wasserman's collection of paintings by Vuillard and Degas—he could not care less. He has studied the other senior agents, and what he admires is their chameleonic quality, their ability to speak for another person, the artist, and to negotiate superior terms for their employment. That is something he does aspire to, not because it is noble, but because it is interesting. There is something interesting about strapping on the role and assuming the needs of your client, of arguing for them instead of just for your own ordinary self-interest. It is not exactly being a lawyer, but he was not wrong in the way he talked to Earl Zook, there is an advocacy involved, and he can imagine himself doing it, can see himself on the telephone haggling, arguing, playing the game in which—like tennis—you win or lose your points on the chalk. He can see it because it hinges upon the one thing common to everyone, which is the need to become someone else, to escape, even if just for a few moments each day, the narrow prison of his own skin.

★ ★ ★

DOES MY FATHER imagine that even Lew Wasserman, the man who has reached the pinnacle of his profession, feels this way? Is beset by a desire not just for "more," but for something else entirely?

"What are we doing out here, Lew? What is this place?"

"What does it look like?"

On a Saturday afternoon in 1959, Wasserman stands in a musty room, an airplane-like hangar, alongside two other men. My father is not one of them—what happens next does not involve him—but I must tell this story because it sets the tone and the terms of the next half-century to come.

"It's a soundstage," Wasserman says. Rain drums hard on the aluminum roof above. "At least it used to be."

Flanking him are Jules Stein and Taft Schreiber, MCA's most senior brass. They're over the hill in the San Fernando Valley, on a quiet corner of the Universal Pictures lot, a lot that has certainly seen better days.

"Used to be is right." Taft Schreiber gazes up at the ceiling through horn-rims, with his cropped hair the silver-gray of iron filings. "This place is a dump."

"I didn't say it wasn't."

"So whaddya want it for?" Schreiber's been with MCA since 1926. He has no love for Wasserman, who leapfrogged him in the pecking order to become Stein's heir. "You'd have to be crazy to buy this place."

Maybe so. Universal Pictures, the studio, has fallen on hard times. Many studios have. Ever since the Supreme Court decided in 1948 to force them to sell off their ownership in the nation's theater chains, the landmark Paramount Decree, the studios have been reeling, but Universal remains the weakest of all. If they'd once shot monster movies in here, old Lon Cheney, Karloff, and Lugosi pictures, or westerns—the Tom Mix serials Stein, especially, had loved as a boy—this soundstage is just a glorified storage closet now, crammed with bric-a-brac: saloon signboards and sagging latex costumes, wagon wheels and breakaway chairs, all of them layered with dust.

"I've gotta say, Taft's right." Stein, a cherubic little fellow with white hair and rimless glasses—he looks not like a Hollywood shark but like the Midwestern ophthalmologist he, also, is—twists his lips skeptically. "You really think we should buy this place? The Justice Department's not giving us enough grief already?"

Wasserman nods. The DOJ has been pawing around their company's business for more than a decade—ever since a pair of San Diego nightclub owners accused MCA of monopolistic practices back in '46—and lately they've turned it up a notch, nosing around the company's back door like raccoons attacking garbage cans in an alley, which makes his idea counterintuitive. Were the agency to buy a movie studio, the DOJ would go ballistic since this is a clear antitrust violation. You can't be a buyer and a seller at the same time. But there is a difference between blurring a line and crossing it.

"We're not gonna buy Universal Pictures," Wasserman says. His voice draws soft contrails of echo in the room's damp air. "Just the land."

Stein fingers his overcoat's silk pockets. Schreiber paws the ground with his oxford like a stallion. Don't be fooled by Stein's mild appearance: he'd built his company going toe to toe with Al Capone, Moe Dalitz, and Meyer Lansky—you had to, in the band business in those days—and these are not sentimental men. MCA has gobbled up its competitors as calmly as a frog picks off flies. When Stein and Wasserman came to Los Angeles, they'd built up their business not by schmoozing actors or discovering talent—why waste time on the conventional ways?—but instead by buying out their rivals, consuming other agencies until theirs was the biggest one standing. In this sense, Universal Pictures is as ripe for acquisition as anything they've ever considered. It is weak even by the standards of 1959, a year in which all the studios are also beset by the rise of television, and by a steady decline in moviegoing over the last decade. Universal is weak because it has always been weak, because it was founded by a weak man, Carl Laemmle, who'd made the mistake of bequeathing his kingdom's operation to his incompetent son. As a result, the studio had fallen into receivership, passing out of the family's hands altogether and into those of a UK conglomerate. For men like these, Universal—which has a long history of making inexpensive pictures profitable—is like a limping gazelle caught straggling at a water hole, a perfectly distressed asset if ever there was one.

"Just the land?" Schreiber snorts. He gestures around the roomful of sugar glass and cowboy outfits, monster costumes and horror props. "What are we gonna do, rent it out for birthday parties?"

"No." Wasserman stares up at the room's cathedral-like ceiling, the rain accelerating to pound down on the metal roof now with a violence. "We're gonna rent it right back to Universal Pictures. Everything is gonna go on exactly as it is."

★ ★ ★

"IT DOESN'T MAKE sense."

"What doesn't?"

One more dogleg before we return to my father; one more turn of the wheel to create the world through which he and I both shall pass. In the fall of 1958, a man named Leonard Posner—a minor figure, he will occupy our attention for just one moment—starts asking questions. A lawyer with the Department of Justice, Posner is, as they say, straight out of central casting: a short, squat bulldog of a person—if you've ever seen an old Warner Brothers gangster movie, you know—with a five o'clock shadow and the smoldering stump of a nickel cigar clenched between his teeth.

"What doesn't, boss?"

"Packaging." In a conference room in Washington, D.C., surrounded by a cluster of subordinates, he jabs his fat finger at a stack of subpoenaed documents. "What the hell is 'packaging'? Are these people at the post office? Are they just running around exchanging Christmas presents?"

Leonard Posner is a ghost. In the annals of Hollywood history, he barely exists. Scour the margins of other people's biographies and you will find only light mention of an antitrust lawyer who'd come up investigating monopolies in the world of sports broadcasting before going after the Mob. Within a few years he'll drop dead of a heart attack on a street corner in Beverly Hills, but just now he has literally put his finger on a thing that rests at the core of this story.

"I don't know what they're talking about, but I'll tell you what it sounds like, this 'packaging.'" He rests his cigar on the edge of the conference table and takes a wolfish bite of a cheeseburger. He's been chasing MCA for a while—even a company that minimizes its paper trail leaves something—but at last he zeroes in on a lexical detail that intrigues him. "Sounds like the same thing the bootleggers used to do. You want the good stuff, you take the rotgut with it. Real strong-arm shit."

Indeed. When the studios owned the theater chains, they used to force the regional exhibitors to show their weaker movies to gain access to the cream, which ensured they made money on everything. This is why the Paramount Decree exists: to break up the monopoly in which studios had owned both ends of the supply chain. This is what MCA is doing, as Posner sees it: forcing the networks and studios to take their lower-end talent to gain access to their stars.

"Same shit, different business," he mutters, as he reaches over to unwrap a second burger. He's like a furnace running on beef instead of coal. "These people are as crooked as the day is long."

Posner. He only matters as a kind of counterforce here, as a man who exists to chase Lew Wasserman down a certain path. My father will be gone from MCA by the time this clash reaches its resolution, but that path will clear the way for his future. Still, it matters. There are agents, and there are producers; there are artists, and there are businesspeople. Fred Specktor, a businessman, will never be confused about his position. But as Lew Wasserman drives home from Universal Pictures that day in 1959, the green Bentley cutting through the rain with its usual gleaming grace, perhaps he is confused, just a little.

Perhaps—I have no choice but to plunge to the center of him for a moment, this man who is an architect, also, of an industry's future ruin—he remembers how green he'd been once. How innocent he was, when he'd arrived back in '39. Shrewd, yes, canny, but fresh off the turnip truck all the same. He's not much given to retrospection either—he occupies the same eternal present as my father, which happens to be the tense of the movies themselves—but there are times when the past just bubbles up inside him.

This company was nothing when he arrived. MCA had about three clients, nobody important besides Hattie McDaniel. Stein had sent him west—Hattie McDaniel and Ronald Reagan hardly seemed to anyone the building blocks of empire—to do what young men were supposed to, which was conquer. Without connections, without any real resources beyond MCA's music industry money and his own mind, he'd come out here and swallowed everything: contracts the studios wanted out from under, smaller agencies like Associated Artists and Hayward-Deverich, gobbling up almost every competitor until, barely ten years later, they had a grip on the industry's biggest stars: Cary Grant and Jimmy Stewart, Marilyn Monroe and Katharine Hepburn, Ben Hecht and Billy Wilder. He represents people who are a million miles from what you think of when someone says "Hollywood," people like Dorothy Parker and Ernest Hemingway, so why, still, does he hunger for more? When he sits down to play cards with Selznick and Samuel Goldwyn—people he's already beaten a hundred times over because they used to govern this place and now it's all his— he's not afraid to bet his own house, because he can always buy it back and because it isn't just money that drives him but vision. Those days when actors were just wage slaves tied to multiyear contracts, at the mercy of the studio bosses' whims? Gone. He broke those chains, negotiating unprecedented profit participation for Jimmy Stewart on *Winchester '73*, cutting his clients in as producers, hiking their fees. TV? He was the first to see it coming, having owned one of the first two televisions to exist in the entire state of California. Visitors to his office thought it was a novelty, but he knew it was the future, had revived MCA's dormant subsidiary, Revue Productions, and used it as an umbrella to begin producing network shows, which was where the real money was, it turned out. He'd made MCA's senior management obscenely rich, and still, because he is a human being, because a certain restless rapacity burns inside him, he cannot help but hunger for more.

Now he drives his automobile through the eucalyptus dream of Laurel Canyon, the two-lane ribbon that winds up and down the other side of the Santa Monica Mountains, cutting between the banana palms and blue gums, an asphalt corridor that amounts to one tiny seam in the rust-colored sprawl of the hills. He's going to own a chunk of this, also, because Universal's plot runs all the way up here, four hundred fifty acres that even his colleagues can't imagine what he'll do with.

The windshield wipers beat their metronomic time, his tires hiss softly through puddles, and around him there is silence, the better to hear himself think. Somewhere inside him remains the person he'd once been, little Louis R. Wasserman from Woodland Avenue in Cleveland, the Jewish boy who'd watched his parents struggle, who'd seen his own brother lowered into an early grave. That boy had loved the movies, had been enraptured by Douglas Fairbanks and Buster Keaton just like anybody else, but what he really saw in them was an avenue to escape, to redraw himself a little ("Louis"' became "Lew"), the better to become more fully American. Is he a hard-nosed businessman? Yes—to him, packaging isn't racketeering, it's leverage: driving a hard bargain to put even his lesser clients to work—but he makes the mistake of every bright-eyed capitalist when he assumes that his self-interest and everyone else's (in fact, isn't he doing Metro a favor when he convinces them to take Eva Marie Saint alongside Cary Grant and Alfred Hitchcock? Isn't that making their job a little easier?) are the same. Somewhere inside him remains that child who was bullied on the schoolyard for his stutter, but he rarely thinks of it. Because when you've come as far as he has, when you own the very world through which you pass, as he does right now, you are no longer just a person, but a process.

He turns right on Sunset Boulevard (no, no: you're still a person, with memories and dreams—feelings, even—but these things get harder to access), snaps on the radio so he can hear the news. Stein is right to question what he's up to—this land is going to cost a fortune—but he knows well enough to trust Wasserman's process by now. When Wasserman had offered $50 million to buy Paramount Pictures' pre-1950 film library last year, Stein was perplexed, until it turned out he'd already structured the deal to pay for itself by pre-selling all those movies to run on television so that everything ahead of them was pure profit. This is who he is: a person who is always out in front. Somewhere inside him now, too, there is my father, a piece of flotsam lost in the body of a whale. Once upon a time, he'd been just like my father himself: Dr. Stein's little flunky, pushing a mail trolley around MCA's offices in Chicago, but now he is a fully fledged adult, a killer executive who understands there are no puppets, and there are no strings, there is just acquisition, the dull hum of capital coursing through his blood.

The rain starts to taper. He stares through the spangled glass down the corridor of Sunset and snorts. "Mobster." As if Leonard Posner's rubric can explain him really, as if he isn't something new, just as the world is new, the sun breaking through the cloud cover on the horizon to paint the sky an opalescent orange above the grassy pavilions of Beverly Hills. He knows what Posner thinks—the DOJ's so far up his ass it's a wonder he's still able to taste his own food—but he knows what a real mobster is. A mobster is a person like his friend Sidney Korshak, or like those guys he'd seen hanging around outside Kornman's chophouse when he was a boy. A mobster is a shakedown artist. He doesn't have any interest in that. Sure, he knows people who do—any business where you deal with organized labor, as the movies naturally must, puts you in touch with such people—but shakedowns aren't what he's about. The DOJ hated the Paramount library deal, and they'll hate this one, also, because MCA owns too much already, but it isn't really even about "ownership." When he calls himself a paper pusher—"I'm just a humble paper pusher" is what he tells interviewers who ask him how he does it—he isn't being sarcastic or modest. The world is paper, and all he does is arrange himself among its many symbols, the better to ratify reality as dream.

West, he rides, west, west, the Bentley's tires gliding down wet asphalt. His movement through the world is just like anyone else's. He knows, as he rides in this cool, quiet car with just the creaking of his body and the armature of his thoughts for company, that you can structure your life the way you structure a deal, and once you've done so everything around you opens up just like a flower, and it is as if you are an artist after all.

★ ★ ★

WHEN MY FATHER goes home on weekends, he enters a different reality, one that exists merely blocks away, but which seems— how to explain it?—comprised of an alternate material, heavy and gray like Dorothy's Kansas.

"Where have you been?"

"Working."

"At what?"

Reuben Specktor isn't a cruel man, but he is an uncommunicative one. There are facets of his own experience he can't quite confront, let alone express, and so when my father enters the house on Bedford Drive, the last to show on this particular Friday evening, Ruby is already boiling in his seat.

"You know what I do, Dad."

"So? You couldn't be here a little sooner?"

Reuben Specktor doesn't understand the movies either. He doesn't detest them—he likes going to the pictures as much as anybody, likes to sit and smoke his Chesterfields in the dark—but they aren't real to him, which means his son may as well have taken a job inside the funny papers.

"Maier here works for Hughes Aircraft." He looks approvingly at his son-in-law, a dark-haired cherub from Chicago. "He was here at six o'clock."

It is true. Maier Margolis, the man who has recently married my father's younger sister, works for Hughes and is not just a PhD candidate in engineering at UCLA, but also an observant Jew. He is everything, in other words, my father is not. He grins sweetly—impossible to resent, his hair is neatly parted, his mouth as softly pouty as Spanky's on *The Little Rascals*—while Marcia, the sister, reaches forward and starts to circulate the challah. From my father's perspective, the scene is the usual: Marcia and Myrna, the twins, seated on one side of the table, with him and Maier on the other. But as he strides in through the dense smell of brisket, he sees the challenge. Who is the real son, the seating seems to ask, him or his brother-in-law? He takes off his jacket and drapes it over his chair. My grandmother, Stella, comes in, small and golden, with her cat's-eye glasses and copper-colored hair, but Ruby shakes his head. Once upon a time, perhaps, Ruby might have been easier—I look at old photographs of my grandfather and see a young man who had been a bit of a dandy, his hat lightly cocked over a smile that radiates both mischief and confidence—but by now he has sunk firmly into his age. His narrow head perches atop a thickening torso, his white hair recedes, his eyes glare through black-framed spectacles. Not yet sixty, he seems to my father as old as Methuselah.

"Good to see you, Pop." The rough, synthetic weave of Ruby's jacket feels as gnarled as tree bark as my father reaches over to touch his arm. "Gut Shabbos."

The gulf between them is unbridgeable. Each views the other like a departing ship, vanishing through fog. The difference being that for my father Ruby can loom back up before him with a terrible immediacy: he might think he has escaped into open water only to find himself tangled in the kelp, crashing upon the rock of his ancestry. It is like this now, as the little dining room with its traditional décor, its bell-and-pomegranate table runner and hammered silver candlesticks; the living room with its barren coffee table and walls lined with Judaica, books with Hebrew titles and worn, gilt spines all conspire to oppress him. The light of the movies doesn't penetrate in here.

"Who wants to say the berakhah?" My grandfather looks at the twins, which is his way of provoking my dad, which in turn creates an opening for Maier.

"I'll say it, Reuben, if you'd like."

Sweet Maier, with his jowly face like a gentle-tempered hound's, his dark eyes attentive and penetrating. My father has no quarrel with him, nor with his sisters—Marcia the ethereal, black-haired, and lovely swan; Myrna the lonely one with the crooked smile; the two like mismatched siblings in a fairy tale—but his battle with Ruby is endless.

"So?" After the blessing, Ruby speaks. His voice is throaty and fricative, his accent still carrying its trace of Ukraine. "Did you meet any movie stars today?"

"Dad." One of the twins leans forward, touches his wrist.

"Did you learn any new addresses?" he continues over Marcia's objection. "Did you wash Clark Gable's car?"

He looks at my father and sees frivolity. A real person builds things, or, if they have chosen to pursue a life of the mind, studies law, or literature, or medicine. Only a fool would waste his time chasing movie stars.

"Why can't you be more like Maier here, a worker?" He sparks up another Chesterfield. "I don't understand what you do. Other people have sons they can be proud of, but you, you're nothing. You're a bum."

A rare cruelty, coming from a man who is fundamentally decent. But when Ruby looks at my father, what he sees is an affront to the real. Real isn't Hollywood. Real is Hughes Aircraft. Real is when they come for you in the middle of the night, when they dress you up as a girl—the better for you to avoid conscription in the Russian army if you are caught—and smuggle you off in a wagon that smells like hay and horse manure, away from your village and your extended family, some of whom, like your uncle Levy, you are never going to see again.

As for my father, gazing through the silence and the smoke, the haze of my grandfather's cigarette that hangs above the table like that of exploded ordnance, what he sees is a nightmare from which he can only run. "Nothing?" Lew Wasserman can yell all he wants but ultimately it's like getting barked at by your sergeant in the army: it stings but doesn't scar. My grandfather's words define a world in which he'll never be good enough, a nullity that leaves him no choice. In the smoke my father can read, perhaps, the name of Ruby's shtetl—Kapaygorod—and the stories of all his relatives, the ones who had dispersed to Portugal or São Paulo or Montreal, because he's heard those stories over and again. Cousin Max is a successful tailor now in Philadelphia . . . Uncle Julius was pistol-whipped by a mobster in a cigar store in Brooklyn . . . Bubba Ruchel bought a five-pound bag of sugar whenever she got depressed. But this particular story, my father will only ever tell me once.

("You think I'm tough on you sometimes?" I can still hear him, all these years later. I will be nine years old when I ask why we rarely visit my grandfather. "You have no idea what my father said to me once.")

Can you blame him for looking up to Lew Wasserman? For taking the first available avenue of escape himself? Like Wasserman, the boy from Woodlawn Avenue—or, indeed, like Ruby Rubenstein, as my grandfather was called before he landed in Montreal and took the name of another branch of the family—he yearns to become someone new. To do the American thing and enter a world of illusion, a dream factory in which real people can nevertheless lose their real shirts, and which happens to be the only world that offers him a chance to really live at all.

★ ★ ★

"I DON'T REMEMBER."

On the day Ronald Reagan takes the stand to testify before a grand jury in the federal building at 300 N. Los Angeles Street, in February 1962, my father is long gone from MCA. The circumstances surrounding his termination will remain forever vague. Even decades later, he won't talk about it, but it happened in late 1960.

"Mr. Reagan, I'm going to ask you again." (All this vagueness, all this slippery indeterminacy. Is an agent a buyer or a seller? Is Hollywood just in the business of making movies, or does it traffic in other, still greater mythologies?) "Did you in fact have a meeting with Lew Wasserman in July 1952 in which you promised, as president of the Screen Actors Guild, to grant MCA a waiver that would allow your membership to appear in television programs produced by the agency?"

"Sir, I have meetings every day. You can't expect me to remember what was said at one that happened a decade ago. Like I told you, I simply don't recall."

Is my father just a corporate soldier or an actual human being? Which will he become? If I'm going to get to the bottom of him I need to tell you how MCA falls apart, which begins with one of Posner's deputies, a man named John Fricano, hammering Lew Wasserman's clients on the stand. Ronald Reagan is evasive, just as he will be in a different courtroom twenty-eight years later, but he is hardly the only one. Hollywood has built itself around a series of managed oblivions, and so might America, which will forever take its cues from this place, from the chiseled cheekbones of its men and the silver tongues of its women. If Leonard Posner came here to unwind corruption, a corruption that springs as he sees it from Hollywood's venal soul, he has a surprise coming.

"Next witness . . ."

"We'll call Paul Newman."

None of this will go as Posner hopes. By the time a grand jury convenes in the spring of '62, he has been building his case for years. He has rooted through MCA's files and interviewed its employees, rivals, and clients, those few who will talk, for half a decade. And if Wasserman's own hand remains invisible, Posner nevertheless recognizes what he sees. It's the same thing he saw when he was prosecuting the Mob: the company may operate with a soft touch, insinuating itself into every secretarial pool in town, sending gifts to typists and valets, people who might be willing to slip them information to which MCA ought not to be privy, but what really greases the wheels for them is intimidation. And what the agency is doing, not just "packaging" its clients and selling these bundles to networks, but cutting itself in to receive lavish producing fees on top of their ten percent commission, is unethical: straight-up monopolistic shit. For MCA to buy up studio libraries and land, those huge deals Wasserman has been putting together these past few years, only enhances the point. You can be an agency, or you can be a motion picture studio, but you cannot be both things at once.

"Well, sir, I'd like to be helpful, but I just don't know." Paul Newman is less combative than Reagan but no more helpful, with those blue eyes that burn with a persuasive clarity. "My wife's the one who handles all the accounting in our family. I'm just an actor."

Golly, gee. Look at him smiling up there, not insolently, but as sweetly as a small child. Last year he had played Fast Eddie Felson, a pool shark ready to wager his soul against the devil at four in the morning, in Robert Rossen's adaptation of *The Hustler*, so what part of this is supposed to unnerve him? It doesn't matter what he says, Posner thinks. It only matters what the jury believes, and how far these witnesses can persuade them. So it is with Tony

Curtis, Lucille Ball, Rita Hayworth, Cary Grant. Each of these people comes in and stuns the jury, twenty-three ordinary members of the American public, with their poise, their wit, their humor, and their beauty. They are like human beings—they *are* human beings, as Posner fights valiantly to remind the jurors: just people—and they are like gods, radiant and expensively dressed, whose little blemishes (Lucille Ball has a mole at the base of her left earlobe; Tony Curtis has a blackhead on his chin the day he takes the stand) only manage to enhance their loveliness. Had Posner thought he could compete with this? Does he think he can walk in here and win on the strength of the facts, defeat the movies with anything as meager as the real?

Still, Wasserman is running scared. Posner knows it, knows the agent has been shuttling back and forth to D.C. these past few months trying to put the arm on Posner's bosses, weaseling his way into a meeting with Bobby Kennedy. He knows that MCA has recently announced a plan to spin off its talent agency into a separate entity, thereby allowing its television production branch to persist independently. But all this tells Posner is that Wasserman knows he's been caught with his hand in the cookie jar. Spinning off his talent agency to his own employees, pretending that the agency (seller) and production company (buyer) will thus remain separate entities, is like a gangster placing his assets in a trust controlled by his girlfriend. It's a scam, born of desperation.

"Lew Wasserman is like a father to me." Tony Curtis takes the stand, playing the part of sentimental ingenue, slumping in his chair to suggest just the right note of gentle piety as his voice seems to crack. "I owe him my entire career."

Tennessee Ernie Ford gets up and acts like a hillbilly, while Audrey Hepburn is as gossamer and graceful on the stand as she was in *Breakfast at Tiffany's*. Leonard Posner is a likable man. The jurors find him truthful and regular, like a person who—he reminds them of this, as plainly as he can—earns five grand a year while each of the attorneys in the seemingly endless parade MCA trots out to oppose him earns twenty times that. If only that was what these ordinary Americans, these jurors, wanted. Honesty.

"So you're telling me, Mr. Warner, that even though MCA has been a thorn in your side for more than twenty years, you consider Lew Wasserman a friend?"

Americans don't want honesty. They want hypocrisy. They want lies, like children who've been brought to the circus. Jack Warner, that old showman who still owns the studio he'd built long ago with his brothers, knows the score.

"Yessir."

"Why is that exactly? How can someone who opposes you at every possible turn be considered a 'friend'?"

Posner must have imagined he finally had it in the bag with this witness. Jack Warner is as hostile to Wasserman's interests as anyone who's ever lived. The old man used to run this town, before the agent, a person who's probably cost him more money than anybody, stole it from under his nose.

"A man's got to eat, doesn't he?" Warner leans back in his chair and grins. With his little Chiclet-teeth and his bushy eyebrows, his pencil-thin mustache and pinstriped suit, he looks like Groucho Marx run into a buzzsaw. "You think because Lew Wasserman costs me money that makes him my enemy? No, no—we do business all the time. He's my friend!"

An agent can be anything he wants, perhaps: can be both enemy and friend. Posner thought he had it all figured out, but this courtroom, with its drab tans and dull-waxed linoleum floor, is no match for these people. Plain speech, logic, the law: Hollywood defies every last bit of it. Fricano paces and questions; Posner fumes and glowers. But this fight seems lost almost before it begins.

★ ★ ★

WHO IS MORE honest? Lew Wasserman wonders. Bobby Kennedy and his feds, with their ideas of rectitude and black-and-white morality, or those like Jack Warner, who know it's all a charade? When Wasserman lies awake at night—is it a charade for him, also, alone in the dark in his study? Edie sleeps in a separate bedroom now, down the hall—he knows it is decision time: that all those flights he's taken to Washington are for naught. They are going to hammer him until things get so uncomfortable there'll be no point in carrying on anyway. As he lies in the brittle blue silence of four a.m., he waits for the hour when the networks will begin to broadcast again, when he will rise from the couch and switch on the three sets he keeps side by side so he can monitor them all at once.

These fucking hypocrites. These Yankee cocksuckers don't understand any of it, how his job is merely to create jobs. When MCA had revived Revue Productions and started assembling shows for television, this was what it was for: to create employment opportunities for their own clients, with whom they had a fiduciary relationship. This is his job, to procure employment for other people. He doesn't control anybody! He's just a humbug, he's no mighty wizard! Lying there in his pajamas, seething— these people have no idea how it works—he's just about ready to burst a blood vessel.

Dawn is breaking. He sits up. He and Edie live on Foothill Drive now, in a house north of Sunset that more befits his stature, filled with fine art, surrounded by lush gardens and koi ponds and glass walls. But it was Edie who'd wanted this, Edie who'd proposed, as was her way, that they enjoy the fruits of his labors. Otherwise, they might have gone on exactly as they were: nothing to call attention to itself, just as he has always preferred. *He* is a hypocrite, sure, but at least he knows it, which is more than one can say for the Kennedys. When you play the part to the hilt—the aggrieved American businessman telling the papers that you're just a bureaucrat, not some nefarious puppeteer—you can almost believe it, and upon this "almost" hangs the measure of your reality.

When I am a small child, a decade from now, my mother will tell me a story, that of the *Fisherman and His Wife*. In it—you know this story, too—a poor fisherman catches and re-catches a magic flounder, who grants him a series of wishes in exchange for being let go. The man wishes for a cottage, then for a palace, then for a kingdom, finally for an empire, before, in his fathomless misery, he realizes there is nothing he wants more than the simple poverty from which he came. This story will haunt me throughout my childhood. It haunts me now, as I consider this austere and terrible man whose decisions will continue to carve up the world, shaping those hierarchies that preside over Los Angeles and beyond.

★ ★ ★

LEONARD POSNER WILL be sandbagged just like everybody else. So will my father, who, when he hears the news, will set his turkey sandwich down—he'll be in the Brighton Coffee Shop on the corner of Camden Drive—and whistle like hell has just frozen over. Posner's cat and mouse with Wasserman goes on—MCA announces its plan to buy Universal Pictures itself, having already snapped up the land, and on June 13, 1963, Posner delivers his report on the grand jury's findings, recommending indictment in a case that now seems cut and dried—but even he is flabbergasted when he arrives at his office barely a month later and stares down at a memo that has just come in from his bosses.

"Jesus Christ." He cannot help but laugh, because he can almost appreciate it. If only it didn't mean Wasserman is going to slip through his fingers yet again. "The stones on these sons of bitches. My God."

A telegram goes out on July 24 to MCA's clients and employees alike. Every actor and director, every agent, secretary and mail boy receives the same message. Without a warning, Wasserman and the board are leaving them all high and dry.

> Dear ____: *Effective immediately MCA Inc and all of its domestic subsidiaries . . . will surrender all of their guild, labor union and other franchise with respect to their talent agency functions . . .*

High and dry, as the news sweeps through the halls of 360 N. Crescent Drive like a fire, creating chaos, creating ruin.

"What the hell am I gonna do?"

"What are you— What am *I* gonna do? My wife just had a baby!"

Yesterday, a Monday, these people had jobs. This morning, a Tuesday—"Black Tuesday," it will be termed in the industry's newspapers, the *Daily Variety* and *Hollywood Reporter*—they do not. You can understand how Leonard Posner would be unhappy—he'd thought he had them on an antitrust violation, but by dissolving the agency instead of merely spinning it off, there is suddenly no violation to prosecute, since it's no crime to own a motion picture studio on its own—but it's nothing compared to the shock and disorder that runs through Lew Wasserman and Jules Stein's stately seat of power. My father may be outside the fray himself—having hooked onto a small agency across town called Kumin-Olenick, he can afford to simply raise his eyebrows and then go back to his lunch—but let's take a moment to think of that beautiful building, that wondrous fiction whose other inhabitants had thought their reign would last a thousand years, like the very courtiers of Vienna.

"What are we gonna do?"

Secretaries sit at their desks, sobbing; agents roam the halls, ties unknotted, bottles of scotch dangling from their hands, drunk at ten o'clock in the morning; telephones burp and shrill, while voices plead from the interior offices.

"Come with us! I know a guy at William Morris."

"Look, I've already got something. Arthur Park and Herman Citron are setting up their own shop."

"The fuck do you care where Marlon's going?" Is it Jay Kanter who speaks, haggling with another reluctant client? "I asked what *you* wanted to do."

Imagine for a moment the carnage, because it's going to repeat itself over and over. Black Tuesday. Just another stupid massacre in an industry that will remain forever full of them, one more bubble to erupt in the annals of American capitalism.

"Of course I didn't see this coming. What are you talking about?"

Agents haggle with their clients; the clients—actors and writers and filmmakers—whisper to one another because it is not just some talent agency that is dissolving, but all of Hollywood being redrawn, with alliances being formed or discarded accordingly.

This is going to happen again. Only young people believe their luck is never going to change. Young people and young industries, and, let's face it, young nations, too. All of them think the world they have conquered is going to stay conquered, that what's theirs will remain theirs forever.

★ ★ ★

MY FATHER GOES to the movies. On a Sunday afternoon he drives to Grauman's Chinese, heading east along Franklin Avenue. On the other side of Nichols Canyon, Lew Wasserman has commissioned a tower. He never liked Jules Stein's building: his vision of the future is sleek and modern, an obsidian-black high-rise jutting up sixteen stories on the lot in Universal City. His influence hasn't ended—on the contrary, it is just beginning, and will find its echo in things my father and his future colleagues do twenty years hence—as Universal Pictures soldiers on, now under his and MCA's umbrella. But just now it has come to rest on a hot summer afternoon, the blacktop steaming as my father pilots his

Austin-Healey down the corridor that runs parallel to Sunset Boulevard. The radio blares. For him, Hollywood is only Hollywood; Los Angeles is merely itself. He doesn't know that when Lyndon B. Johnson comes calling to offer my father's former boss a post in his cabinet a few years later as secretary of commerce, Lew Wasserman will decline, because he knows where the real seat of the nation lies. He knows that on those 450 acres of land he has purchased, there is endless room for development: for a theme park and a shopping complex, for a golf course and hotels, for licensing and marketing opportunities—the true lines of the American horizon—of which the industry's old pharaohs never dreamed.

My father will never enter that tower as anything other than a guest. His time is his own again, which is great, but it does leave him somewhere close to where he started. He's a junior agent now, but a junior agent without clients is like a priest without parishioners. Kumin-Olenick is a nice place—they handle Hope Lange, Jack Elam, Dick York—but it is no MCA.

He is still a young man. He is not yet thirty, as he strolls over the boulevard's brass-and-terrazzo stars, the theater's pagoda-like marquee (*The Man Who Shot Liberty Valance*, it reads. JAMES STEWART. VERA MILES.) looming into view ahead.

"Freddy!"

"Oh—hey, Irv." He's standing in the Grauman's courtyard waiting to buy his ticket when an acquaintance coming out of the previous showing, another former MCA man, clocks him and walks over to say hello. "How's the picture?"

"Terrific."

My father cannot remember this person's last name. They are all named Irv, or Stewart, or Ronnie, these sharp-eyed young men with whom he'd brushed elbows in the MCA mailroom. Still, he seems to be doing well, as my father notes his wristwatch (expensive, an Omega), the girl on his arm (attractive), the spring in his stride even on a Sunday afternoon.

"How's Lee Marvin?" my dad says.

"Terrific. I'm going to sign him."

Bullshit, my father thinks. "Where are you these days?"

"Famous Artists. I hear you're over at Julian Olenick's place."

"I am. I like it."

"We should have lunch."

The two men trade cards. In this business, you should know your rivals, you should cultivate your friends. Tough to know sometimes which is which.

"I'll call you, Freddy."

My father enters the theater. The man's manner rubs him a little the wrong way, and so he tucks the business card in the pocket of his windbreaker, where he will not rediscover it for several months. He sits back and watches the picture: James Stewart plays Ranse Stoddard, a small-town senator who has built his political career upon a lie. According to the lore, he has rescued his town from the terroristic reign of sociopathic gunman Liberty Valance—played by Lee Marvin—who has in fact been killed by Ranse's rival, Tom Doniphan (John Wayne). That doesn't stop Stoddard from trading upon his myth, however. "When the legend becomes fact, print the legend," goes the film's most famous line, one that everyone knows is also applicable to Hollywood itself. When the story is more attractive, why bother with the truth?

My father enjoys the film. He walks out two hours later into humid twilight, passing between the tourists who crouch in the theater's courtyard to scrutinize the palm- and footprints set into its famous squares of cement, moving down Hollywood Boulevard, stepping over the stars again—*Constance Talmadge* and *Rudy Vallee, Linda Darnell* and *Ezio Pinza*, names that feel eternal—on his way to the little white coupé that sits at a meter up the block.

Sunday, Sunday. He doesn't know that the card in his pocket will change his life, that when he calls the man and has the lunch it will result in his moving over to Famous Artists himself, which will result in another fateful encounter, and so everything rests upon a choice, made at the last moment, to hit the four forty-five showing instead of the two-fifteen. He climbs into his car and starts the ignition. Away from his father, away from Lew Wasserman, he feels unfettered, happy and free in a way he never quite will again. Everything that follows will amount to complication, to both the realization of and the foreclosure upon his dreams.

He drives home to a little apartment on Orlando Avenue, the room in which I will one day soon be conceived. The sky bursts into orange flames above him, his car's hood shines a dying gold. The radio plays the Crystals, Claudine Clark, and the Drifters, a song, "Ruby Baby," that reminds him, of course, of his father. He arrives home humming (*"Ruby, Ruby, Ruby, Baby"*—Ruby slippers just like Dorothy's) and he makes spaghetti, standing in his tiny kitchenette with the checkerboard tiles and straining it, Jack Lemmon–style, through a tennis racket he holds over the sink. He stares down at its crooked strings, the strands of pasta sliding through, half-caught, dangling over the pale basin, and knows that they are just like he is: half-in, half-out, half-snared, and half-free, captured inside the spreading American net of the movies.

2. NOBODY

1963–1967

MY MOTHER IS WAKING up. In her bedroom on Chelsea Avenue, in a carved-up duplex in Santa Monica, she stands and paces through the morning's cloud-bound whiteness, the fog that has drifted in off the Pacific. All over Los Angeles, in Santa Monica and West Hollywood, Toluca Lake and Valley Village, there are women like her: beautiful women with headshots in their closets and refrigerators clustered with Tab soda and cottage cheese, women with stage names they hope will launch them to stardom. My mother has had such a name, also, as she was once Katherine McKenna (modeling), then briefly Katherine Froelich (marriage), before reverting to her birth name, McGaffey. But at twenty-seven, she has given up those dreams. Her headshots are up in an attic somewhere, glossy black-and-whites in which she appears almost doll-like, although in real life her smile is warm and convivial, her eyes a piercing, seawater green. No man has ever accused her of not being pretty enough, not even the husband who'd left her, alas, for other reasons.

In the kitchen, before the rumble of rush-hour traffic begins, she sits at a narrow table and reads, bending over a Signet Classic. If she could, she would read all day, or—she cannot quite admit it to herself—write. She would write. She cannot admit it, because though she admires the boldness of her favorite writers—Jean Rhys and John Dos Passos, James Joyce and Elizabeth Bowen— she remains privately timid, and does not yet fully possess her own mind. Still, she bends over her paperback, smiling and shaking her head, picking up a pencil here and there to underline; her imaginative life unknown to the people around her, the ones at work, but inside it's lively, burbling, and clear. She reads until she can feel the light changing—she looks up to see the fog is starting to burn off—then stubs out her cigarette and races to get dressed.

It is barely more than a studio, this place, with its cramped and shady sitting room, its crooked kitchenette. She grew up in splendor, as for a while her parents had owned a house on Mc-Cadden Place that had previously belonged to Judy Garland, but now she and her mother barely speak. Her older sister, Marge, is a secretary at Hughes Aircraft in Fullerton, her older brother, Don, a municipal worker in Pomona, and she remains in exile from the expensive world into which she was born, a world that had dissolved itself even before her father died, as the family had lost all its money. She is alone, divorced, employed inside the motion picture industry, and she knows that the job she has, secretary, isn't going to lead anywhere but that she doesn't particularly want it to. She likes movies fine, but she isn't obsessed or enthralled by them. Sometimes she wonders, as she picks up the telephone and catches the sound of a familiar voice ("Hold on one moment, Mr. Brynner, I'll connect you") whether they sound as strange to themselves, these people who buzz in her ear all day. It's not that they aren't friendly or polite, it's that even when they flirt, they seem mostly to be talking to themselves. Perhaps this is her quarrel with the movies, why she likes them less than literature: because they are like one-way glass, where fiction is a welcoming room, one that bursts into life the moment you step inside it.

She dresses quickly. Her oblong, Scots-Irish face may be too idiosyncratic for the screen anyway, the hollow cheekbones and sharp eyes, the straw-blond hair worn in a low-slung and slightly disheveled beehive. Over the course of her life, she will assume a succession of roles—wife, mother, activist, administrator—some of them closer to her original dream than others, but none of them will suit her perfectly. She will carry with her a certain ambivalence, trying things on and abandoning them, moving on to whatever is next. Decades from now, her closet will hold a leotard and several pairs of shredded ballet shoes; a baby grand piano will sit in a corner of her living room, its keys dusty; the scraps of her life as a serial spouse and parent, both of which may prove more challenging to her than a layperson's mastery of dance and music, will litter her house and yet it will be books, walls of them, that dominate, not one of them bearing her own name.

Oh, well. There is plenty of time left to make her mistakes, plenty of opportunity for her yet to miss. Her life is like any other young person's: still golden, more so than most because she has grown up with all the advantages of whiteness and money, with private schools, with swimming pools and a beach club membership from which her father, the late Mac McGaffey, had ultimately resigned in liberal protest of the fact they didn't admit Jews. Her trauma—poor Mac had dropped dead right in front of her when she was just fourteen—is ordinary. Nothing marks her, nothing evident to the naked eye: her divorce was clean and left her anything but heartbroken once the circumstances were clear to her. But the quickness with which she grabs her purse, darts back into the kitchen for her cigarettes, races through the clutter of her sitting room and then out, down the front walk to her car: all of this suggests not a person who's simply afraid to be late, but rather one who is running: who remains, always, in flight.

★ ★ ★

"IRA STEINER'S OFFICE?"

She sits at the end of a long row of secretaries now, perched outside a corner office at 9255 Sunset Boulevard.

"One moment, Mr. Lancaster. I'll put you through."

The women line up in almost identical profile—all of them pretty, most of them pale, heads angled against telephone receivers and hovering over typewriters, hands clutching cigarettes, coffee cups, and cans of diet soda—flanking a long corridor on a high floor of a mid-century modern tower. The carpet is mustard-colored, the air gray with smoke.

"Ira Steiner's office?"

Flight, too, is in her blood. This city is also famous for its other dominant industry, aviation. Her uncle Neil had owned a small company that designed planes for private ownership, a prototype called the McGaffey AV-8, back in the thirties. Her great-grandfather, a lumber magnate who was one of the wealthiest men in New Mexico, had died in a commercial crash in 1929, among the first in American history. And yet here she is working for a medium-sized talent agency, having gone to UCLA instead of to secretarial school like her mother suggested because, according to Helen McGaffey, the only future that means anything must involve her finding a husband. Helen, my grandmother, is a blueblood, an old-line American whose ancestry can be traced all the way back to John Alden of the *Mayflower*. She and my mother are just at the beginning of a quarrel that will last several decades. Here, at least, my mother feels insulated. The hungry young men and women of the Ashley-Famous Talent Agency are a far cry from Helen's prim, Protestant frigidity.

"Ira Steiner's office?"

The repetition of it might bore her to death. But she is good with monotony, in fact likes a little numbness, as she does crossword puzzles, sums and figures (her father was an accountant), driving, anything that invites hypnosis, an anonymizing process in which it is possible for her to disappear. When she was seventeen, she'd taken a blade and slashed at her wrists. Two pale scars commemorate this event, which she will never explain to me. Eighteen months before this, her father had died. They'd been sitting in her family's house on Esparta Way shortly before her sixteenth birthday, waiting for the *Sammy Kaye Variety Show* to start, when Mac got up to prune his flowerbeds in the twilight. He'd stepped out the sliding doors, his hulking, football player's body—he'd been a star at Cal Tech—looming against the evening sky. She'd looked back at the TV a moment and then heard it: his shoulder slamming against the doors, hard enough to crack glass.

"Ira Steiner's office?"

All these years later, she can still see his body crumpling to the concrete terrace, the shears dangling from his hand; his final words—"It's like a wake in here"—ring in her ears, and the channel of blood that ran from his head, redder than you can imagine, often paints her dreams. But it's not this that makes her feel she could vanish from this earth, and no one would miss her.

"One moment, I'll see if he's in."

Not this, valve damage—her father's heart like a ticking bomb, thanks to rheumatic fever he'd had as a boy—but something else, something I will never wholly understand.

★ ★ ★

DOWNSTAIRS, IN THE bar in the lobby of the building, she sits in a booth with a few of her girlfriends. It is December 1963, and the men from the office who surround them are not blackbirds—they are looser, less uniform in their blue, khaki, or dove-gray suits— but they are cut from a similar cloth: sharp, Jewish, attractive but uncomfortably brash.

"Kathy! Hey, Kathy, c'mere!"

A friend, a sandy-haired agent with whom she'd gone on a single, perfunctory date before he'd drunkenly confessed he was gay, pops up like a buoy from a booth across the room and waves her over. The agent is jammed into a narrow two-top, and the man sitting opposite is different somehow: shy, almost pensive as he glances up at her, tugs on his cigarette, and smiles.

"I want you to meet someone." The friend peers up at my mother, who stoops slightly—at five-ten, she is taller than many men in the room—as she looms over the booth. "Kath, do you know Freddy?"

My father eyes her. He may seem quiet, with a feline circumspection, but she has seen him around the halls, and she knows that he is opinionated, as aggressive as he needs to be in his dealings. Still, there is something thoughtful, oddly sensitive, about him. Most of the time, as she eavesdrops on the junior agents, she notices how they are overeager, like dogs three feet away from a T-bone steak: all they want is to close the deal at any cost. But when she passes Fred Specktor in his little windowless office, she can't help but notice he is often listening, leaning back, tugging on his cigarette for a long moment before offering his counter. ("What about three weeks? It'll be a little tight, but if that's what you have to offer, I can let you have him for three.") He doesn't just beat people up. He looks for the equitable solution.

"Hello."

She sits. Whether he has coaxed their mutual friend to invite her over or if the friend—what this man knows, she realizes, is how to get what he wants without always having to ask for it directly—

has simply taken it upon himself, she does not know, but he has noticed her around, also, she is certain of it.

"You want something to drink?" he says, glancing at her empty glass.

"Sure."

"Same thing?"

She nods, but he is already up out of his seat, halfway to the bar while she sucks the gin-tasting straw, the muddled lime that rests in a puddle of melting ice. It's early. They're down here drinking at four-thirty because it is almost Christmas, and the office is closing for the holidays. The jukebox plays the Ronettes' version of "Frosty the Snowman." She watches him cross the room then lean over the bar to order, his tan jacket hitching up slightly as he bends so she can admire the cut of his suit, a meticulousness that stops just shy of being fussy. He says something to the bartender, who laughs, then lifts two fingers by way of telling him to stop the pour.

"So." My father sits back down, pushes one drink over to her.

"So."

The friend has vanished. This is a setup, she realizes: her friend had agreed to play Cupid on my father's behalf. She scans the room and sees the man flirting with another girl, resting his hand for a moment on her bicep while she looks back with exaggerated shock.

"What have you got there?"

"Where?"

(Why do men do this, she thinks, as she watches the other agent. She understands the need to remain in the closet, but when Bob Froelich burst into tears one night after they were married six months and told her he felt like he was drowning, she wondered why he had taken it this far. Did he really need to get married? Wasn't there some other accommodation he might have made with reality, or with his own desire?)

"There." (Perhaps not. Not even the bohemian provinces of the motion picture business are yet that liberated.) "That book that's falling out of your purse."

"Ah." She looks over, but he is already across the table to pick it up.

"*Dubliners*." My father frowns, scrutinizing the paperback. "You read this?"

"Is there something the matter with it?"

He holds the book by the edges, respectfully—delicately, even—but also with a certain strangeness, like it is a rare object that belongs under glass.

"James Joyce." He shakes his head, then breaks into a wide grin. "I don't know anybody who reads this."

"You don't?"

"No!" The smile widens. "What do you think people in this business read? Screenplays. Army Archerd's column if they think they might be mentioned in it. They don't read literature."

"What do you read?"

He freezes for a moment, then laughs. "Screenplays, Army Archerd's column. Too many hard words and I start to get a headache."

She laughs, too. Her first husband was a reader—with Bob, she could stay up and discuss Ibsen for hours—where this man, plainly, is not. She likes his candor though. He's not trying to pull anything over.

"No hard words in this, really." She grins and flips it open. "See? It even starts like a children's story."

My father is not a reader—not like she is—but he retains a thoughtful intelligence. He is acute, if not highbrow, in his tastes. When she comes to work over the next few weeks carting *The Man Who Loved Children*, *Lolita*, *The Ambassadors*, he will wonder that she is a person of enormous potential, someone who wouldn't necessarily have to waste her life in the movie business. For him, this industry is an escape. For her, it could be slumming.

"Tell me something," he says, watching her smoke. "Where'd you go to school?"

"Who says I went to school?" she teases. "What if I'm just carrying that thing around to impress?"

"Who are you going to impress? Most people here don't know James Joyce from the guy who wrote *From Here to Eternity*."

"I impressed you, didn't I?"

He shakes another cigarette from his own pack, his hand brushing hers as he reaches across the table for her matchbook. Her brand is L&M; his, Pall Mall. She drinks another G&T, her third, out of a Collins glass, while he nurses his second dry martini, its sliver of lemon rind bobbing weightlessly as he sets it back down.

"Where were you?"

"What?"

"You know," she says. "A couple weeks ago. Where were you?"

"Ah." My father tilts his head, exhales. "Right."

The room is dark now, empty and quiet. Their voices are hoarse from trying to speak above the former din. The bartender puts on *Sinatra with Strings*. My father cannot tell her the truth, which is that he was sitting that morning in his car, waiting outside a house in the South Bay where he'd taken a girl to have an abortion. That feeling, the heat of the leather upholstery on his back, the twin senses of sickness and of shame as he sat with the sun beating down, had been vivid enough already. He'd been queasy, hungover even before he reached over and snapped on the radio. ("A bulletin now from the United Press . . . President Kennedy and Governor John Connally of Texas have been shot . . .")

"Home," he says. "I was out sick that day. You?"

"Upstairs," she says. "Handling Mr. Steiner's calls as always."

There is a beat, a lurching pocket of silence between them. Perhaps she has not detected his fib, but she can feel it. The girl was not a steady, just a one-night stand with unplanned consequences, but that sharp smell of burning tar as he waited on a broad, flat avenue in El Segundo, a recently repaved strip in a residential subdivision, still lingers. That place, with its almost identical houses painted in beachfront colors, matte blue and salmon pink, unnerved him with its smooth featurelessness, its strange suburban opacity.

My father reaches across the table and puts his hand atop hers. (Could he live in a place like that now, so ordinarily American? Has the business changed him that far already?) "You wanna go somewhere?"

It is an insidious thing, this industry of theirs: its illusions are too quick to become one's own. His last girlfriend was Stella Stevens, who'd co-starred with Elvis. Once you've watched your partner kiss the King onscreen and then come home to kiss you, it changes things, redraws the boundaries of your reality. It deforms you and renders you vulnerable to boredom, makes you impatient with a life that is merely human-sized.

"Yeah." Her smile is wide and toothy, but her eyes narrow so tight her delight seems closer, somehow, to pain. "Let's do."

They collect their belongings—his jacket and briefcase, her sweater and purse—while the bartender mops down the bar with a rag and Sinatra sings "That Is All." In a moment, they will step out into a cold and clear December night. They will turn to one another with their breath drifting skyward and they will lean forward, and their story will begin in earnest. But for one last moment they are just colleagues, strangers who've collided in a bar and who might, still, part without consequence.

★ ★ ★

WHAT MAKES THEM this way? What makes them so perfectly ill-suited for each other, so doomed even before they begin? Two young people meet and fall in love, then decide overnight to start a life together. That's not just my parents' story, but rather that of generations. My father will rarely speak of their courtship. My

mother, too, will say little, even in the journals where she copi-
ously records other aspects of her life. But I know them. I know
that in the early days of 1964 their relationship moves quickly, not
just because they are mutually attracted but because each sees
in the other a symbolic value: my mother is a gentile, which crys-
talizes my father's conflict with Ruby, although his parents will
embrace her even before she converts; he is a liberal young Jew,
which represents a break for her, also, even if her mother isn't an
anti-Semite.

"Listen to this."

"What is it?"

They are in her living room in Santa Monica. Most nights
they are at his place on Orlando, but today, one of the early afternoons of spring with the windows flung open, they are at hers. He
sprawls on the couch while she crouches to sift through a stack of
LPs with worn Vanguard Records sleeves, hunting until she pulls
the one she wants.

"Just listen."

He likes the fact she can surprise him, that there are things—
music might be one—about which she knows more. He closes his
eyes against the sound of crackling vinyl. Aviator sunglasses on
the table, soft-pack cigarettes and keys, as he leans back blind
and inhales, hoping to taste everything he can of this moment:
notes of quinine, tobacco, sea air, lemon.

"What is it?"

He likes jazz and rock and roll—Ray Charles, Sam Cooke,
Jackie Wilson—and she likes . . . whatever this is exactly: a music
that is all treble, in which weedy voices fight over skeletal acoustic
guitar and banjo.

"Folk music," he says, opening his eyes to see the sleeve she is
holding: *The Weavers at Carnegie Hall.*

"Yeah."

"You like Bob Dylan?"

She shrugs. Dylan is fine, but he doesn't excite her the same way this does because it is so blunt: because it is plain-spoken and political, and because it came first, before Dylan.

"Listen."

They sit in silence as the Weavers sing "Pay Me My Money Down" and "Rock Island Line," and then she takes the record off and puts on another, Sonny Terry's *Folk Blues*.

"What do you like about it?" my father says.

"You don't like it?"

"I do," he says. "I asked what *you* like about it."

"My mother hates it," she says, after a long pause.

"Really?" He laughs, delighted by this blunt, primal reason. "That's why?"

It is. But my mother has not said much yet about Helen Mc-Gaffey. She loves these songs for their politics, which happen to stand in direct opposition to her mother's. But there is more to it than just politics.

"What's she like?" he says.

She winces as if she has just bitten down on a lemon. "If we're going to talk about my mother, I'm going to want another drink."

"So, fix another." My dad leans forward, strikes a match against the rough, wooden surface—ridged and gray like an elephant's hide—of the low coffee table. "I'll have one, too."

My mother disappears into the kitchen, then returns ninety seconds later with fresh glasses. When my father meets Helen, he will charm her without really trying and she will decide he's acceptable husband material, but he will understand, even beyond what my mother tells him now, the problem.

"She's a Bircher."

"What?" He takes the skinny glass, shifts to make room for her on the couch. "Really?"

"Yep. My brother and older sister, also. They all are. My whole family." She takes my father's filterless cigarette and tugs on it herself, then coughs. *Too strong*. "They're all gonna vote Goldwater."

"Jesus." He exhales. He is—the term is not quite an oxymoron yet—a liberal Republican, though he'd voted for Kennedy and won't pull the lever for another conservative candidate again until 1980, which will mark the last time he ever does. "That's bad."

She takes another, smaller drag off his cigarette and nods. "It is bad."

Mere voting patterns aren't the problem, however, nor even the fact that Helen is a cold, cold woman: a widow in her late fifties who seems at least twenty years older. Misery is carved into the folds of her sour, Calvinist face. When she'd married Mac McGaffey there was wealth from both his family and hers, an old money line in Shaker Heights, Ohio, but God knows where it all went. Since being widowed, Helen has worked selling yarn at Bullock's department store, and now as a secretary for a man named Jack Morehart, who owns Pacific Ocean Park, the amusement facility on the Santa Monica Pier, but it's not just politics but rather a deeper, revanchist bigotry that bothers my mother so.

"You'll meet her," she says, exhaling contemptuously—*hssss*—and stubbing their shared butt in the ashtray. My mother, the baby of the family, has a reputation among the McGaffeys for being spoiled, but if she's been spoiled by anything it isn't Helen's icy simulacrum of love. "Soon."

Indeed. But as they sit in this room on Chelsea Avenue, neither of them is in any hurry to get there, to leave this oasis of gin and tobacco and newness and sex. The future seems to them unlimited, like their lives will forever be this only more so, and they will always remain both modern and young. Mac McGaffey, "Papa Don" as the family called him, was a liberal, easygoing man with a penchant for practical jokes, but he's been dead now a dozen years. Helen has gone on to embrace Christian Science along with the country's radical right wing. THE JOHN BIRCH SOCIETY IS NOT A SECRET SOCIETY. ASK THE DRIVER OF THIS CAR, reads one bumper sticker on the back of her aging blue Plymouth; CUBA FREE IN '63! reads another. My mother's siblings have also gone around the bend with their fervent anti-communism, their Birch Society attachments—recently, her brother has moved his own family to Utah, the better to commune with other society members—which makes her love for songs about the Wobblies, about union strength and leftist politics, understandable. In the shadow of the Civil Rights Act, which will be enacted in just a few months, she is aware that she and Helen have different feelings about this as well, and it is this, the stark fact of my grandmother's racism, that troubles my mother the most. She is nothing like her family: she has fought to get as far from them as possible. Perhaps she will get far enough. When my father proposes, in just a few weeks, she won't hesitate for a second to say yes.

"Play it again," my father says as the Sonny Terry record ends, and then pushes off the couch to go flip it. "Play it, Sam."

Every love story is a tragedy, even a minor love like this one. The room slowly grows dark, shadows creeping across the carpeted floor as they sit drinking and talking, trading confidences and histories and stories about the past, sculpting themselves into whoever they want to be until the music stops. In every photograph I will ever see from these years they look so happy: two people with gentle faces who adore each other, my father with his bare arm wrapped tenderly around my mother's neck; she with her face turned and tilted up toward him like she is in the middle of saying something private, words of love that I will never, strain as I might, quite be able to hear.

★ ★ ★

IN THE SUMMER of '64, they are married. By the end of that year my mother is pregnant with a girl, just as she has always wanted, and so, for a moment, they are happy. They go to the movies just like everybody. If the twentieth century is the filmed century, they are right there at the heart of it. They gape at *Goldfinger* and at *A Hard Day's Night*, stare up at Elizabeth Taylor and Richard Burton. The big hits this year are *Mary Poppins*, *My Fair Lady*, and *The Carpetbaggers*; the stars are Rex Harrison, Richard Harris, Anne Bancroft, Natalie Wood. If there is something missing from these movies, and there is, my parents don't quite know what it is. Only—

"Ouch!"

"What is it?"

My mother shifts in her seat, doubling over in the dark. "Cramp, I think," she whispers through clenched teeth. "Cramp."

No cramp. When she gets up in a moment to dart out to the restroom, she will find she is spotting. When they arrive at the ER later that night—her bleeding hasn't stopped, and she is nauseous and dizzy—it is too late. Their baby is lost, early in her third trimester. She stays at the hospital, Saint John's, overnight, the ambulances shrieking down Santa Monica Boulevard below. It is the blood that startles her most. There is so much of it.

In November 1964, my father leaves Ashley Famous and goes to work for a company called Artists Agency Corporation. My mother returns from the hospital and, instead of maternity leave, takes a job working for a producer named Michael Garrison at CBS. In the spring of 1966, when she is pregnant again, she quits. My father is making enough money now to support them. He is what they call a "servicer" now, someone who handles the finer points of deals for the senior agents and their stars. All day he drives around to the studios and to casting offices to find out what parts are available, fetching this information back to his superiors. He closes deals for Peter Falk, James Garner, Alan Arkin, modest agreements for which he earns three- or low-four-figure commissions. He drives around in his little Austin-Healey, which he soon replaces with a Jaguar the silver-gray of gunmetal, carving his way onto the lots—Twentieth Century-Fox; MGM: these are the two he covers—only to spend most of the day being rejected. Occasionally he takes on a client of his own, a young actor he discovers or decides to hip-pocket—someone he sees in a play, or cold calls after he admires their cameo appearance on *Wagon Wheel* or *Trackdown*, one of the popular TV shows—but so far this has amounted to nothing.

"Fred Specktor."

He pulls up to the studio gate now at the Fox lot, gazing up at the security guard through his aviator shades.

"Who?" The guard squints at his clipboard. "I don't see you."

"Look again. There should be a drive-on."

"Nope."

"S-p-e-c-k-t-o-r," he says patiently. "Look again."

"I don't—Oh," the guard says. "There you are. They left out the K."

"Right."

My father waits for the white bar to lift. How tired he is of this, of being an unknown player, invisible to the naked eye. Unlike Lew Wasserman, he wants to be seen; at the very least, he would like to stop spelling his name out to strangers. But for now, here he is, another misprint, as nameless as the baby girl whose body lies in Westwood Village Memorial Cemetery, whose existence would almost certainly have precluded my own.

★ ★ ★

MY MOTHER SITS underneath a white umbrella at the Beverly Wilshire Hotel, by a swimming pool shaped like an amphora. Shopping bags at her feet from Saks and I. Magnin; keys to the house she and my father have recently purchased in Holmby Hills in her purse; wedding ring on her finger. The accouterments of adult life are piling up. In a few months, my mother will be pregnant again. Perhaps this is why she likes to come here to read and to drink iced tea, basking in the freedom and anonymity only a hotel seems to offer.

"Miss?"

When she was an actress, a casting agent had told her once that she looked like Amanda Blake, of *Gunsmoke*. At the time, it annoyed her—who wants to be compared to someone else?—but now she enjoys it, the sense she might be a card pulled from a limitless deck.

"Hey miss? Sweetheart?"

Not everyone enjoys this freedom. She looks up to see a man is speaking to her, a dark-haired fellow whose beauty is practically blinding, perched on the edge of one of the poolside chaises.

"Settle an argument for me," he says, grinning with the ineffable confidence of the genetically fortunate, a smile that opens every door.

"What is it?"

She recognizes him immediately. It is Warren Beatty, the actor. She gazes at him over her book, which rests flat on the glass table in front of her.

"My friend here"—he gestures to a fellow perched on the edge of the chaise next to his, an older, owlish-looking man in tortoise-shell glasses—"says you're in casting, which is why you have that big book. I say you're an actress. Which is it?"

She smiles back.

"Neither I'm afraid."

"Neither? Sweetheart, why is that?"

She likes Beatty as an actor—liked him in *Splendor in the Grass*, is aware of him now as someone who has thus far failed to live up to that picture's promise, having since starred in a string of duds—but finds him oddly unthreatening, handsome but not attractive.

"Well, why not? Honey, you're—"

She bursts out laughing. She holds up a hand, the one with

her wedding band. Beatty looks down at the ground for a second, pantomiming shyness, then looks back at her, still smiling.

"Now come on, pussycat, I don't mean anything here. I just wondered if you'd like to sit and have some iced tea with us."

She laughs again. The man sitting next to him has the sun-kissed look of a Miami retiree: nut-colored, white-haired, with a little pot belly and a cigar between his fingers. Only a certain air of industriousness, a pile of scripts by the chaise, tells my mother he's not a vacationer.

"Sorry, Charlie." She turns her attention down to her book. "I've got everything I need right here."

When she tells me this story years later, it will be just a blip. Sitting in the dark at the Mann's National Theater in Westwood, waiting on a showing of *Reds*, she will say, "I met him once, not long before you were born." But just now it is something else: evidence of the porous world she and my dad together have entered, its weird commingling of reality and dream.

"Warren, c'mon," the older man says, as she looks back down at her book now; as the man's cigar smoke distracts her just enough to hold her out of it a moment, so she catches a scrap of what he says next. "I think George Stevens is a great idea for this script if you'd like to try him . . ."

She sinks into her novel. It is the Random House hardcover edition of *Ulysses*, the one with the green jacket and the author's initials embossed in black on the cover. All her life she will remain attached to this book, the same copy she bought in college, with her undergraduate notes scratched in pencil in the margins, which she will read over and over. In her dreams, she is a writer, and if it will be a while yet before this aspiration reaches its brief fruition, she is there in her mind already as she sits with her head bent, eyes drilling down into the page behind amber-tinted sunglasses. The chapter she is reading now is the one in which the Citizen accosts Bloom in a pub, abusing him with anti-Semitic remarks. When I am first learning to read, a few years from now, she will buy me *D'Aulaires' Book of Greek Myths*. She will read to me the story of Polyphemus, the Cyclops, with which this chapter of *Ulysses* is associated; of how Oedipus tricks him by claiming his name is "Nobody," the better to escape from his capture. Just now a warm wind picks up ("Nobody! I'm Nobody!"), and the canvas awnings above the hotel patio stiffen, the umbrella above her head snaps. A series of little waves, as delicate as the goosebumps that lift upon her skin as she reads, go rippling across the surface of the pool. And she disappears into her dream, becoming nobody, too.

★ ★ ★

THE TWO MEN keep talking. The older one is an agent, my mother had noticed—she'd recognized the argot, and the manner—and so even as she reads she cannot help but eavesdrop, feeling their conversation crowd the margins of her awareness.

"You think I should do it?" Beatty says.

"Warren, we've been through this. It's a good script."

"Good, sure. But should I do it?"

The actor's dilemma. The agent's, also: when to push, and when to lean back. My mother doesn't know the agent's name, Abe Lastfogel, or that in a few years he will become my father's boss. But she has stumbled across one of those hinges of Hollywood history that will come to change everything. The actor is coming off a recent flop, an arty experimental semi-noir called *Mickey One*, and will soon head off to London to shoot *Kaleidoscope*, a frothy spy comedy in which he feels no great confidence. He knows it's fake James Bond.

"You really think it's good?" He nods at the script in the agent's lap, lowering himself down on the chaise and looking at the older man like an anxious bird. "Do you?"

Should he or shouldn't he? You'd think it wouldn't matter much what an actor chooses to do, and that this story, my parents' story, wouldn't depend much upon what this actor, in particular, chooses. But you'd be wrong.

"Yes, Warren, I do." Lastfogel peers through the cirrus of his cigar smoke, looking at the actor with a patient smile. No cold fish Lew Wasserman, he. His manner is warm and avuncular. "Uncle Abe," they call him in the halls of the William Morris Agency, where he works. "Same thing I thought when I read it six months ago."

The project they are discussing, the script in the agent's lap, is one that will unlock doors for both my parents, that will make their future careers possible. Oddly, it strikes Abe Lastfogel, who's been doing his job since Lew Wasserman was in diapers—1913 was the year he went to work as an office boy for William Morris in New York—as almost old-fashioned. Almost. He was around for all those Jimmy Cagney shoot-'em-ups, for Edward G. Robinson dying in a hail of bullets on the street, and this picture, like those, is a gangster story. Truthfully, he isn't wild about the script, which has a modish, *up yours* attitude, a frankness about sexuality (does Beatty really want to play a homosexual, as the lead is currently written?), and a graphic violence that is practically obscene, with gouts of blood seeming to spout across every other page, but he can sense its potential. Right now he doesn't see how this picture could ever get made—it is just too violent—but he is an adaptable man. Like every agent, and every artist, he is a bit of a chameleon, and so decides to give his famously indecisive client the gentlest possible nudge.

"Look, let's see if we can put a director on it, someone who won't scare people. I don't think Jack Warner's gonna want anything to do with your Frenchman."

"It doesn't have to be him."

"Then we need to find someone else. Someone Jack's comfortable with."

"Jack hates me."

"Warren, that's in your head."

A tennis ball thwacks in the distance, its metronomic to-and-fro keeping irregular time. My mother shifts, her cheek resting against her palm. This book she is reading, it, too, was considered obscene, once, and so this is her dream now, her future that's being decided in this conversation taking place not fifteen feet away; in the murmurings and chatter of the guests and swimmers; in the little ripples that cross the pool like precursors to a much larger wave, her future is being written.

★ ★ ★

A MOVIE IS like a message in a bottle. It takes years sometimes to make shore. On a spring afternoon in 1963, two young men are having a conversation, the same one that happens thousands upon thousands of times each day all across America.

"What should we see?"

"Well, what's playing?"

One stands and one hunkers, scowling down at the newspaper folded open in his hands. Together they are crowded into their shared office at 448 Madison Avenue in Manhattan.

"Crap," the one who is sitting, whose name is David Newman, mutters into his paper. "A whole lot of nothing."

"And that's news how?"

These two are civilians, not movie people. They are the audience men like my father, and like Lew Wasserman, hope for the movies to reach. And like a lot of young people in 1963, particularly on the coasts, they find much of what's in theaters these days to be lacking.

"It ain't news," Newman says. He is short, sardonic, and brooding. With an unlit cigarette dangling from his lip, in a black turtleneck and black boots, he looks a bit like Lenny Bruce. "*Son of Flubber*? I'd rather blow my brains out than see this shit."

He tosses the paper aside in disgust. The other man stoops to pick it up. Tall, sandy-haired, and quiet, Robert Benton is an art director at *Esquire* magazine. He is so silent sometimes people wonder if something might be wrong with him, until he lets loose with the kind of quick, cutting insight that can shut everyone else up in a hurry.

"That bad? It can't be that bad." His voice carries a trace of Texas twang. "Let's see."

One day, Benton's and my father's paths will cross—my father will cast his clients in Benton's future movies more than once—but for now he and Newman, a writer, work together. They are what will be referred to in the future as "creatives," media people, hipsters who, like young folks since time immemorial, seem to have a quick answer for everything. Everything—except this.

"*Ufff,*" Benton says, staring at the paper. "This *is* shit."

"Told ya."

They're not so young: Newman is twenty-six and Benton thirty-one, a year older than my father. Still, these two might look at my parents as squares, and are, for whatever reason, one step ahead in their embrace of the new. Perhaps this is because they are artists instead of suits. My dad may like to blow a little reefer on weekends, my mom may soon snag a copy of the Byrds' first LP, but they are on opposite sides of the desk, and these two are leaning into the present a little harder.

"*It Happened at the World's Fair. Papa's Delicate Condition.*" Benton throws the newspaper back onto the desk in disgust. "I'll show you Papa's Delicate Condition."

"Told ya. No research for us today. It's all work and no play."

"Shut up," Benton says. "I'm taking a walk. I gotta get out of here."

"Suit yourself. If any of those movies makes you slit your wrists, I'm not responsible."

Their office is crammed with detritus—a pair of wind-up chattering teeth; a copy of Robert Lowell's *Life Studies*; photos of their shared icons like Audrey Hepburn, Sonny Liston, a character actor named Timothy Carey—that represents their common humor and private vocabulary, a language they have evolved in the service of an article they are writing called "The New Sentimentality," which they hope will serve as a clarion call. Or not. In their general abreaction to earnest sincerity, these two more resemble members of my own generation, Generation X, but all the same. They have an ethos, an aesthetic they are developing. How they will deploy it is an open question.

"I'll report back," Benton says. Then he strides off down the hall, turning left at reception, heading for the elevator and the street.

* * *

THE NEW SENTIMENTALITY. It's just what it sounds like. When they publish the article in July of 1964, "The New Sentimentality" will prove to be one of those documents—part manifesto, part inside joke, and part acute cultural observation—that kicks up once or twice in every generation whenever some hipster decides to pick up their pen and codify what they see. For Benton and Newman, the "Old Sentimentality" means Eisenhower, Gene Kelly, John Wayne, and Frank Sinatra. It means the America they see as dying. The New Sentimentality means Antonioni, the Beatles, Alfred Hitchcock, Lenny Bruce. It means what is fresh, and cosmopolitan. It means a world that is just now being born.

"New Sentimentality . . . has to do with you, really just you, not what you were told or taught, but what goes on in your head, *really*, and in your heart, *really*," he and Newman will write in their article, and this is it exactly. Benton is looking for something that will express what it feels like to be alive. John Wayne doesn't. The movies he just pooh-poohed in the paper don't either. When he was a young boy in Waxahachie, Texas, cinema was a refuge. He'd sat in a theater and watched *A Place in the Sun* and *Singing in the Rain* over and over until he'd all but memorized them. Images have always felt more accessible to him than words because he is dyslexic, and so he finds in the privacy of the movies a respite from his own shyness. He and Newman go often. They play hooky from work, taking excursions they call "research." He'd come to Manhattan for the same reason he goes to the pictures: to get lost. To feel himself as one person among the millions, to the point where he can be anyone at all.

You can be anyone at all. Isn't this why we all love the movies? You can be anyone (well, maybe not anyone: as he cuts up Fifty-Ninth and then up Broadway, Benton observes that more and more of the faces around him are brown and Black, and—being a person of some sensitivity, whose articles have appeared cheek by jowl with, say, James Baldwin's—he knows that these faces are largely, still, excluded from the movies. When Hollywood does make pictures about race, like *Paris Blues* and *A Raisin in the Sun*, it does so in ways that are decidedly Old Sentimental), and you can be no one: Cleopatra and Tom Jones; General George Custer and an American psychiatrist; a socialite played by Tippi Hedren and a sociopath played by Tony Perkins; you can be the darkness and you can be the light; you can be the dreamer, as well as the dream.

He walks uptown, lost in thought as he moves up Broadway, past its luncheonettes and cigar shops, bookstores and bars. The boy from Waxahachie likes this place because it is democratic and, daydreamer that he is, he can feel himself vanish inside its flow of traffic. The movies are like this, also: you come alive in the dark, are free to be yourself—your whole self—as you are liberated from the mediocre constrictions of being an ordinary body in space. The city hums around him—engines, radios, car doors clanking and slamming, arguments, umbrellas opening and closing against a rain that keeps threatening—and he perceives both none of it and all of it: the external weaving itself into his being.

He crosses Eightieth Street, his pulse quickening as he spots the marquee a few blocks ahead, a boxy black sign with black lettering that reads THE NEW YORKER. This city may be full of theaters—he loves the Lyric, the Thalia—but he returns to this one more than any other because it shows European and Japanese movies, films that are the only cure for the garbage that seems to be eating Hollywood alive. He's already seen the one that is playing there now almost a dozen times, but he doesn't care. He is going to submit to it again. He pays for his ticket and then crosses the lobby, passing under a banner that depicts yesterday's stars— Peter Lorre, Greta Garbo, Katharine Hepburn—before hurling himself into the silvery light of the Lethe.

Jules et Jim will screen so many times in so many theaters the world over—in the decades ahead its life will remain ongoing, eternal—it is tempting to take it for granted, but let's imagine, for a moment, that it is still new in the world: that we have stepped inside the theater with Benton to encounter it as something contemporary, as fresh as a cold Sancerre. It is black-and-white, the way so many American movies were until recently, when certain technological processes—Eastmancolor, Panavision, CinemaScope—began to make color both cheaper and more attractive. The screen shows a planetary silver, as pale as the moon, shot through with the oblique shadows of a Paris street. You can smell the beach when the characters visit, and when Jeanne Moreau arrives, caught between the bruised smile of Oskar Werner (Jules) and brooding eyes of Henri Serre (Jim), she is fluid and incorruptible, slipping through their grasp like light sparkling in a jar.

Benton comes in in the middle. What does it matter, since he'll stay when the showing ends and stick around for the next one anyway, as the movie is for him inexhaustible, a story that, like all great stories, never ends but just goes on, forever refreshed because there's always something you've missed. A plot like that of a nineteenth-century novel—as *Jules et Jim* indeed is adapted from a novel, by Henri-Pierre Roché—with the tragic violence of *Madame Bovary* or *Anna Karenina*, only modern, so modern, which is why it cuts Benton so deep. It is set in the past, in the shadow of World War I, but it is emotionally contemporary, so ringingly of the hour in its view of men and women and of their conflicting longings, their self-betrayals, their wish to be both captive and free. Even his most recent ex-girlfriend, a woman named Gloria Steinem who'd recently written a piece for *Esquire* about the pill, had loved it when he'd taken her to see it, because Moreau's character is so unfettered, and because these people—the women in the film especially—are so frank and so real, completely unlike those in American movies. Compared to this, Rock Hudson and Doris Day may as well not even have genitals when they appear onscreen, all dolled-up in their Pepsi Cola colors. *Jules et Jim* isn't explicit, but it is emotionally honest in a way Benton finds shattering. American movies (not all of them: he likes Hitchcock, for example) are bullshit next to this. And because he knows he is not alone—because he also loves *The 400 Blows* and *Shoot the Piano Player*, Vittorio De Sica's *Shoeshine*, and Antonioni's *L'Eclisse*, Godard's *Breathless*, and Kurosawa's *Stray Dog*—he understands he is being offered a set of conditions, a grammar and a feeling that, he realizes, he can use. By the time the afternoon is finished, he will know just what to do. Benton and Newman want to polish off the Old Sentimentality? The two of them are going to need to do it themselves.

★ ★ ★

WHEN MY MOTHER sits down to write her first screenplay, almost two decades later, she will model portions of it upon the story of *Bonnie and Clyde*. Her script will be based on a news item about a pair of young hitchhikers, a Florida carjacking gone wrong, and she will borrow some of her original opening's mood from the 1967 film about the two legendary American bank robbers. Benton and Newman don't really know what they're doing, but they base their own script on a book, John Tolland's *Dillinger*

Days, and on the tales Benton had heard growing up in Waxahachie, where Clyde Barrow and Bonnie Parker were locals. They
write quickly, the two of them getting together at night to drink
beer and play bluegrass music while they huddle over a single
typewriter, the story pouring out of them even though—in fact,
because—they don't even know what a screenplay should look like.
They bang out seventy pages, then give them to a friend, a theater producer named Elinor Jones, who is the only person they
know who has any connection with the movies, and who somehow manages to get the pages to Benton's hero, François Truffaut.
Astonishingly, he agrees to do the film, only to change his mind
and hand the project over to his friend Jean-Luc Godard, another
hero. But as Godard is trying to extract Benton and Newman's
message from its bottle—his vision of the film is so different it
may as well be another movie altogether—the screenplay lands
in the hands of Warren Beatty. Some say it is Truffaut who gives
it to the actor just to get rid of him, as when Beatty flies to Paris
to pitch himself for the director's adaptation of *Fahrenheit 451*,
the two don't exactly hit it off. Others will later insist Beatty first
sees the script when it passes through the hands of an executive
on the set of *Mickey One* several months earlier. Either way, the
actor loves it. He loves it not because it is conventional, another
hagiographic retelling of ancient gangster mythology—one more
American myth that is already an American cliché—but because
it is something much more exciting. Because it is fraught with
modern sexuality—in one draft, Clyde is bisexual; in another, he
has a threesome with Bonnie and their getaway driver; in the
final, he will be impotent, a detail that appeals to an actor who
is sick of playing to his image as a Lothario—and because it is
voluptuously violent in a way that feels new. This is not a picture
in which people trade rat-a-tats with cap pistols and gasp out
their final words on dry ground: it is a slaughterhouse in which a

volley of machine guns is emptied into multiple bodies, in which skulls are blown open and blood runs across the screen in dense puddles. But this, of course, also represents a problem. American cinema is governed by the Hays Code, which limits what you can depict onscreen, prohibiting adult language, sexuality, and violence. So what exactly is the actor proposing to do here? What good is a forward-thinking movie if no one will allow you to make it?

But then again, what good is a Hollywood that doesn't reflect the will of its artists? On the other side of the country, my mother remains trapped inside the restrictiveness of her upbringing. It's not that she's prim—she's just as full of obscene dreams as anybody else, and when she reads *Ulysses*, the bawdy parts are the ones she loves best—but she grew up in a world in which women didn't swear, and so she blurts out things like "shoot!" or "fooping around" when she gets upset, sanitized substitutions for the things she really means. (You can't say "fuck" or "shit" in the movies either.) As she moves through Los Angeles in the spring of 1966, growing ever more pregnant by the hour, she doesn't necessarily yearn for a less restrictive world, but she's going to need one. In order to become an artist, she's going to need those conditions that will allow her to be free.

So, too, will my father. As he travels from office to studio lot, studio lot to screening room, he knows what he needs are clients of his own, clients whose mood is equally modern. He can't just walk around sweeping up the old guard's leavings forever, closing deals for people he doesn't even represent. He's going to need to find younger people, talent with a style that will guide him into the future. One day, he sits down at a screening—he is not at a first-run theater but at a repertory house, a place that shows mostly European and art cinema—when a man in the next row looks back over his shoulder and spots him.

"Heya, Freddy! Where you been hiding?"

"Oh—hi!" My father says, nearly spilling his popcorn as he settles into his narrow seat. "How ya been?"

The man is an actor. In fact—it takes my father a split second to recognize him, as he's grown his hair, and his sideburns are a little shaggy—he's someone my father represented briefly only a few years ago, back in 1962. In his striped T-shirt, reeking faintly of marijuana, he looks like one of the Beach Boys gone bad.

"Can't complain." The actor flashes a wide, lupine smile—a smile that, in fact, had been a bit of a problem when my father had sent him on calls, as it marked his look as unconventional—and arches his eyebrows. "You still at Kumin-Olenick?"

"Nah. I'm at AAC these days. You?"

The relationship didn't last. One day, after he'd taken the actor to see a casting director, the latter had tugged my father out into the hallway to scold him.

"I'm at Bob Raison now."

"Ah, good, good. Raison will take good care of you."

("Freddy, you can't do this to me." The casting agent had slung his arm around my father's shoulder. "It's not that the guy's not talented, but there are no parts for people like him. He's not employable." It was the kind of rejection that stung for weeks, because the casting agent was questioning not just his client's future—wrong, my father knew: the parts would eventually shape themselves to the actor instead of vice versa—but my father's acumen.)

"It's great to see you, Freddy."

"You, too."

Maybe there are still no parts for actors like this, or the ones that exist—Roger Corman movies, biker films from American International Pictures (AIP), and cheapo westerns—are too marginal to dine out on, but my father believes in this man's talent. He's got a volatile, almost malevolent quality, but so did Montgomery Clift. He'd be as vital to this moment as Marlon Brando was to the fifties, if only someone would give him a real job. They'd met in an acting class on Cheremoya Avenue, which my father had attended for the same reason he comes to theaters like this one: not because he is an actor or a cineaste—he likes these European pictures, but not the way Robert Benton and my mother both do, with a devotion born of being artists themselves—but because he needs to go where talent collects if he hopes to find and represent it. If my father's early career has a marker it is this man, the actor who, in a few years, the rest of the world will come to recognize as a generational star.

"Who was that?" My mother returns from the bathroom and slides in next to him. She's showing now, her pregnancy visible even as the theater lights dim and she settles into her seat, then offers my father a sip of her Coke.

"Nobody," he whispers, as the projector starts to whirr and *Un Homme et une Femme* blazes up on the screen, bathing the room in silver. Nicholson is the man's name, Jack Nicholson. "Just somebody I used to represent."

★ ★ ★

WHO'S GOING TO guide my parents through the gates, open the door to where they both need to go? Who's going to ensure that there are parts for the actors my father will in time represent, that they aren't just oddballs and misfits relegated to the fringes of Hollywood? ("I dunno," the casting director had said to my father. "He's just so . . . intense.") It turns out it is Warren Beatty, who crawls across a mustard-colored carpet in July 1966, just a few months before I am born.

"Colonel—

"Get the fuck up, Warren."

My parents are not the drivers of change, they are merely its beneficiaries. But neither their careers in Hollywood nor my own will be possible—my mother will never write a thing; my father

might end up selling cars in Encino; I will grow up having nothing to do with the movies myself—if the business does not come to
align, at least a little, with their tastes.

"Listen to me, Colonel, I need you to listen! This movie is everything!"

"Get the fuck up."

It's the same old battle, between the dying and the new. Jack
Warner isn't actually dying, he's just getting ready to retire, hanging on to his studio by his fingernails as he stares down at Beatty
with disgust. The actor has come into his office with two writers
to pitch a movie and instead wound up literally on his knees. He's
trying to kiss Warner's loafers. Anything to get the old man to
give in.

"Not until you say yes."

Jack Warner has seen a lot in his time, from fascists to com-
munists and everything in-between. He's an old right-winger,
sure, but he's also a man who led Hollywood to oppose the Nazis
to begin with—who fought against the Hays Code's explicit ban
on anti-Nazi content in the thirties—which is why, for one moment, I want to take his side, to imagine his incomprehension as
he stands in his Savile Row pinstripes, shrinking back from the
kneeling actor like he's afraid he'll receive an electrical shock.

"What are you selling here?" he snaps. Beatty's modish, open-
necked shirt and shaggy hair make him uncomfortable, also.
"Why is this picture so important to you?"

People have been coming in here to kiss his ass since time immemorial. To run a studio is to hold the world in your hands, after
all. But Beatty's gesture feels like parody to him, like all of a sudden he's the one being mocked. Then again, the world itself seems
to mock him these days. Outside the window of his office those
corridors of the lot that used to bustle with activity, with gaffers
and grips and cameramen, and with the stars who had belonged
to him, are all oddly silent. The beige water tower with his stu-

dio's initials on it seems to mock him, too, jutting uselessly into a cloud-free sky. The studio, his life's work, is about to pass from his hands.

"It's a gangster movie, Jack." The truth is, Beatty isn't mocking him at all. He's a student of film history, one who's gone out of his way to work with directors like Elia Kazan and George Stevens. He reveres the Old Hollywood Warner represents. "You used to make those better than anybody."

"Used to."

Indeed. Jack Warner may be a dinosaur, but he's also a businessman, a pragmatist. It turns out he has one more meaningful gesture left in him.

"Why would I make one now?" he snaps. (A businessman, a pragmatist, and a failed artist. Before he and his brothers left Youngstown, Ohio, to launch their first film distribution company, he was a vaudeville performer, a song and dance man.) "This kind of picture went out with the tango."

Beatty struggles to his feet. Benton and Newman are watching from the couch, agog, but it's Warner's show, his and Beatty's.

"Because it's not the same movie, Jack! It's an homage! It's—"

Fuck it. Warner waves him off. *OK.* Anything to shut Beatty up. The truth is, his heart's not in it. He built this studio, cutting his own brothers' throats to do it, but he's on his way out. Let these weirdos do what they want, so long as they can do it for a price.

"One point five?" he says.

"One point six," Beatty counters. "And you know Arthur and I"—he means Arthur Penn, *Bonnie and Clyde*'s director—"will bring it in on budget."

Warner sighs. An actor producing his own projects. He doesn't like that either. Things were better when he had total control. In this case, he hasn't even read the script, but what's one more story in a career that numbers them by now in the hundreds, if not the thousands?

"Go ahead," he says. Staring out at the water tower pointing up into the Burbank sky like an alien silo, the initials on its side his final tiny hedge against oblivion. "Go make your movie."

★ ★ ★

WHO OWNS THIS place? Who owns the movies now that Jack Warner, like Sam Cohn and Louis B. Mayer and David O. Selznick, all the old moguls who built this industry to begin with, is going if not already gone? Lew Wasserman still runs MCA Universal, and Darryl Zanuck is on top again at Twentieth Century-Fox, following his years of exile—he'll be out for good in a few years—but everyone else is dead or in a rest home. Which is no tragedy, as they were mostly bullies, abusers of power, as almost anyone who ever gains power will turn out to be. But as Warner stands by the window of his office, he cannot help but feel regret all the same.

He, too, is not given to introspection. Almost no one who works on his side of the desk in this industry is. But he is about to sell his kingdom, this studio he built with his brothers Harry, Albert, and Sam—to a company called Seven Arts, who will then spin it off to Kinney National, a parking lot consortium out of New Jersey. The movies, which are in his blood, the blood of a performer, belong to someone else now. They belong to American conglomerates.

Maybe it makes no difference. Maybe a studio was always just a corral, a place where artists could be domesticated and their unruly spirits broken, so it makes no difference at all who owns it. Maybe, as Beatty goes off with his skeleton crew to shoot a movie he has meticulously engineered to remain under his own supervision, an arrangement that would've been unthinkable in Warner's heyday, it belongs now to the artists themselves, without whom Jack Warner would be nothing. But he doesn't believe this. The money comes first. Always, the money comes first.

He stands by the window and lights his cigar, staring out at the pale bricks of the bungalow rooftops, the vacant soundstages with their butter-colored walls, the very absence of everything that used to be his. There's no need to be sentimental about him, this aging potentate with his bald crown and tiny-toothed smile. He's about to pocket $32 million. What difference does it make who owns a studio?

Still. History uses all of us in ways we don't expect. He's no champion of the future—when Beatty delivers his film, Warner will hate it; he will not understand why the actor has created such a bloody and boring mess and he will bury the movie, booking it only in limited release—but he does have one key battle left in him. The administrators of the Hays Code are giving him grief because *Who's Afraid of Virginia Woolf?*, a Mike Nichols picture that's already in the can, contains language—"Screw!" "Monkey nipples!"—you wouldn't think would upset anyone older than a kindergartener. Rather than cut it to conform to the Code, he's going to release the picture with a label denoting it is For Adults Only. As it happens, Warner is not alone, because over at MGM they're fighting to release Antonioni's *Blow Up*, which contains full frontal nudity, but *Bonnie and Clyde's* release will be a mighty blow to the crumbling wall that stands between the movies and the future. When this wall falls, it won't be Warner who kicks it down for good—a bare few months from now, Jack Valenti, a man Lew Wasserman has finagled away from President Johnson's cabinet and helped to install as head of the Motion Picture Association, will dismantle the Code and replace it with a ratings system—and it won't be for the sake of freedom of expression. It will be for money, for his aging showman's instincts that tell him, at least this far, exactly what an audience wants.

He is almost gone. Standing in front of his window, painted by late-afternoon sun, he is like an insect batting against the transparent barriers of empire, his reflection encased in glass as in celluloid, his dream of immortality vanishing, written, as we all are, in water.

★ ★ ★

"LET'S GO TO the movies!"

"What, now?"

"Yes, now." My mother folds the paper open, scans the Family section of the *Los Angeles Times*. "The Shapiros canceled. We have a sitter. Let's go!"

Ah, my parents. They are like all young mothers and fathers now, harried and tired and, yes, happy together, hovering over a newspaper for a moment in their living room, flitting like hummingbirds in the day's late light.

"*Bonnie and Clyde*," my dad says, reaching already for his jacket because, of course, they have so very little time. "Let's see that!"

"You think?"

"Yeah, yeah," he says. "Supposed to be great. I should see it for work."

October 1967. Is it supposed to be great? The reviews upon the picture's release a month and a half ago were mixed. *Newsweek* calls it "squalid." The *New York Times* says "cheap . . . sleazy . . . moronic." Still, these are just opinions—*Newsweek* had also published a counterpoint a few weeks later—and there is a certain buzz around the movie, so off they go.

One more snapshot of my parents in their innocence, one last evening before I join them onstage. They see the movie at the Vogue Theater at Hollywood and Las Palmas, next door to Musso and Frank. Its marquee juts out, glows yellow over the worn gray marble of the pavement below.

"Hurry up!" My mother's heels clack along Hollywood Boulevard, ringing against the ceramic tile stars. "We'll be late."

By now, I have arrived. "The Fred Spectors [sic] expect the stork in December," read an item in the *Hollywood Reporter* on July 5, 1966, and then, on December 23 in *Daily Variety*, "A boy for Mr. and Mrs. Fred Specktor. Father is talent agent, mother nonpro." Now that they are finally spelling his name correctly, my father is most of the time exhausted. As he settles into his seat, feeling drowsy on the heels of his evening gin and tonic, he wonders if they shouldn't have stayed home.

But their lives are about to change. The lights go down (can my father imagine that one of this movie's stars is a part of his future fortune, that Gene Hackman will be the first real marquee player he ever signs?), and the screen lights up with black-and-white images, photographs punctuated by the click of a camera shutter. There is austere silence behind the credits before Rudy Vallee's voice fades up singing "Deep Night."

"Huh," my father whispers. Already it is different than he expected. But what had he expected?

My parents are attending this movie as minor minions, lowly foot soldiers in a business that belongs, still, to their elders. But in a few weeks Pauline Kael will proclaim the film's greatness in the *New Yorker*, calling a film old fuddy-duds like the *Times*'s Bosley Crowther had dismissed "the most exciting American movie since *The Manchurian Candidate*." By the end of the year, Beatty, and Faye Dunaway, who plays Bonnie Parker, will be on the cover of *Time* magazine, with an article announcing the arrival of a new American cinema, a "New Hollywood," of which my parents will prove to be very much a part. But this season there is also *Point Blank*, and *Cool Hand Luke*; there is *Reflections in a Golden Eye* and *The Producers*, *Bedazzled*, and *The Graduate*. All of a sudden it's not 1963 anymore, and the movies, that great repository of the American self-image, have begun to depict people who look and feel more like my parents.

"Longing is what makes history on a large scale," Don DeLillo will write, three decades later, in a passage that will haunt me when I am embarked upon my own voyage through the industry as an adult. So what is it my parents long for, sitting here in the dark? For my father, I suppose, it is simple: he yearns for material success, the same thing American men have aspired to for decades. For my mother, it is a little more complicated. She longs for self-expression, longs to find a way, outside of marriage and motherhood, to become and articulate who she really is.

"Hey, booooy?" Faye Dunaway fills the screen now, gazing from her bedroom window at Beatty down on the street. "What you doin' with my mama's car?"

My mother is no Faye Dunaway—her own dream of stardom died a long time ago, before it had time to blossom—but she cannot help but notice that this movie, on its face the story of two famous bank robbers, is really about a wish for fame. Bonnie Parker and Clyde Barrow are not famous yet, they are losers, a waitress and a yokel about to go on a spree. But this telling of their story is really about their own self-mythologizing. About their desire, which is stronger even than death, to one day be famous, so their names might live on.

Two hours pass: two hours of wind and violence and poetry and light. Then they sit in the stunned silence that follows the film's final volley of bullets, the fifty-eight seconds of film that had taken four days and sixty camera angles to get right.

"Did you like it?"

At last my father speaks, but my mother just shivers. A movie about the movies, about the abiding power of fame itself. But she's not ready to talk yet, to parcel out her feelings about this film, which will remain one of her favorites forever. They walk out onto the street, her ears still ringing with the thunder of automatic weapons, her thoughts painted with the sight of Beatty and Dunaway spasming like puppets, of their cadavers ripped with holes,

Beatty's eye blown out and Dunaway leaking blood. They walk up Las Palmas to where my father's current car, a gold Cadillac convertible sedan, sits alone at the curb.

"Pretty good," my father says as they climb inside. He is thinking of Hackman, his performance as Clyde's brother Buck, which has its own kind of electricity onscreen. "Pretty, pretty good."

My mother turns on the radio, tuning it until she stops on Buffy St. Marie's "The Circle Game." She loves this song and will play it over and over throughout my childhood in various versions—Joni Mitchell's, Tom Rush's, Ian and Sylvia's—because it speaks to her, with its words about the turning seasons and the carousel of time, the repetitions of experience.

"I loved it," she says finally, after a silence long enough my father almost wonders if she has fallen asleep. "I absolutely loved it."

Indeed. But he will never know what she is thinking, what she must force herself immediately to forget: that the two of them are wrong for each other, that their marriage will end like so many others, like that of almost everyone else they know, in tears.

She knows, and she does not know. This is just something that churns below the surface of her thoughts, reflecting itself in restlessness and agitation, in the slight peevishness with which she lights one more cigarette as they ride home in silence. They climb the steps of the front walk on Warnall and my father walks ahead to pay the sitter and to look in on me while she goes upstairs alone.

"How's the little shaver?" she asks when he returns, referring to me by a nickname coined from the plastic shaving set that is one of my favorite toys. She is in the bathroom brushing her teeth.

"The little shaver is sleeping," he says. "As the good Lord intended."

Outside, the streetlamps spray the asphalt white. The massive mulberry tree that grows in the front yard crowds the bathroom window. My mother stares through its branches for a moment, hunting for the moon. The movies are a circle game, also. They will repeat themselves over and over, and only rarely, like right now, will they strike her as truly new. She hangs over the sink and spits, then straightens. She remains full of *Bonnie and Clyde's* strangeness and violence, but has gone too far down the path of her life to change course now. She looks up to see herself in the mirror and realizes she is foaming, rabid, white saliva frothing out of her mouth like an animal's.

3. PLAYERS

1969–1973

"FREDDY!"

My father hoists me off the ground, throwing me over his shoulder like a sack of potatoes. We're in line at the counter at Hugo's Delicatessen. It is New Year's Eve 1969, a week after my third birthday, and we are running errands, picking up champagne and prosciutto, when the man behind us taps his arm.

"Hey Freddy, whatcha got there? Looks like you bought a new bag since I saw you last."

This memory, among my earliest, exists in vivid, revolving flashes like a magic lantern's. Dangling over my dad's shoulder, I peer up at a man whose face is wide and sinister, whose bright grin is bracketed by long sideburns.

"Jack!" My father turns. "If it isn't the man of the hour!"

"Is that all it's been? Jeez, I thought Cannes was a few months ago, but I'll tell ya, it's hard to keep track."

Later, years later, I will piece all this together. Right now, I am absorbed in looking at the man's face. He glances at me—smile widening, brows arching over his aviator glasses—then back at my father.

"The picture is fantastic," my dad is saying. "Dennis should be very proud."

"Oh yeah? Freddy, that means a lot coming from you."

When I am older I will know that this is the man my father represented only briefly, the actor for whom he'd been told there were no parts, but for now Jack Nicholson is just a werewolf in a polo shirt and canvas shoes.

"You still at AAC, Freddy?"

"Not for a while now," my father says. "I'm over at William Morris these days."

Childhood memory is like a funhouse mirror, warped and unreliable. But I remember this room with its mud-colored floor and its low-hanging brass fixtures, its potted plants and loitering adults, a woman in a macramé hat clinging to Nicholson's elbow, and a long line of people behind us, winding around the dining area and out to the street.

"Great to see you, Freddy. Happy New Year."

Unreliable, but vivid, as my father carries me out to the parking lot, his bags laden with provisions, with booze and melon and meats.

"Pop?"

"What?" My father sets me on the ground, hoists the bags into his Cadillac's trunk. "What is it, sport?"

"Was that man Lon Chaney?"

He laughs. "How do you even know who Lon Cheney is?"

How, indeed? Like so much of childhood, it is mysterious. But the movies are imprinted within me. Their detritus—the posters; the glow-in-the-dark, snap-together models of Universal Studios monsters; a Mickey Mouse wristwatch—decorates my room. My father slides me into the car, cranks the ignition, and lowers the top.

"You wanna listen to the Beatles?" He squints at me through smoke-gray lenses. He's gained a little weight, grown a mustache. In his Canadian tuxedo, he looks like a Jewish cowboy, like a cross between Sonny Bono and Tevye the Dairyman. "Let's see if we can find some Beatles."

He is a gentle parent, more tender than his own had been with him. He is my favorite person, at least until those years arrive when he will be, for a while, my enemy.

"Let's go home, sport." (Sometimes "squirt," other times "little shaver.") "Your mother's making a rack of lamb."

He aims his Cadillac west on Santa Monica Boulevard, gliding through the golden afternoon until we turn right on Club View Drive. My body slides on the bench seat's burning upholstery. The radio plays the Jackson 5.

"Is Mike Roosevelt coming?"

"Yes," he says, laughing. "Mike Roosevelt's coming. We're having company."

"Mike Roosevelt's coming!" I announce when we get home. My mother is in the kitchen. Her hair is cut short like Jean Seberg's. "Did you know Mike Roosevelt is coming?"

"Rosenfeld," she says. The room smells of rosemary and mint. "His name is Mike Rosenfeld, sweetie."

"Mike Roosevelt," I say. "His name is Mike Roosevelt."

My father is arranging wines—Bordeaux, Beaujolais—on a sideboard in the dining room; my mother is cutting cubes of cantaloupe to go with prosciutto; my infant sister, curly-haired and olive-skinned and all of six months old, crawls on a blanket in the adjacent den until my father steps in to scoop her up.

"Mike Roosevelt," my father says, grinning as he strides back in with her. "Like Theodore, or Franklin Delano. Our friend's gonna make a great president someday."

I lie on the floor, paging through a copy of *D'Aulaires' Book of Greek Myths*. Too young to read, I can spend hours staring at the book's illustrations. Later, I emerge from bedtime's exile to stand in the doorway of the dining room in my pajamas, drawn by the noise and hilarity.

"Go to bed, Matthew."

"No, no," my mother says. "Let him come out and say his hellos."

"Go to bed." It is Rosenfeld—one of my father's colleagues at the William Morris office, the architect of my parents' future fate, of the move that will splinter our family forever—who speaks, his mouth twisting slyly. "How can I convince you go to back to sleep?"

I stand in front of him, silent. He's doing a bit.

"Should I hypnotize you? Are you asking to be mesmerized?"

Lovely man, with a lovely face: clever and rabbinical, box-jawed, and chestnut-bearded, with the conspiratorial smile of a cartoon hound.

"Will this convince you?" He eyes me for a moment and then plucks a quarter from behind my ear, the classic parlor magician's trick. "Or do I need to do it again?"

"Do it a few more times," my father says. "I'll take the commission."

Laughter ripples around the table. There are my parents; there is Mike and his wife Marilyn; there is baby-faced Beau Bridges, an actor my father has recently signed; there is Larry Peerce, black-haired and goateed, a director more like a community college professor than any young Hollywood nabob; there is an agent named Robert Shapiro and his wife Sandi. These are the people my parents love.

"Bedtime, honey." It is late—the clock is ticking toward midnight—as my mother gets up to lead me off, away from this room with its French doors and rich overhead glow, its empty green bottles and champagne glasses fizzing still with the dregs of earlier toasts. "C'mon."

I want in. Can you blame me? The grown-ups are having an obvious good time, the air hazy with dope- and cigarette smoke, the doors leading onto the patio cracked, the dog, Susie—another terrier, now that their beloved Spencer has passed—dozing, stoned beneath the table.

"Of course, I didn't wanna do it," Beau Bridges says. From the night-lit cocoon of my bedroom, next door, I listen to them carrying on. "Fred kept telling me I should, but then I read the script."

"I told you to do it, too, Larry," my father says.

"You did."

"What is it?" Marilyn Rosenfeld speaks.

"*Love Story*," my father says. "There's gonna be a book, and it's gonna be a movie."

"It's hokey."

"Maybe. But it'll be a bestseller," my father says. "And the movie's gonna be a huge hit."

Maybe. But what do any of them know, other than that the rules that used to govern the business are in flux? My father is thirty-six; my mother, thirty-three. These are young people still, parents of toddlers, without lines in their faces or silver in their hair. ("Jack? You saw Jack today? How was that?") The future is unwritten ("Talented, yes, but a star? You think Jack's a star?"), but the past is suddenly useless, a compass without a needle. Bridges has lately done a western called *Adam's Woman*, which flopped, and has just wrapped another picture in New York City with Hal Ashby called *The Landlord*, of which, who knows? I hear him now, croaking out words with his lungs full.

"I was never gonna do *Love Story*," he says. "I don't know if I'm a leading man."

"What are you talking about? Of course, you're a leading man."

"Why should I want to be a leading man? I'm an actor. Shouldn't I be looking at the best parts?"

"The best parts are the leads," Rosenfeld says.

"You would think that. You're an agent!"

"The best parts are the parts that pay the best," my father says.

"Horseshit! That's horseshit, Freddy!"

Another round of laughter shakes the room.

"I figured if I said it out loud, maybe I could get myself to believe it," my dad says. "Let's open another bottle and see if we can really get to the bottom of this."

Candlelight flickers across their faces. Bridges looks like a surfer, with his guileless eyes and his open smile, his golden-blond hair cut in a teardrop fringe.

"What are we drinking, Fred? Is this the '57?"

They are so young. They are not yet at the apex of anything. Their reflections skim the surfaces of the French doors behind them, as ghostly as the starlight that lacquers the windows of their cars parked out on the street, and they believe it will go on like this forever, that the movies they make in the future will all be hits and they will be richer, and they will remain secure in their attachments as spouses and lovers, colleagues and friends, loyal together until the end.

"It's the '55, I think, it's—Kath? Kath? Oh, shit," my father says, as the room lapses for a moment into silence. "What time is it? Did we forget to sing 'Auld Lang Syne'?"

★ ★ ★

LET'S GO BACK a few months, to early October 1969. Let's talk about my mother, and an afternoon in Roxbury Park, on the southern edge of Beverly Hills. My sister is not with us yet—any day now my parents will go back to the adoption agency to pick her up—but she is very much on my mother's mind as she sits on a park bench watching me play in a sandbox alongside a group of children. Soon there will be two, she thinks as she sits with her handbag and stroller, cigarettes and book, not reading just now but gossiping, talking with the other mothers.

"You heard about Shirley?" one of them says.

"What about her?" My mother exhales, smoke pluming from her mouth. "She's usually here by now, no?"

"She's in jail."

"In jail?" My mother's eyebrows twitch. "What do you mean she's in jail?"

"Hand grenades," another woman says. "She's in for possession of hand grenades."

Traffic sluices along Olympic Boulevard. A green light filters through the trees. My parents have lived their entire lives within a five-mile radius. Other than when my dad was in the army, they have rarely ventured outside of west Los Angeles for more than a week at a time. One could throw a baseball from here onto the lawn of the house in which my father grew up, but not even in her most militant daydreams is anyone throwing grenades in drowsy Beverly Hills.

"You're not surprised?" the woman says.

My mother shrugs. When she tells me this story years later, she will act as if it is no big deal. Perhaps it isn't, to her. The friend in question is an actress named Shirley Douglas. She and my mother aren't close, but for the fact her son, Kiefer, was born in the same hospital at the same time I was. Kiefer will grow up to be an actor like his father—he will use the father's last name, Sutherland— but Shirley is an activist. According to the feds, she is running those grenades for the Black Panthers.

"Wonderful." My mother shakes her head and smiles. (Five days later, the case will be tossed and Shirley exonerated, but my mother can't help but remain admiring under her flip, sardonic shell.) "That's really great."

She is thinking of her daughter, the one who has not yet arrived. When she and my father had told her mother that they planned to adopt a baby girl and name her Johanna, Helen McGaffey greeted this news with her usual coldness. Johanna, my sister, is Black, and for a long time my grandmother will refer to me as her grandson but to Johanna as "Kay's daughter." Years from now she will repent and apologize, and she and my mother will reconcile, but what difference does that make now?

"Did anyone bail her out?" She fishes in her purse for a cigarette. "Is she just sitting there in lock-up?"

My mother is no activist. Where Douglas is a committed leftist, who belongs to a group called Friends of the Black Panthers, my mother merely leans that way. But there is a yearning in her voice when she speaks.

"Someone needs to bail her out. Has anyone talked to Donald?"

She sits in the shade at Roxbury Park. The sunlight flings its dancing coins onto her shoulders, as she looks up through the trees. The sky is the vapor-blue of velour. She could get pregnant again if she wanted to. She and my father are adopting by choice, not necessity. But I know she hungers obscurely for something more, that my mother is not meant to be a Hollywood housewife. For now, though, she is here, seated on a park bench with a Graham Greene novel and a packet of True, watching her older child play. She wears a gingham shirt, and when the wind picks up it whips her blond fringe so from a distance she seems almost to glimmer, lambent as a match. When she goes home, she will write in my baby book: "Matthew's memory is phenomenal . . . his strongest area of development continues to be language." She will write this and really be writing about herself, also, about the aptitudes she possesses but has not yet mastered. She will prove to be an ambivalent parent, troubled by many things she cannot know yet, but for now she is loving and attentive. An airplane drones lazily overhead; the voices of children playing are as distant in their

discord as gulls'. And not even a hand grenade will disturb this
suburban boredom, this blanket of calm beneath which anyone,
let alone this young mother, might yearn with everything she has
for more.

★ ★ ★

BUT AREN'T THEY just liberals? Aren't they—perhaps my mother
and father will both read the article that appears in the June 8,
1970, edition of *New York* magazine by Tom Wolfe, the one in
which he famously describes a soiree at Leonard Bernstein's pad
on Park Avenue to fete the Black Panthers—just "mau-mauing
the flak catchers?" Is this just "radical chic?" Perhaps. But as my
mother moves through Los Angeles with her left-ish politics and
her brand-new biracial baby (my sister's biological mother is the
daughter of a Holocaust survivor, her father a musician, drummer
on a handful of R&B hits), she is in tune with the mood of her own
time and place. When my father straddles his brand-new Yamaha
and roars out of the garage onto Comstock Avenue—no helmet,
just his shaggy hair and mustache fluttering in the breeze—does
he imagine he's Peter Fonda in *Easy Rider, Captain America* setting off on his last, wild ride? No, no. It's just that he, too, is in tune,
for once, with the times, and that his external world is affected by
the movies just as the tides are by the moon. Unless it is the other
way around. After he books Beau Bridges to do *The Landlord*, a
film about the feckless son of a wealthy white family who decides
to buy a brownstone in a Black neighborhood in Brooklyn, he
signs Bernie Casey and books him in Martin Scorsese's *Boxcar
Bertha*. He signs a television director named Billy Graham and
sets him up to make a feature about interracial love called *Honky*;
soon thereafter he starts to represent the great actress Cicely
Tyson and books her onto a picture called *Sounder*. It's not that my
father specializes in representing Black talent, or even in progressive themes, but rather that Hollywood has relegated that talent

to its economic periphery, where he, also, happens to exist. That it has at least begun to acknowledge that talent, even if its reasons for doing so are purely market oriented, is to my father's benefit.

The studios remain anything but progressive—*The Landlord* is written by Bill Gunn, who goes on to direct a movie called *Stop* in 1970, which is one of the first directed by a Black filmmaker for a major American studio in the modern era, only Warner Brothers will shelve it on the eve of release for being "too experimental"— but my father is happy to represent Black talent and other talent alike. He signs his clients not because he wants to change Hollywood, but because he believes in them, in everything they have to offer. Many of these clients are inherited, as when his friend Bob Shapiro moved across the Atlantic to run William Morris's office in London, my father took on Shapiro's existing American roster, but they are at least his own. He specializes, really, in up-and-coming talent, people who haven't, for whatever reason, fully broken through. And so one day he sits down and writes a letter to an actor, someone he has been keeping an eye on since he'd first spotted him in Alfred Hitchcock's *Marnie* in 1964. "I'd like you to come in for a meeting," he writes. "I'd like to see if we can find you some better parts." The actor arrives in his office a few days later, carrying a stack of index cards bound by a rubber band, wearing a sweat suit and a pair of canvas shoes so ragged they look like they've been run through a shredder. He eyeballs my father with the look of a man who is impatient with being jerked around, who carries in his heart a sliver of contempt for those businesspeople who presume to judge an artist's talent.

"Mr. Specktor."

The contempt is hard-won. Like Jack Nicholson before him— Nicholson, who is his friend—the man is used to being turned down. He shifts from foot to foot, long and skinny like a nervous horse.

"Sit," my father says. "You want something to drink?"

"Coca-Cola, if you've got it."

"Hey, Linda? Will you bring us a couple of Pepsis?" my father yells.

The actor snorts. Lean and explosive, with a profile as stark as a knife's, he looks like he might kick the walls of my father's office to pieces if the agent so much as looks at him funny.

"So," my father says. "I've been following you for a while and I think you can do better."

"You do, huh?"

"I do."

"How exactly do you think that?" the actor says. "Because I've been knocking around for more than a decade and I don't have much but a handful of Corman movies to show for it. What can you do that my current agent can't?"

He has a point. Beyond his tiny part in *Marnie*, Sydney Pollack has recently used him in *Castle Keep* and *They Shoot Horses, Don't They?*, and he'd started his career at the Actors Studio in New York, where he'd done *Sweet Bird of Youth* for Mr. Kazan. But the last ten years have mostly been *The Cycle Savages* and *The St. Valentine's Day Massacre*, B-pictures so crummy you'd be hesitant to show them to your closest friends. Recently, he'd taken a picture called *The Incredible Two-Headed Transplant*—a cheapo horror flick as dire as it sounds, like *Frankenstein* for morons— because the $3,500 he'd gotten for it helped him pay for his second wedding. He doesn't lack ambition, but what can my father do for him?

"Look," he says, lobbing the stack of index cards—it is an inch and a half thick—into my father's lap. "Take a look at these."

"What are they?"

"Read 'em."

My father does. He unbinds the stack and notes that each card has the name of a filmmaker written on it. Monte Hellman, John Frankenheimer, Alan Pakula.

"These are people you want to work with? I know Monte. I'll call him right now."

The actor smiles. He has a long face, narrow cheekbones: there is something pinched, a little too taut, about it—the eyes are close together—but he is a good-looking man. His jaw is unshaven, his coppery hair a little long, but he's no hippie: Coca-Cola is all he drinks. He doesn't even smoke dope, despite having played heavy drug fiends in *Psych-Out* and *The Trip*.

"Those are people I can't work with. All those fuckin' guys turned me down."

"Oh yeah?" My father kicks his foot up onto his desk. "I guess that tells us something, doesn't it."

"Sure does. It tells me I'm not very employable."

"Nope." He shakes a cigarette out of his omnipresent red pack. "That's not what it says at all."

"Oh no?" The actor tugs from his long-necked bottle of Pepsi. "You've got a funny way of reading the tea leaves."

My father lights up. His office is as tiny as a travel agent's, with only a tiny window behind him to let in any natural light. A heavy Rolodex, almost comically large in this context, dominates his desk like a Ferris wheel. The air is cirrused with smoke.

"You met with all these people?" he says. "They had you in to read?"

"They did."

"Well then, they like you." He stares at the man who is about to become not just his client but his closest friend, a second self to pilot him into the decade ahead. "You just need an agent who's strong enough to close the fuckin' deal."

★ ★ ★

BRUCE MacLEISH DERN. His godfather is Adlai Stevenson; his uncle, the poet Archibald MacLeish. He is not precisely a part of the New Hollywood—his politics are largely conservative—

but he is contiguous with it. Lately he has finished shooting *Drive, He Said*, a picture in which he plays a college basketball coach struggling to connect with his star players, one of whom has been radicalized by the Vietnam war. Nicholson, who directed the movie, is one of his biggest champions. ("You're fucking brilliant, Dernser. You're gonna win an Oscar for this.") But the picture opens and flops. It premieres at the Cannes Film Festival, where no one asks him to go—Nicholson and Karen Black, the film's other leads, are there—and Mick Jagger's goddamn baby starts crying in the middle of the showing and no one applauds and that's it. The picture dies in theaters. My father books him as a lead in a visionary sci-fi eco-thriller called *Silent Running*—it's mostly him and a trio of robots named Huey, Dewey, and Louie—and then lands him a part in a western called *The Cowboys*, in which his character shoots John Wayne in the back. It's a heavy scene, as Wayne rarely dies in the movies he makes and never like this, gunned down in the street like a dog. But neither film is a hit, which leaves Dern exactly where he started. My father sends him up to San Francisco to audition for a gangster picture—Francis Coppola is casting an Italian crime drama, wants him to play an Irishman named Tom Hagen—but he hates reading sides and so he walks out. The actor has a chip on his shoulder, but my father likes that. It represents the chip on his own shoulder. My father is no artist, but part of what makes him effective at his job is a tendency to identify with his clients. He needs to become them, to sublimate himself almost as thoroughly as they do when playing a part onscreen. For the next few years, my father will be closer to Dern than to anyone. He will be closer in some sense than he is even to his own wife and children, because the actor also represents his own best shot. "No more television," my father tells him. Meaning it's big screen or bust. He's going to need to find his new client a real star part. You can't let your bread and butter be shooting John Wayne, and there's no way he's going back to doing exploitation movies either.

"Brunto." My father calls him up one day, addressing his client by the nickname at which they've arrived. "I think I've got something for you."

"Oh yeah?" The actor's voice crackles down the line from his place out in Malibu Colony. "Better be something good, Nun. Andrea and I can't spend the summer eating rice and beans."

"Nun" is the nickname Dern has given my father, for unknown reasons. My mother is "Rin." My sister and I are "Toosoon" and "Notyet," respectively.

"I want you to see Curly Bob Rafelson," my father says, reaching for his lighter. "He's got something for you to read."

"What's that?"

"A script called *The Philosopher King*." My father's humid exhale seems to blow directly into Dern's ear. "Jacob Brackman."

"Huh," the actor says. "I like Curly."

"I know you do." Rafelson had been one of the producers on *Drive, He Said*, and he and Dern had hit it off. "He asked for you specifically."

"No audition."

"Nope."

What a strange pair he and my father make, the actor shirtless and bronze, prowling the cool nest of his living room with the telephone in hand, its long cord snaking away behind him; the agent leaning back and breaking into the day's third pack of smokes, brushing the muffin crumbs off his lap.

"Two parts," my father says. He and Dern will come to resemble each other more than you could imagine, even physically. "One for you, and one for Jack."

"Huh." The actor stares through the room's slatted blinds at the beach, the waves hissing softly on the shore beyond the glass. "So I'm gonna play second fuckin' banana to Jack?"

"Nope."

"Nope? Jack just got nominated for an Academy Award. I don't see any statuettes on my mantel, so unless Curly's crazier than I think he is, I'm gonna take the short straw."

"That's not what he has in mind," my father says.

"Well, what does he have in mind?"

Dern is competitive. He's an athlete, after all. At Choate he'd broken records for the five-hundred-meter dash, and now he's an ultramarathoner, lives on the beach because he can step onto the sand and run twenty or forty miles in a single day. He's my father's very opposite, but he is a great actor—at heart, he is a theater actor, and likes nothing more than being onstage instead of before a camera—and he hopes, just like his friend Jack, to become a star.

"Go see Curly Bob," my father says. "He'll get you sorted out."

★ ★ ★

"CURLY" BOB RAFELSON. He'll also play his part in shaping my father's fate, but right now he sits in an office at 931 N. La Brea Boulevard, an office that is more like a playpen, with its Wurlitzer jukebox and alpaca rugs, its sterling silver bowl of dope that sits right out in the open, and squints through yellow-tinted shades.

"So?" Where Dern is long and skinny, Rafelson's built like a lumberjack, the type of guy whose silences have an almost hostile quality. "You in?"

Dern likes Bob Rafelson—they've been in touch ever since the actor was still doing stage work in New York—but this place makes him uncomfortable. Rafelson's a hippie, one-third of a company called BBS Productions, which he shares with a fellow named Bert Schneider, whose office is just down the hall. Together with their other friend, Steve Blauner, Bert and Bob had made a killing with the television show *The Monkees,* and then an even bigger one when they took a flier and decided to finance *Easy Rider.* Their mechanics needn't concern us too much, but for one thing.

"Sure, but—Curly, you want me to play Jason?"

"Yep."

"Why is that?" Dern stares across the desk at Rafelson's chaotic auburn curls, his flattened, antagonistic face like a boxer's. "That part feels written for Jack."

"It was."

"Then why do you want me to play it?"

The Philosopher King is about two brothers, one of them (David) saturnine and depressed, the other (Jason) dazzling and charismatic. The latter is the sort of part that always goes to the established star, which, having almost won an Oscar for his performance in Rafelson's *Five Easy Pieces*, Jack Nicholson now is. But everybody wants to be somebody else. That, again, is the fundamental promise of the movies. Rafelson's an artist, and so given to flights of intuition. He knows his film, which will be retitled *The King of Marvin Gardens* before it shoots, will benefit from subverting its audience's expectations, that everyone will expect Nicholson to play the more charismatic role, so why not knock them off balance before the movie even starts?

"Don't sweat it," Rafelson says. Why not knock the actors off balance, too? He likes friction, complication, and difficulty. He likes Ozu—the poster for *Tokyo Story* that hangs on his office wall is there for a reason—and he likes Jodorowsky's *El Topo*. He thinks most American movies of the last fifteen years are for squares. "Just say you're in."

"I'm in."

"Great," Rafelson says. "I'll call Fred to make it happen."

Everybody wants to be someone else. Dern would like to be Nicholson, to have his friend's suddenly turbocharged career. My father would like to be Dern: the athlete, the all-American, the talented actor. And Rafelson? Well, some part of Rafelson, perhaps, might like to be more like—

"Bert!" After Dern leaves, he pushes up from his seat and shambles down the hall, searching for his partner. "Ayo, Bert!"

"What is it, Curly?"

He jostles down the hall, past the hippies and dope dealers and freaks who crowd BBS headquarters, a building he and Bert (and Steve: BBS stands for Bert, Bob, and Steve) had bought with their own money. All they want is to do their own thing, to make the movies they want to make. Bert's father is the president of Columbia Pictures, so their problem was never access. It was independence.

"Am I interrupting something?" Rafelson barges into Schneider's office at the far end of the hall.

"Not today," Schneider says. He lolls behind his desk with an aristocratic ease, the body language of a person who is used to having every door open itself in front of him. "What's up?"

"Dern's gonna do *Philosopher King*," he says. "I thought you might like to know."

"I do like to know."

"Then why do you sound like someone just took a dump in your favorite pair of shoes?"

Bert and Bob. They're a curious pair—where Bob looks like a merchant marine, Bert Schneider is faun-like, lanky, and beautiful, with high cheekbones and a Jewish afro—but they are united by a mutual contempt for authority.

"Not at all," Schneider says. They started this company when they realized the problem with American movies wasn't talent but distribution. They wanted a place where artists could control their own fate. "I'm happy for you."

"You're happy for me? Buddy, this is our company, which makes it our movie."

"I know."

"Yeah? So?"

We'll come back to these two. All that matters is that Bob, the filmmaker, is an artist and Bert, the producer, is a businessman, just like Lew Wasserman before him. And just like Wasserman before him—don't be fooled by the groovy shirt, he got into this business to make money—he wants something else.

"So, I'm happy," Bert says. "I think it's great, Curly."

Something else, but it's not what Wasserman wanted. He's got all the money he needs—more than he wants, even—and he's not much interested in real estate or power, which he understands are just capitalist carrots at the end of a poisonous stick. He spins in his chair and looks out at the sun-blasted corridor of La Brea, three stories below. We'll have to see what he wants, this man who holds a key to the Hollywood my parents are moving through. We'll have to see what it is that turns Bert Schneider on.

★ ★ ★

"MRS. ALLEN? COME this way."

My parents, too, want to be other people, and on weekend afternoons in 1971 they take to the stage, leaving my sister and me at home with a sitter while they walk through one empty apartment after another.

"As you can see, we've re-done the kitchen. The linoleum is new, the dishwasher's a few years old, but it's a Philco, it'll last forever."

"Nice."

"If you come this way, I'll show you the other bedroom. Mr. Allen?"

"Huh?" My father's voice echoes over from the apartment's front room, where he stands studying the street's drab panorama of lawns and antennae through a single-pane window, running his fingers across its cheap plywood frame.

"If you come with me, I'll show you and your wife the back."

For today's playacting purposes, they are childless; sometimes, they are graduate students; they are a lower-income couple just getting started in life. Their footsteps clop against exposed laminate flooring, this unit part of a triplex south of Olympic Boulevard, not far from Century City.

"What do you do, Mr. Allen?"

"I'm in sales." My father changes it up every time—"I'm a medical student," he'll say, or, "I work at Hughes Aircraft"—and sometimes he uses his father's birth name, Rubenstein, to see if the landlord might discriminate against Jews also. But his performance is never convincing. He's too hesitant, and he fumbles small details.

"And you, Mrs. Allen? Are you a homemaker?"

The landlady's performance, as someone hoping to appear at least a decade younger than she is, isn't very convincing either, but my mother merely smiles.

"Oh, yes." In her plaid skirt and poodle haircut, this landlady seems airmailed from 1953, so my mother may as well lay it on thick. "I wouldn't have it any other way."

She takes a Method approach. In her purse there is a copy of Marjorie Karmel's *Thank You, Dr. Lamaze* ("Oh, not yet," she'd told the landlord who'd spotted it at the previous apartment they'd visited, "but soon, we hope. Right, honey?"), and though she is jonesing for a cigarette, and has been for hours, she won't smoke one now. ("You know what the surgeon general says. May as well get used to it.")

"Any pets?"

"No, ma'am." She enjoys this, performance without the threat of attention. She'd do this every day if she could, even without an end in mind. "My husband is allergic so we can't."

This landlady, with her pointy little face, her faint rosacea. My mother loathes this woman more than any they've encountered yet today. Too shy to be an actress, too unsure of herself in regular life, my mother is in full command of her performance today, twisting the taps in the kitchenette, pretending to test the water pressure.

"Where do you work, Mr. Allen? Will there be much of a commute for you?"

"Santa Monica," my mother leaps in to cover his hesitation. "He works in Santa Monica."

She glances out the window to where her car, a red Volvo sedan less conspicuous than my father's Caddy, sits at the curb, then swivels and springs for the kill.

"When is the unit available?"

"Right away," the landlady says. "With a deposit and two months' rent, you could move in tomorrow."

"Is that right?" My mother's voice sharpens. "Tomorrow?"

"Yes, of course. We'll need to run a credit check, but it's yours if you want it."

"Is that what you told the family that was here Thursday afternoon? Mr. and Mrs. McCleary?"

The landlady freezes.

"Mr. and Mrs. McCleary," my mother repeats. "The family that was here two days ago. You told them the place had been rented. Remember?"

The landlady turns and walks away.

"What happened?" My mother's voice echoes off the apartment's cheap molding and exposed floors as she follows the woman into the living room. "Other tenants didn't work out? You signed a twenty-four-hour lease?"

"Kath." My father touches my mother's wrist. "Let's go."

"Housing discrimination is illegal," she shouts. Not so shy now. Her rage spirals out of her, rising to become almost an entity in itself. The mousy housewife of thirty seconds ago is gone. "But I'm sure you know that, lady. You know about the Rumford Act, right? Black families have the same right to housing as everybody else!"

My father pulls her onto the landing, guiding them down the narrow white stairs that lead down to the street. My mother knows the ins and outs of the Rumford Act, which was nullified in '64 by California Proposition 15, until the U.S. Supreme Court declared the nullification unconstitutional, because she is a founder of an organization called the Westside Fair Housing Council, which works to identify and to fine discriminatory landlords. She clutches the wrought-iron railing. She doesn't trust herself not to stumble, she's so mad. At the bottom, she lights the cigarette she has been craving all day.

"I don't think I can do another one," she says, steadying herself with one hand against the steering wheel after they have climbed back into the car. She is shaking still. "I'm done."

"It's OK." My father reaches for his sunglasses on the dash. "We'll file a report in the morning."

Outside, the sky is opalescent and cold, the pale, striated yellow of a winter twilight. She pounds her palm against the steering wheel.

"D'you think it makes a difference?"

"I do."

"Do you?"

She means not just this work, but her life. Nixon is president, and Reagan is governor. Sam Yorty, whom she hates more than anyone, is mayor, and Ed Davis, who is no better than Reddin or Parker before him, is chief of police. So, what difference does any of this make? Fines. What is the point of her dream of a more equitable world if the people like her mother are still in charge?

"Let's go home," my father says. This upsets him, but not so acutely. He's in the world of art, where, he thinks, everything matters, but also nothing does. A movie could flop and his client, Bruce Dern or anyone else, might suffer. But the sun will rise tomorrow morning in any case. The world he works in may be rotten—it's Hollywood—but there are good things in it, and gifted people. He can only try, within reason, to do the right thing.

They drive home, my father still steeped in thought (the right thing, which is not always the altruistic thing: sometimes "right" means right mostly for him), my mother smoking in silence. After they have grilled spareribs out on the patio, after they have watched *Story Theatre* and *Wild Kingdom* and then packed their children off to bed, she turns to him in the kitchen.

"What is it?" he says.

She bursts into tears. They're doing the dishes, my father soaping up the long-tined fork my mother had used to turn the ribs on the grill.

"What is it, Kath?" He sets the fork down. "What's wrong?"

He is not great with emotion. Like so many men of his generation, he is embarrassed by displays of strong feeling. But it is also true that my mother's register here is extreme.

"That bitch," she sobs. She is shaking like a very young child, barely able to get the words out between breaths. "That awful bitch of a landlady is what's wrong."

My father picks up the fork and dries it, then puts his hands on her shoulders. When Mac McGaffey died, her mother had walked over to the piano without a word of consolation for her daughter and started playing a hymn, not one word then or since; so when my mother grieves sometimes it is like a lifetime of sorrow pours out of her all at once.

"Imagine," she says finally, wiping her runny nose with her palms as she straightens up. It's like a thunderstorm has run straight through her. She mops her nose, and my father stands with the wet imprint of her face on his shirt. "Imagine, that fucking cunt wouldn't even rent a place to our daughter."

★ ★ ★

"FREDDY."

"What is it?" My father rolls over. He cups his hand over the receiver, as it is early. "Brunto?"

"You got a tux, Nun?"

"Yeah, I've got a tux." He sits up. "Why are you calling me at seven a.m. to see if I own a tuxedo?"

Dreams, dreams: those dreams of stardom, and of success. From the next room, there is the sound of the shower running. My mother is already awake.

"Y'know that goddamn basketball movie I made last summer?

The one nobody saw? Jack called this morning to say the National Society of Film Critics is giving me an award for it. Supporting actor."

"Ah. Brunto, that's great."

"Get yourself to New York tomorrow night if you can. Bring Rin. Apparently, there's a wingding at the Algonquin. They're giving out statuettes."

My father rises, dresses. He flies to New York City the next day. My mother, sister, and I do not go. There is no time, after all, to find a sitter. He meets up with Dern at the actor's hotel, to which Bruce and his wife have decamped after six weeks in Atlantic City. The actor still bears the imprint, the toothbrush mustache and a bit of the reckless swagger of his character in *The King of Marvin Gardens.*

"Is this what it's all about, Freddy?" In the cab over to the ceremony he turns to my father. "Awards?"

Not for my father it isn't. Not for Dern either, although the recognition is gratifying, of course. The character he plays in the movie he has just wrapped—the time in Atlantic City was spent on location; the film was shot mostly on the derelict Boardwalk in wintertime and at a crumbling hotel called the Marlborough Blenheim—is a petty crook, a hustler who spends the film trying to rope his brother into a real estate deal. A line from the film echoes in his head as they ride through Midtown. "Jason's no business-man . . . I think he's an artist." But which one are you when they start handing out statuettes?

"Look!" My father walks alongside him and his wife as they enter the ballroom on the Algonquin's third floor, passing through a small crush of photographers before they spy the BBS table. "Look who's here."

Dern scans the room, waving to Jane Fonda—in a few years, he will play her husband in *Coming Home*—and to Burt Reynolds, taking in the crowd before he zeroes in on the same thing my father has. There is Bob Rafelson, and there is Bert Schneider, and there is Jack Nicholson, and between Jack and Bert there is another man, one who has already spotted Bruce and is on his way over to say hello.

"No kidding," Dern murmurs, his smile widening in response to the man's own. "Huey, Dewey, and Louie, I'll be damned."

Hollywood. It is a world of strange bedfellows, inexplicable alliances. If MCA was an octopus, whose tentacles circled the globe, then the world my parents now occupy is even stranger, and more insurgent in its reach. The man walking toward my father is Dern's friend—they have known each other for some years, and even if their politics are largely opposed, the actor thinks of him as one of the greatest he's ever known—and he is Bert Schneider's friend, closer to him than anyone in the world. My father knows him only from the papers, and from the nightly news.

"Bruce," this man says, for it is Huey P. Newton in the flesh. "It's good to see you, brother."

"How's the food?" Dern says. In a room full of famous people, it is Newton who draws everyone's eyes. He is handsome like a movie star, possessing both magnetism and notoriety. "Better than it was in prison?"

"It's a little better." Newton grins. "Yeah."

His voice is so soft my father finds he almost needs to lean in to hear it. His manner is surprisingly gentle. His Afro is cut short, and even after thirty-three months in the Men's Colony in San Luis Obispo, twenty-two of them in solitary, Newton remains muscular and solid. In his black tux, he has the casual ease of a person at home in his pajamas, but that's only because he has both earned this ease and cultivated it as a way to inhabit spaces like this one. He leans over to shake my father's hand, this man who is neither a businessman nor an artist but something else altogether.

"Come on," he says, clapping Dern on the shoulder, beckoning my father to follow. "Let's go get ourselves something to eat."

★ ★ ★

STRANGE BEDFELLOWS, AS I say. But Hollywood has always created those, with its alliances between filmmaker and financier, warm charisma and cold calculation. As my father sits staring across the table at Bert Schneider and Huey Newton, he is on the outside. For it is no ordinary friendship, no transactional matter of radical chic or stolen valor, that seems to unite these two, but something much, much deeper. Even if Bert's checkbook keeps the Movement afloat, if he pays for Newton's apartment on Lakeshore Drive in Oakland, and for his furniture, and into the People's Free Food Program and all the rest, it is not just political aims that draw them together. It is love.

Love? Look at them now, the revolutionary from Monroe, Louisiana, and the rich young man from Westchester, New York; the one who taught himself to read at eighteen, the other who got expelled from Cornell because who needed an education when you were already wealthy? This room is full of improbable couplings, of actresses sitting with critics; directors hobnobbing with executives, but these two seem to only have eyes for one another. See them whispering like naughty children, Huey's face solemn over his rum and Coke until Bert leans over and his face explodes into a gleeful smile. They love each other, they do—when it is time for Newton to flee the country in a few years, when the government starts pursuing him again, he will turn to Bert, who understands him better than anyone, and Bert will arrange his passage to Cuba—but how, and why? How do these forces of revolutionary freedom and capitalist art, forces that also tug at my parents, conspire? Together they huddle at the limits of human imagination, that place where art and commerce end, and something else, something lacking even a name or a form, begins to take shape.

★ ★ ★

"IT'S CALLED *I Never Thought of It That Way Before.*"

"Oh yeah?" Bert Schneider straightens up and tips his head back, feeling the alkaloid burn drip down through his sinuses as he pushes away from the glass table in his living room. "That's great. *I Never Thought of It That Way Before.*"

"Yeah," Huey says. "It's an allegory. It's about me and Eldridge."

There is a movie that will never be made, one of the thousands that wash through Hollywood every year, fireflies, ghosts. Most of these pictures, the unmade, will never mean anything to anybody, but this one does.

"It's about two brothers who live through the riots and become TV reporters, one with a camera, the other with sound."

This one does mean something because it represents an alternative future for Hollywood, a utopia that almost—almost—comes to pass.

"So it's like *Medium Cool,*" Schneider says.

Almost. But "almost" is everything here in the world of Hollywood, and of history.

"Not like *Medium Cool,*" Huey says. "*Medium Cool* is good, but it's not real even if it pretends to be. This is about the struggle. It ain't *Shaft.* It's about the real."

"Right."

Bert Schneider's house is up in the hills. The two men are at a party, alone for a moment while the chaos unfurls in adjacent rooms. From outside, the hot tub cantilevered out over the hillside on the terrace, they can hear women giggling, the hiss of a canister of nitrous oxide.

"Who stars?" Schneider says. The lights of the houses opposite sparkle vaguely. He runs his finger across the table's glass to collect white residue, rubs it against his gums. "It's not like you can make this kind of picture with Sidney Poitier, or even with Jim Brown."

"Right."

"Not if you want it to be real."

How do the movies accommodate the revolutionary's impulses? Why is even Huey P. Newton caught up in their net? For Bert Schneider, it is simple: he was born to them and now is tired of them and here, on a warm spring night in 1973, he is ready to throw them away. This is the thing that has troubled him for the last few years. He and Rafelson had created BBS as a place for artists, a place to make movies the studios wouldn't touch. But now he finds he is sick of the movies altogether. He cares about the Movement, not about the pictures.

"Who directs?" Schneider says. "Who understands the struggle enough to get behind the camera?"

He is ready to throw it all away. Perhaps I overrate him, perhaps ("I want to be like Jesus Christ," he is fond of saying, "but with better participation") he is just another slumming rich kid, because only a rich kid could ever be so avid to be rid of what he has, but I don't think so.

"Paul Williams," Huey says, meaning not the architect or the singer or the actor, but the filmmaker of that name, the one who is also his friend. "Paul Williams says he's interested."

"Paul Williams would be great."

BBS will make only one more movie—a documentary called *Hearts and Minds*, based on the Pentagon Papers—and Bert Schneider will cause a stir when he gets up to collect an Oscar for it and then reads a congratulatory telegram from the North Vietnamese ambassador onstage. He will walk away after that and his company will dissolve and the dream of a Hollywood that is dominated by its artists will disappear, but right now it is, however tenuously, alive.

"A million-five," Newton says. It is alive for him, too. When he was in the hole, the soul breaker in Alameda, with nothing but darkness, rats, and roaches for company, he taught himself to control his mind, to slow his thoughts and speed them up and edit them any way he wanted. "Film clips," he called these altered quilts of memory and desire, for the movies have entered him to the bone. "That's what it will take."

"A million-five," Bert shrugs. "That's easy. We can do that."

In this Hollywood that is fully governed by artists—the one that exists only in my dreams—my parents will stay middle class but happy, and agents will never run the show. Bert Schneider will go on to produce the one other movie whose prospect excites him the most, a biopic of Charlie Chaplin, and BBS will continue to thrive forever. But right now a reel-to-reel tape player turns in its lacquer cabinet, the air filling with the weightless sounds of Timmy Thomas, just organ and mechanical drums. And even Huey P. Newton, who loves the pictures as much as anyone, who loves *El Topo* and *Black Orpheus* and the Orson Welles adaptation of *Macbeth* most of all, those movies that taught him you can survive everything, even death, Huey P. Newton is a part of this dream, too.

"Beautiful," he murmurs, and it is, it really is, this Hollywood that exists—*you can survive everything, even death*—without ever fully being born. "Wait till you see this picture." He bends down now to the table himself. "It's gonna be like nothing you've ever seen."

★ ★ ★

MY PARENTS ARE sleeping. My father sprawls on his back like a bear. When Newton was in prison, he'd consoled himself with the memory of his older brother's books, Melvin's copy of *Plato's Republic*, with which he'd taught himself to read. He'd thought often of the parable of the cave, Plato's prisoners who see not the world but only shadows flickering across a wall. My parents are like those prisoners, trapped inside the limited light of the movies.

My mother rolls onto her side. ("A studio is a place where fiction is made, but the Black Panther Party is out to create nonfiction,"

Newton will soon write in his autobiography, to be published in a few years, and perhaps this is true. But a studio, Hollywood, is also a place where history is made, and my parents are prisoners of history, also.) Her arm juts out off the edge of the bed, reaching into space.

The floor judders, the windows begin to rattle and bang in their frames. It is February 9, 1971. My father opens his eyes to a resounding crack that sounds like the crunching of bone. It's like there is something inside him that's breaking, followed by a cascade of smashing glass.

"Kathy, what—"

My mother bolts up. She, too, hears the symphony of shattering dishware from downstairs. They turn to each other on the heaving bed and even before it is over—twelve seconds—they know what it is.

"Jesus." My mother speaks into the brittle silence that follows, a stunned predawn hush. "That was a bad one."

They know. California natives both, they know. It is six a.m. on the dot. Even before they go downstairs to turn on the news—the television won't give them anything but static—they know it is an earthquake, the worst to hit Southern California in forty years.

"Mom!" My voice, from below, splits the dawn light, and she is up out of bed, crossing the room on bare feet before my father can shake off the remains of his sleep. "Mommm!"

The ground rumbles again. An aftershock. The parquet tiles of the dining room feel unsteady, like the deck of ship. She races to my bedroom, where I am standing in my pajamas, having been shaken out of bed.

"What was that? Mom, what was that?"

One more early memory, perhaps the first for which I possess narrative clarity: my mother sweeps into my room on the morning of the Sylmar earthquake and hoists me onto her hip, carries me down the hall beneath an ugly chandelier that has always filled me with mysterious anxiety, picks up my sobbing sister, and carries us both back to the kitchen, which is strewn with glittering glass.

"Wait!" she says. She deposits us in the den, switches on the television, which is just crackling snow—the broadcast signals are out—before turning back to that room full of broken crockery. "Wait here."

First memories: of sitting on the edge of the couch, staring at that field of rioting pixels; of my mother pushing a broom across the kitchen, moving cautiously like a soldier pushing a sweeper through a clearing, stooping to light a cigarette off the kitchen stove's gas burner; of my father emerging finally, coming down inside the morning's fragile light to tease me.

"What did I hear you saying, sport? You didn't like the earthquaker? Is that what you said to your mother? The earthquaker?"

He laughs and picks me up, carries my sister and me into the breakfast nook, where we sit with the few plates my mother has managed to rescue from the carnage, my father smoking over his cup of watery coffee, my mother in the next room cooking French toast in an iron skillet. The dream isn't over, not quite. *The King of Marvin Gardens*, that masterful examination of failed utopias and American rot—all the brothers in that movie want is to shape their own kingdom, Staebleravia—hasn't flopped. Huey Newton is free from prison, still years away from being gunned down by an associate on a street corner in Oakland. My mother's radical friends are beating their drums, raising money, raising consciousness, planning a rally they expect will happen on May Day, protesting the war. I sit at the kitchen table, legs dangling over white linoleum. My mother enters with an enormous platter, a narrow trail of blood—she has cut her foot—smearing across the floor behind her. She sits, forking out our food. The clock on the wall above the table is stopped and will remain that way for weeks.

"History is a nightmare from which I am trying to awake." Years later I will read these words in my mother's copy of *Ulysses*—her favorite passage—but history is sometimes, too, a dream you hope will go on and on and on. In the one I am having, Huey Newton will live on to a ripe old age, Bruce Dern is the huge movie star he might have become, American movies are filled, still, with abstraction and ambiguity, and the four of us—my sister in my father's lap, fidgeting with his mustache while he cuts up her French toast; my mother gazing pensively out the patio door, staring at her boxes of rosemary, oregano, and mint while a cigarette smolders between her fingers; me, attacking a breakfast that tastes like ambrosia—remain forever together, exactly as we are right now.

THE TOWN

4. ROYAL

1974–1980

WITH A RAZOR BLADE clutched between thumb and index finger, under a panoptical arrangement of movie posters signed by the people they feature—Bruce Dern in *Silent Running*, Jeff Bridges in *Thunderbolt and Lightfoot*, Marty Feldman in *Young Frankenstein*—I cut a pill in two, sawing cautiously to split it down the middle. You might say I am becoming a citizen—I place half the pill on my tongue, the other back in its glassine baggie—of the motion picture colony myself. I tuck the baggie in my pocket, crouch back down on the floor, and wait for something to happen.

1977. The very air is pregnant with radiant potential. I seem to have entered a kind of arcadia. (Three pills, purchased on the playground this very afternoon, each one thicker than aspirin and with rounded edges, stamped with the words "Rorer 714.") I lie on my back on the coffee-brown carpet in my bedroom, upstairs in the new house my parents have recently purchased in Santa Monica. I watch the movies and they, now, seem to watch me back, which in time will prove to be a treacherous bargain.

"Matty, what are you doing?"

My sister comes into my room. I look up at her, her face inverted, looming over me like a long-stalked flower.

"Relaxing."

"Can I relax, too?"

This arcadia, it is a dangerous place. This paradise into which I have awakened—three blocks to school every morning, tramping beneath the coral trees and kiwis, the milky fog burning off into a lemon haze—is ruthless, gladiatorial, and cruel. Every pocket holds a bowie knife, every fist is looking for a face to punch, every empty swimming pool is an invitation to shatter my skull.

"Get the fuck out of here, Johanna."

"Please?"

"Only if you flip the record," I say. I don't feel anything yet. "Go on."

Many of the kids my sister and I now go to school with will die before they're fifty. There will be overdoses, homicides, liver disease; there will be disappearances into the California State Penal System, car crashes, and hemorrhages. Many of my friends seem, already, half-vanished. Bob Badour, my fellow fifth grader, shows up in class whenever he feels like it, Marlboros rolled in the sleeve of his white T-shirt, eyes empty and red. One day, Santa Monica will be a playground for the ultra-rich, but not yet.

"Relaxing is boring."

"Relaxing isn't boring," I say, "it's—

Led Zeppelin roars in my ears. An aqueous wave of sensation rolls through me, my ten-year-old body going slack.

"What?"

I struggle to move my tongue, splayed on the floor like a starfish.

"Uhhh," I say. "Johanna, will you . . . change the . . . record, please?"

I lie still. Twilight paints the blue bodyboard in the corner, the LPs, and comic books—*X-Men, The Avengers, Conan the Barbarian*—scattered on the carpet around me.

"What's the matter with you?"

"Nothing."

"You look like you're gonna barf, Matty."

She crosses the room. For a moment I seem to dolly up to see us both, consciousness lifting out of my body so I can see myself, stapled to the floor; my sister crouching by a stack of records against the wall; my skinny, tan frame, naked from the waist up, wearing only a pair of corduroy shorts.

"*Meddle*?"

"N—no." Pink Floyd will make me vomit, that I do know. "More Zep."

Movies are the place where America goes to dream about itself, and this—this room, this antechamber—is where I go to dream about myself. The next few years will move slowly. Though I will remain fucked up an alarming percentage of the time on skunk weed and occasional pills, the adult world will not seem to notice.

"*Presence*," my sister says, lying back down next to me.

"Wise choice."

Johanna is eight. I am ten. Precocious, perhaps, but by the standards of our place and time, my sister and I are ordinary. The boys in my class speak of "'ludes" and "yellowjackets," "Colombian" and "Panama Red"; the girls feather their hair like Farrah, filing across the playground in thigh-hugging shorts.

"Ahmm," I say, as "Achilles Last Stand" trickles out of the speakers. "'Tea for One' sucks."

"'Tea for One' sucks," my sister says.

"'Hots On for Nowhere' rules."

"What about 'Stairway to Heaven'?"

"That's not even on this record, Johanna—what are you even doing here? Get out of my room."

She grabs the record and scampers off before I can stop her. I flop back, panting, woozy. I think about the boy who sold me these Quaaludes, with his heavy Pendleton shirt and deep-set, raccoon eyes, brown curls exploding around his brown face. Soon, he will vanish into Santa Monica's world of drugs and unknown conclusions. My back stings with sunburn; my sinuses are thick with seawater; my elbows and knuckles are raw where I've scraped them against concrete. I roll onto my stomach and try to push up on my palms, only gravity defeats me. I lie face down like Buster Keaton doing a pratfall, Charlie Chaplin even after the camera stops.

★ ★ ★

SOMETHING IS HAPPENING to my parents as well. This new house is only a symbol. In 1975, they pay $125,000 for it, which is certainly a step up—the last one, in Holmby Hills, set them back only $37,500 a decade ago—but it is no palace, a three-bedroom, Greek Revival–style residence in a neighborhood none of their friends will touch. Santa Monica? Santa Monica is nowhere, a sleepy backwater filled with nursing homes and dingbat apartments, stucco boxes built on little stilts. Ancient Mustangs and Camaros rust in their rickety breezeways. This isn't Hollywood, it is surfers, senior citizens, working-class families, and retirees. Only north of Montana Avenue, where my parents buy, is there the inkling of a more prosperous future, and still not much. Back in the 1920s a developer had imagined Santa Monica as paradise by the sea, and after the war it had lapsed into its existence as a bedroom community, affordable housing for aerospace workers commuting to the South Bay. But now Lockheed Martin is reeling from a loan crisis, Douglas has merged with McDonnell and moved to St. Louis, and Hughes, where my uncle Maier works, is wobbling due to defense cuts, and so Santa Monica has lapsed into semi-decrepitude.

What are my parents doing here? What do the migration patterns of such Hollywood workers, middle-class ones who don't live in splendor on Malibu Beach or in the canyons, tell us about the state of the industry? Why is my father, who's doing okay but lacks star clients, moving backward rather than forward, enrolling his children in a mediocre school district, buying a house in a neighborhood that is worse than the one they are leaving behind?

Let's look at that neighborhood, at the silent corridor of Montana Avenue in the morning, its small businesses—dry cleaners, a small bakery, two pharmacies, a Union 76 station—practically moribund. There is the Aero Theater, its marquee jutting low over the street; there is Miller's Market, whose owner still lets retirees shop on credit; a few blocks east there is a malt shop—my mother used to go there in high school—called Sweet Sixteen, where a basket of curly fries still costs thirty-five cents. It could be 1952, if you'd like it to be. Wisps of white fog hang over the sidewalk, lingering in the air like smoke. Men and women arrive to unlock the metal gates and glass doors of their shops. Threadbare awnings flutter in the breeze. Something is going to happen here. Outside Duck Blind Liquor a man sits in a car with a gun in his pocket. A few blocks south, a group of shirtless seventeen-year-olds smoke a bowl in the backyard of a derelict apartment complex, gazing hungrily at the crater of an empty swimming pool. My father wakes up and heads off to work, carrying his briefcase down the front walk, on his way to encounter for the millionth time the reality of experience at the William Morris office. But not for long.

Something is going to happen here. Something is going to happen right now.

★ ★ ★

"FREDDY!"

My father is in his office. This is in the fall of 1974. For him, a soft year: Bruce Dern, coming off *The Laughing Policeman*, is gearing up to do a picture called *Smile*; Beau Bridges has signed on to do *The Other Side of the Mountain*, which will be directed by my dad's client Larry Peerce. These are solid pictures—*The Other Side of the Mountain* will be a hit, *The Laughing Policeman* an underrated gem—but nothing that will change anybody's life.

"What is it, Mikey?"

He looks up. Mike Rosenfeld, whose office is right down the hall, is standing in his doorway, clutching a sheaf of papers.

"Contracts came in for Peter Strauss. Starger's office sent 'em over this morning."

"Great. Let's see."

Rosenfeld doesn't budge.

"What is it?"

He glances down the hall and then ducks inside. He drops the papers on my father's desk and leans in, sotto voce.

"You heard they fired Weltman?"

"They fired Phil? What the hell for?"

Two men, both on the sunny side of forty. Rosenfeld is a year younger, but they both—suddenly—find themselves staring down the barrel of middle age. They have spouses, they have school-age children, they work for the largest talent agency in Hollywood, and they are asking themselves the same question. *Is this it?*

"They ran the numbers on him," Rosenfeld says. "They 'fed his numbers into the computer' and didn't like what they saw."

"Jesus." My father snorts. "That's how they do it now?"

"That's exactly how they do it. You know that."

Two men, with their thickening waistlines and mounting responsibilities: Rosenfeld, with his rabbinical beard and wry, sweet smile; my dad with his heavy black mustache, which is beginning to show—much to his chagrin—strands of silver.

"Fuckers," my father mutters. He is aware of the computer, the IBM/System 3 he passes every morning—it is the size of a refrigerator, with its own dedicated room—as he trundles down the hall, but this is a new one. Agenting has always been a personality-driven business, and the numbers don't always tell the entire story. "Those motherfuckers."

They are both of an age where it is easy to sink into inertia, to become, once and for all, a schlepper. Weltman is twenty-five years older, so it was almost gold watch time anyway, but still.

"Sam did it." Rosenfeld lowers his voice again. "Fuckin' Sam Weisbord dropped the hammer, fired his best friend face to face. Can you imagine?"

My father shakes his head. No, he cannot imagine. Sam Weisbord, their boss, is a royal asshole, but even he is supposed to abide by the idea this place is a family, no? Weisbord and Phil Weltman were friends for fifty fucking years—even before they became Uncle Abe's lieutenants, as children—and Sam just cuts his throat like it's nothing.

"What a prick," he says. This agency has always pretended to be gentler than MCA, but this is a lie. "What an absolute prick."

Sam *is* a prick: a grumpy little health nut who's always haranguing people about the restorative powers of wheat germ and power walking. Nobody at the agency likes him. But Abe Lastfogel has always asserted that what matters is not gentlemanly appearance, but gentlemanly conduct. You don't kick people when they are down, you don't steal your competitors' clients. You try to behave decently, and not just dress that way. My father likes this. He's no naïf, he knows this is a rough business—these are just ideals—and he is aware this place doesn't always feel so very familial. But it's an ethos, at least, that he can agree with.

"Thanks for letting me know," he says, picking up the papers Rosenfeld has dropped on his desk. He and Weltman were not close—not like Weltman and Rosenfeld, Weltman and a bunch of the younger guys in the TV department to whom he has been a mentor—but my father is a loyal man. If you can work for this company going on forty years and just get tossed out the door without even the dignity of a normal retirement, what point is there in working here? Why get up and come to the office at all?

★ ★ ★

LOYALTY. HOLLYWOOD IS a funny place to look for that, as everybody knows that a person here will sell his or her own grandmother for a dollar, but nevertheless . . . My father and Rosenfeld are pals, actual and abiding friends. My father would never stab Mikey in the back. Sam Weisbord and Phil Weltman were—if you are to take the word of Frank Rose, the William Morris Agency's excellent historian, as offered in his book *The Agency*—like Damon and Pythias, the two Greeks whose friendship illustrated the ideal. Hollywood may be a soul-pulverizing place (certainly no one here is jumping up to die in someone else's stead, like Damon did), but it is a town of relationships, a place where alliances are formed out of love as well as necessity. Sometimes, those alliances can take irregular shapes.

"So what do we need to get a line of credit?" Sometimes it's two people, sometimes it's five, as it is right now, a few weeks after Phil Weltman's firing. Mike Rosenfeld hunches in a crowded booth in an otherwise vacant chophouse on Pico Boulevard. "One of us is gonna have to go to the well."

Five guys: Mike Rosenfeld, Michael Ovitz, Ron Meyer, Bill Haber, and Rowland Perkins. This will become one of Hollywood's most famous origin stories, and because it will affect my father directly, I am forced to tell it again. He is not here today. He is in the dark about what his colleagues are planning. But this will determine the shape not just of his life, but of an American geography. Watch.

"I've already talked to my guy at City National," Ovitz, the quiet one, says. "All we need is collateral. Anyone got a house they're not afraid to lose?"

A round of anxious grins circles the table. All of them hunch low in the booth like jockeys, like they are ducking observation even though the room is empty. Billingsley's Steakhouse may as well be in Bakersfield so far as Hollywood's concerned. When my father takes a client out on the arm, they go to Chasen's, they go to Musso and Frank. But this dusty little room with its Naugahyde booths and burgundy carpet, its dim lamps hanging low over the tables, serves an early bird special. The waitress is wearing a name tag. It's why they chose it.

"Anyone?"

Ron Meyer, on Ovitz's right, speaks. "I'd do it, but my wife would kill me."

Outside, their cars, company vehicles belonging to William Morris, are parked a few blocks away, discreetly hidden on residential side streets. The parking lot of Billingsley's is empty beneath its shabby revolving sign. A valet stands under the restaurant's red awning with his hands in his pockets.

"I'll do it," Rosenfeld says. "What do I have to lose, besides my life savings?"

Rowland Perkins, gangly and pale with early silver hair, and Bill Haber, famously eccentric, are present, too, but let's focus on the big three. Until now everyone has assumed Perkins, the oldest and most senior of the lot, will be the ringleader of this new company they're planning, but right from the beginning it doesn't shape up that way. Ovitz is still in his twenties, but he's got a natural command. There's an intensity, which everyone around him struggles to match. Meyer, his foil, is warm and gregarious, with a beachcomber's tan and a chaotic mess of brown curls. The two of them had been planning to leave on their own until Rosenfeld let it slip that a couple other senior TV agents were contemplating the same. Hence, they've all banded up.

"All right," Ovitz says. Mythology will have it that they are catalyzed by Weltman's firing, Five Musketeers teaming up against an injustice, but this isn't entirely true. They are leaving for the reason such people always do: to become the masters of their own fates. "I'll get into it with the bank. Talk to your clients, but only the ones you're sure of. With everyone else, play the long game. It'll take a minute to get our ducks in a row."

December 1974. All of them are like passengers preparing to jump out of a burning plane. Meyer knows he's on borrowed time already—when he'd mouthed off in a staff meeting wondering why William Morris was signing over-the-hill talent while Freddie Fields over at Creative Management Associates snapped up Barbra Streisand, Weisbord reamed him out and he's known ever since they're going to fire him—but the rest of them? They are operating on faith.

"Whaddya think, fellas? Three ninety-five for the prime rib sandwich? May as well splurge while we can still afford it, huh?"

These are all working agents, TV guys who lack even my father's modest seniority, but they are half a step ahead of him where it counts, in boldness. They don't have significant savings. They don't have well-known clients. They barely have reputations. They've busted their asses at William Morris for years—Meyer had sold menswear for a while, then worked for Paul Kohner Associates before coming over; Ovitz had gone straight into WMA's mailroom from UCLA—and have nothing to show for it. Nothing except this foolish notion that they're going to start their own company. Best wish them luck, as they're going to need it.

★ ★ ★

PANIC. PANIC IS loyalty's bedfellow. Panic is what makes the wheels of industry turn, panic and, as strange as it is to say of so famously venal a place, love. Love and a little bit of envy are what my father feels when he discovers that his friends are on the move.

He arrives one morning just a few days into the New Year—it is January 7—to find Rosenfeld's office empty, completely cleaned out.

"What the hell happened?" He corners his friend Ron Mardigian, a senior agent from the literary department, outside his office. "Where's Mike?"

"Weisbord tossed him this morning."

"What are you talking about?"

"It's a bloodbath," his friend says. They stand, smoking, in the mustard-colored corridor, its vacancy reinforcing the dull, bureaucratic feel of this place, its executive chill. "They fired Bill Haber and Rowland Perkins this morning, also."

It's true. Weisbord has caught wind of the upstarts' plans— their contacts at the bank weren't as airtight as they'd hoped—and fired them all summarily, catching them with their pants down. Ovitz is out of the office, on the slopes in Colorado, and Meyer is down with the flu, but the others have been frog-marched out of the building without even their cars, company vehicles that are repossessed on the spot, to ferry them home.

"Jesus." My father turns and walks back down the corridor to his office. What more can he say? Rosenfeld was his closest colleague. "Linda, will you get me Beau Bridges?" He glances at his secretary as he passes. "He's at the hotel."

What more can he say? He's a loyal person. He's no buccaneer. He's not unhappy at William Morris, but some part of him still imagines another life. He is prudent, even cautious—too cautious, at times—but there is also a part of him, a libertarian, American part, that hates being told what to do. Two weeks later, on January 20, he opens his copy of *Daily Variety* to see his friends' company has a name.

"Creative Artists," he says out loud, staring down at the advertisement that plasters the periodical's entire back page. "Huh."

The ad is cheeky. The new agency's logo is curvy, red-on-white with a sense of voluptuousness and motion, where William Morris's is blue-on-black, the *W*, *M*, and *A* superimposed on top of each other, so it looks like a metal gate. The new ad, down to its printed date of establishment ("Since 1975") seems to be mocking his current employer's solemnity, its self-serious air of tradition. But William Morris has been around since the turn of the century, before the movies themselves even existed, and my father's loyal, dilatory soul can't help but feel attachment to it. He wishes his old friends well.

"Artists," though. Attachment or no, he cannot help but notice this faint shift in emphasis. "Creative Artists." It's as if his friends have recognized a key point, that the essential thing is not the company ("William Morris") but the people they represent. Being a man of some sensitivity, who loves his clients precisely because they *are* artists, he likes this.

"Fred?" Linda's voice sounds out from the hall. "I have Richard Crenna on line two?"

"These are good men." Sam Weisbord will put a smiling face on it in the trades when he is asked to comment on his former employees' defection. "We bear them no animosity." In the staff meeting my father will observe that he makes no remark on the matter at all, as if the departure of five junior agents is otherwise beneath his notice. *We wish them every success.*

Sure thing, my father thinks. ("Freddy, he was piiiisssed," Mike Rosenfeld tells him over the phone. "He called me Benedict Arnold and all sorts of shit. He lost his mind.") But this is a gentleman's business, real or pretend, and this is how things are done here. Does he envy his former colleagues? Not really. Ron Meyer was earning a few hundred dollars a week here, a sum that was both a fucking pittance and an insult to someone of Meyer's capability, but now? Now he's earning nothing.

"Richard, how are you?" (Those poor bastards over there, in absolute free fall!) "The offer came in last night from the network, and I think we can do a little better . . ."

★ ★ ★

MY GRANDFATHER DIES. It is the strangest thing. My father is lying there in bed, thinking about his dad—thinking about a time when Ruby had moved the family to Kingman, Arizona, for a few years—when the telephone rings.

"Hello?" It's two forty-one a.m. according to the clock on the nightstand, so he knows something is wrong even before he hears my aunt Marcia's voice. "What is it?" He sits up, swings his feet off the bed. "What?"

Behind him, my mother sleeps. His voice is a low, chesty murmur, his anxiety boxed in so as not to wake her. Moonlight slicks his legs as he sits, hunched over.

"Which room?" The hospital is Cedars-Sinai, formerly Cedars of Lebanon: the same in which I was born. "When? Yeah, OK," he says. "OK."

He'd been thinking about those years in Kingman because Ruby is sick. He has lung cancer. This move to the hospital is not unexpected. You get to a certain age—he is forty-three this year; it is December 1976—and you are always thinking about mortality or avoiding that thought.

The clock's red LED numbers glow dumbly in the dark. Ruby's health has been declining for a while—two packs a day for sixty years will do that—but you're never ready for this news even when you think you are. He reaches for his pack on the nightstand, shakes one out, and then—snaps the cigarette in half. He throws the pack out the window. He will never smoke again.

Say goodbye to the old Freddy. Say hello to the new. In the morning, I will step over that crumpled red box of Pall Mall on my way to school, and I will wonder what has happened. But my father's transformation is finally set to begin.

He and Ruby have never grown closer. Most of his life has been spent trying to throw mud in my grandfather's eye, trying to escape the clutching, dead hand of the shtetl here in Hollywood, as far from Ukraine as Atlantis is from the moon. He has not been a bad son—he has taken my sister and me to see our grandparents every Saturday now for years, to the liquor store they own on Santa Monica Boulevard—but he is pierced with the guilty awareness he has been merely a dutiful one. Once they bury Ruby at Forest Lawn in Burbank in a few weeks, after he dies on the twelfth, my father will never return to visit him there, not once.

He sits on the edge of the bed. His body is heavy. At six feet on the button, he hovers around two hundred pounds. His body is soft, his lungs ache, his breathing—like my mother's—is raspy when he sleeps. His skin is pale and doughy, almost alien in its middle-aged softness as he stares over at the brass standing mirror in the room's far corner. Who, by now, has he become? And who will he be now that his mortal enemy, his one true critic, is finally gone?

★ ★ ★

"WHAT WALKS ON four legs in the morning, two at noon, and three in the evening?" This is the Sphinx's riddle to Oedipus at Thebes, but it's no riddle to me why my father changes, what it is that sweeps him up in the spring of 1977.

"Matthew, c'mon." He's at my door at six-fifteen a.m., rapping sharply with his knuckles. "Let's move it."

Walks on two legs? It's high noon in my father's cosmos, and he's not walking now, he's running, shifting anxiously from foot to foot in nylon shorts, a white tee, a pair of New Balance shoes.

"Let's go!"

I've seen this movie. It's *Rocky*. But my father looks different already, leaning out a little around his face, his cheeks losing their pudge. In my room I roll over, lace up my own pair of New Balance and slip on a red nylon windbreaker, stumbling down the stairs behind him and out into the oyster-colored morning. I

don't know where my father has picked up this habit—from Bruce
Dern, presumably—but I do know the movies will soon be full of
middle-aged health nuts, anxious people working out their mortality onscreen. It is early, not just in the morning, but in the cultural timeline that will make running a national trend, and so
San Vicente Boulevard is mostly deserted. My father and I are
solo, stampeding along the green meridian strip that splits the
boulevard, hurtling beneath the coral trees toward the bluffs.

ROYALS, my windbreaker reads on the back, in white, iron-on
letters. Occasional runners appear, like apparitions, out of the fog
and then disappear back into the damp mist behind me. My father is already lost in the distance—it is a weekday so our run will
be short, a quick three-miler—and I am alone with my thoughts
as I churn along Palisades Park in a blur of perpetual motion, racing past the brass balustrades of the Shangri La, the Belle-Vue
Restaurant, the Georgian Hotel. The Pacific thunders, glassy and
gray, at the base of the bluffs. The day breaks open, the sun as
sharp as a yolk overhead.

"Hi!" I say, bursting back into the kitchen, where my mom is
up and already on the phone. "Do we have cereal? Maybe some
Captain Cru—"

She holds up a hand to quiet me. I peel off my Little League
windbreaker, while my father trots upstairs to shower.

"No," my mother says, tugging on her cigarette. (In six months,
San Vicente will be mobbed. We are just ahead of the trend.) "I
want you to test him."

She stretches the wall-mounted phone's cord across the room—
she certainly isn't giving up smoking—so she can tap ash into the
sink.

"I don't care what his grades are like. I want you to have him
tested. Why is that so hard?"

The room smells of citrus, the lemons and grapefruits from the
backyard that rest in a bowl on the table, and salt air. The windows

are cracked over the sink, and the French doors that lead to the patio are flung wide open. The dogs nap outside on a patch of sun.

"What the hell is wrong with these people?" she snaps after she hangs up. It is my fifth-grade teacher, whose voice I heard piping out of the receiver, she is mad at. "They're supposed to know their students."

"What is it?" I say.

But she doesn't answer—she is dressed in blue jeans and a peasant blouse, already made-up although it is early—just nods toward the front hall and the stairs.

"Hurry up," she says. "Go get ready. It's almost time for school."

★ ★ ★

MY MOTHER HAS gone to work in the field of education. In an attempt to forestall her fate, she has taken a job teaching Spanish at an experimental high school in South Santa Monica. This doesn't mean my own teacher has to listen to her, but after much prodding, multiple phone calls along the lines of the one I have just overheard, I am dragged from my classroom one afternoon and tested, administered three hours of standardized psychometrics before I am plunked down, two weeks later, in a classroom with a half-dozen other kids, none of them from my grade. Each of us is handed a Signet paperback copy of *Romeo and Juliet* before our teacher, some hapless twenty-three-year-old fresh out of UCLA who looks barely old enough to shave, spreads his arms and smiles.

"OK," he says. "Let's begin."

MGM—Mentally Gifted Minors—is the name of this program, its initialism just like the film studio's. In the fall of 1977 through the spring of the following year we meet twice a week to read *A Midsummer Night's Dream* and *Othello*, plays that are, naturally, over my head, but this time is really about my mother, just as the move to Santa Monica and the shift to public school says something about my dad. Why is the family economizing? And—what is the fate my mother would hope for me to avoid as well?

"Honey?" Now it is the summer of 1978, and I am running reconnaissance on the school I will begin in the fall, the one at which my mother works, doing double-duty in the summer as an administrator. "Honey, will you run down to Lucy's and get us some tacos?"

This place, Crossroads School for the Arts and Sciences, feels oddly institutional. My mom's office is a cinderblock cube. Its window overlooks the industrial clutter of an alley, the concrete backs of warehouses and storage units. An autobody shop does brisk business in the middle.

"Sure." I take twenty bucks from her purse, pick up my skateboard. "Back in a few minutes."

Outside the sun bakes the asphalt to a gummy consistency. The alley serves as the school's quad, charted off from Olympic Boulevard to the north with razor wire and a wrought-iron fence. One other building, a low, brick fortress opposite the administrative hub, belongs to the high school. The rest of the block is occupied by the autobody shop and a handful of crumbling residences, all of which gives the school the tenuous quality of an encampment.

My skateboard clatters along the alley's pebbled surface. The air reeks of paint fumes and solvent, rings with the sawing and hammering of metal. Men yell in Spanish. There's nobody out here besides these workmen—the administrators are all upstairs in their offices, the students and teachers are on summer break—so I pack a bowl inside a tiny brass pipe and smoke it out in the open, the better to absorb this place for what it is. *Arts and Sciences.* My mother's decision to·lead me onto this frontier—the school has eighty students across grades seven to twelve—is a form of resistance, a push against Hollywood privilege. Crossroads is a laboratory of left-leaning good intentions, and I am a specimen ready to be deposited into its petri dishes. Let's see what happens when we dose this specimen with Robert Frost and the Communist Manifesto . . .

Graffiti scars the faces of the buildings on Olympic, those padlocked bunkers and drab plaster storefronts all cluttered with wholesale overflow, discount washing machines and dishwashers that spill out onto the sidewalk. SMG, PEE WEE LOCOS, VX3 are scrawled in matte-black aerosols, leavings of the Crips and Sureños. I roll up to Lucy's Mariscos and order ten tacos at twenty-five cents per, pocket the change—my mother, who is mysteriously flush these days, won't miss it—then coast back over to campus.

My skateboard clatters across the pavement like a roulette ball spinning inside its wheel. This summer paradise is about to end, but for one last moment I'm still a kid, sunbaked and stoned, my beach-browned arms, bare from the shoulders, swinging in the wind. My world is going to derange me, fill me with wild ideas. Hollywood will claim me too soon, well before high school is over, but for now I am a feral cat, seduced by this campus's curious mood. I will discover in the fall its combinations of chaos and rigor, and I will never be able to view the teachers, or anyone else, really, as figures of authority, not when they're as likely as the students are to roll up barefoot in their battered little beach buggies, brushing marijuana seeds off their corduroy trousers, dragging copies of *Wuthering Heights* and Kafka's *The Castle* into classrooms with baffled Styrofoam ceilings; not when we will only ever say their first names, and we can find them, occasionally, high on mushrooms on the beach at night, their faces glowing like jack-o'-lanterns by the ecstatic light of a bonfire.

There are no adults here. A Hollywood lawlessness prevails even beyond the industry's fringes. I will learn about beauty, and I will learn about fear, discover the truth of a muddled terror that has begun, already, to clutch at my heart.

★ ★ ★

SOMETHING HAS HAPPENED to my parents. Something has happened to their industry, too, something that will open the gates—at last, at last—to a new kind of domination.

"How's our baby?" my mother says on a warm fall morning in 1978. She glances up from her crossword puzzle while the four of us sit having breakfast around the table in our dining nook. My father scowls down at the *Times*'s business section.

"Still up," he, evenly, without raising his eyes. "Still up."

A brittle tension fills the room, almost as if they can will this stock they're watching to keep rising, or as if at any moment its bubble might pop. Is this good luck, or is it, perhaps, a portent of disaster? My father rustles his paper. My mother gets up to fetch a little more champagne—Sunday morning—as my sister busies herself with the comics, and I with the sports pages. The French doors are open. The swimming pool rocks gently in sunlight, its turquoise surface sparkling.

"Seven-four," he says, as my mother returns from the kitchen. "Could be all the way to eight by December."

In April of last year, my parents had gone to a screening. Their friend Alan Ladd Jr. invited them to the Twentieth Century-Fox lot to watch the rough cut of a film. There was no fanfare around the movie—indeed, when the director had screened the first picture for the studio a month and a half earlier, without music or effects, the studio was convinced it had a dog on its hands—but by the time my parents walked out afterward it was clear the picture was no dog. The next morning, my father called his broker and bought as much of Twentieth Century-Fox's stock as he could afford, a few thousand shares, which were then trading around a buck-fifty. Now that stock is up, up, up. It is worth five and a half times what he paid for it.

"You sure you don't want a little more?" My mother tips the bottle toward him.

"Huh? Ah, no." My father holds his hand over the rim of his glass. He's wearing the T-shirt for the movie in question, which is black with the film's logo in yellow letters across the chest: *Star Wars.* "I'm good, Kath. Thanks."

My mother sits back down in her blond wicker chair, nursing her champagne buzz. The elevator, it goes straight to the top. My father hasn't got any star clients, but maybe he doesn't need them, not if the movies themselves are going to perform like this.

"So?" My father looks up from his newspaper now and stares at me. It's not just Twentieth Century-Fox that is booming. It's United Artists with *Rocky,* Universal with *Jaws.* All of them, really. "Whaddya say, sport?"

What do I say? I say that something is happening to my parents, and I don't like it. My mother is drunk at eleven a.m. and my father, hovering over the business section—the studios have new byzantine corporate structures, also, as Fox has purchased resorts in Aspen and Pebble Beach, United Artists is owned by Trans-America, and MGM, now owned by a corporate raider named Kirk Kerkorian, makes more money from hotels than it does from the movies themselves—has a new and unpleasant edge.

"You wanna take a run tomorrow?" His eyes narrow. (Trans-America, Gulf + Western. Who owns the movies now?) "For old times' sake?"

I barely recognize him. He has leaned out completely, lost almost thirty pounds and grown a trim salt-and-pepper beard. He is sharp and spiny like a blowfish, critical where he used to be affectionate.

"I don't think so," I say. "Mom's gotta take me to school."

My father reaches over and twists the cap off a Perrier bottle. The snap of its seal is like the wringing of a chicken's neck. It's all he eats now: chicken and fish. When my mother has a vodka tonic, he has mineral water; while she smokes her cigarettes, he huffs oxygen, heartbeat pumping as he churns along San Vicente.

"Can't hack it, huh?" Something of Ruby lives inside him, perhaps. "Can't handle a little four-miler?"

I can handle it. What I can't handle, I think, is him: the father who is suddenly lost, coursing through the meta-corporate belly of the movies. Over the next few years, he and I will lock horns endlessly, but not until I'm an adult will I understand where he's gone.

"Four is nothing," I say.

"Prove it," he says. "Be up at six."

Capitalism and the American family don't mix. But I don't understand that my father is bracing to make a move of his own. My sister leans over her comics page. The walls of this room are lined with photographs, pictures my father has taken of my sister underwater, learning to swim; the four of us on a ski vacation, perched at the top of a mountain; my mother looking pensive in sunglasses and a scarf. Memory's jewels, these eight-by-elevens, framed in black-and-white. But we have left all this history behind.

"Six o'clock," I say, like I am agreeing to terms on a deal. "I'll be ready."

★ ★ ★

"MICHELLE Y MIGUEL . . . in Cabo San Lucas . . ."

Hey now! There is going to be a wedding! My father is so jazzed you'd think he was the groom himself. He struts around the house like a rooster, humming a tune that sounds like "Strangers in the Night" but with lyrics composed by the man of the hour, one Michael S. Rosenfeld. It is, of course, Michael's second wedding—pity things didn't work out with Marilyn—and it happens in our very backyard. My father sets up a chuppah on a windy Saturday afternoon and the next morning, under the white lattice pergola that shades the concrete patio by the pool, Rosenfeld and his new bride tie the knot.

"Don't they look great?" my father whispers.

"Mmh." My mother appears agnostic. (Have I mentioned that the bride is markedly younger than the groom?) "Sure."

Summer Sunday, 1979. After the ceremony Mr. and Mrs. Rosenfeld will climb into the groom's prop plane and jet down to Mexico. All bets are off today, as my father and his friends are celebrating. Ron Meyer is here, Michael Ovitz. Bill Haber swans by and clasps my father on the shoulder.

"Easy on the Bordeaux there, Freddy. You'll feel it at the office tomorrow."

"We're going to the office tomorrow?" My father grins. "I thought it was a holiday!"

"Only for the groom. See you at the staff meeting tomorrow at eight-thirty."

Ah, yes. My father and his friends aren't merely "friends" anymore, they are colleagues now, again. The dam that's been holding Fred Specktor back—call it "loyalty" or "caution" as you will—has burst, and he is plying his trade at Creative Artists Agency himself.

"Mikey!"

"Freddy!"

Look at them now, the groom and his best friend reunited, embracing there on the terrace in a shower of sunlight and champagne.

"You feeling good, Freddy?"

Look at them, with the sudden exuberance of high school seniors goofing off at the prom.

"Never better, never better. And you?"

A year ago, they were at a different wedding—for it is indeed that time of life where many of their friends are wading in for round two—when my father had an epiphany. The CAA guys? They seemed like they were having the time of their lives, horsing around like cool kids at the cafeteria, while the gray soldiers of William Morris looked miserable. Was this going to be his life?

One where you could barely tell the difference between a wedding and a funeral?

"What do you think, Freddy?" Rosenfeld's rabbinical beard—there is a touch of silver in it now—glistens in the sun. "I feel like I'm eighteen again."

This is what it's all about. This is what it's all been about, the move to Santa Monica, the health kick, all of it, because if you're not living for something—who doesn't want to feel eighteen? Besides, of course, actual eighteen-year-olds—what are you doing? My father can sense the vitality pulsing beneath Rosenfeld's suit, the broad shoulders of a man who—his own airplane! A brand-new lady! A company in which he is a partner and not just a cog!—seems to have it all.

"Don't hurt yourself, Mikey. At our age, y'know, certain muscles don't respond the way they once did."

Rosenfeld grins, that wonderful smile that creeps up one side of his face, always a little sheepish, like Huckleberry Hound's, and my father slaps his back, pressing on through the assembled guests. Maybe he feels he has it all now, too. It's been only a year since he made his move, calling his friend to arrange his escape from William Morris the very next day after that wedding. Or maybe he feels a touch of envy. Either way, William Morris was dull, and CAA is thrilling, filled with a loose and freewheeling energy. My father and his friends—there are maybe a dozen of them now, as the agency is expanding—zoom around town in their sports cars, stride into screening rooms and restaurants in pairs, adjusting their sunglasses like hitmen. The partners drive Jaguars with matching vanity plates, "CAA" followed by their initials. This is living, man. This is fun!

"Kathy? Hey, Kath?"

This is fun, so why does he seem so agitated now, walking across the patio again with its stained plates and empty glasses, its balled-up napkins? It is as if everyone has leapt up from the Pico Rents furniture and fled. He collides with me as he strides into the house. I look up at him with a mouthful of cake.

"Where's your mother?" he snaps. It's like it has suddenly gotten late in a hurry. His face blots out the sun. "Have you seen your mother?"

★ ★ ★

BRUCE DERN ARRIVES one night unannounced. He rings the doorbell and then turns, dropping his trousers so he is bare-ass naked from the waist down, spreading his cheeks so we can see the void at the center of a backside sleeved in ink. He is shooting a movie called *Tattoo*. His body is a canvas, painted from head to toe with dragons and flowers.

"..."

"Shit!" He spins, scrambling to pull his pants up. "Sorry about that, Matthew. Is my agent home?"

"Your agent, or your proctologist?" My father arrives in the vestibule behind me. "Are you having trouble with itching or burning?"

"I've always got problems, Fred. How much time have you got?"

What's happened to these guys. Whither the man who shot John Wayne? What's happened to the movies, which were filled with ambiguity and intimate strangeness a few short years ago, but now are crammed with spaceships and sharks. Don't ask me, ask my father. The year before *Tattoo*, in 1980, Dern had starred in a movie called *Middle Age Crazy*, in which he played a successful architect who flips out the moment he turns forty. The architect trades in his sensible sedan for a Porsche; trades in his suit for an open-collared shirt; trades in his wife, a radiant Ann-Margret, for one of the Dallas Cowboy cheerleaders. Bruce, the man, is having no such crisis—he wouldn't leave Andrea in a million years—but my father? Of my father, I am not, now, so sure.

"Allow me to make the following recommendation," he says one night, turning toward me at the dinner table, lifting his index finger like a man with a brilliant idea. "I think you should—"

"Fred, stop," my mother says, before he can get the words, whatever it is he is about to recommend, out of his mouth. "Leave him alone."

"I'm just trying to give him some advice."

"It isn't advice if he doesn't ask for it. Leave him be."

My father, I think, means well. The didactic manner with which he now pushes me toward everything from skin cream to school electives ("What I would propose . . ."; "I'd like to make a suggestion . . .") is exactly what he does with his clients. In the new and improved nickelodeon of his life, he is the hero, the striver, the American man—is he happy? Or is he freshly adrift?—trying to satisfy himself and his family.

"Kathy," he says. "I think he should hear this."

I don't. But it's not just the pushiness, which will pass, but a new brusque way of ordering in restaurants ("I'll have the fish. Grilled. Plain."); a new car, a Porsche 911 the color of coffee, to which he has affixed a license plate that reads CAA FS. The pedanticism that has overtaken my father will pass, as I say, but in the meantime it drives me insane. I push up from the table and head upstairs, leaving my mother and sister to listen to his lectures on how to live and what to do. Has this, too, come from the movies?

"Fred," my mother says. Has he been replaced by a pod person, like Donald Sutherland in *Invasion of the Body Snatchers*? "Has it occurred to you that you're alienating him?"

"Kath, he's thirteen! He's not going to learn if I don't show him."

Exit, pursued by my father's inexhaustible flood of opinions. Adolescence, the real thing, has begun. In my room, I stop up the doorsill with my wadded-up ROYALS windbreaker—the iron-on *s* has flaked off—and tug the bong from under my bed. I am aware my parents' fighting has nothing to do with me. Their differences have begun to assert themselves at last. My mother spends her spare hours now out in the cabana beyond the pool, where she has begun to peck out short stories on an IBM Selectric typewriter. The stories are caustic, about an entertainment lawyer named Gary Katz and his beleaguered family, and while I don't have to wonder where she takes her inspiration—the son, Jason, is a vacant blond skateboarder who speaks in my own Santa Monica dialect—I know that she is an artist, and my father, an entrepreneur. I know that these are two different forms of American self-invention, maybe the only two that lie within the bounds of the law, and that they are incompatible.

I hunch over the bong, smoking until I can barely see, until the room's dank and lamplit air judders around me in black, epileptic-seeming patches. I stand and remove the posters from my walls, unmounting those signed one-sheets for *Silent Running* and *Young Frankenstein*. They belong to another time. Neither I nor the movies are like that anymore. Through the wall that abuts my parents' bedroom I can hear the nightly news, the murmur of their conversation over the television. ("—you voted for him," my mother is saying). I stare at the now-blank walls ("Well, what was the alternative? Governor Moonbeam?"), then slap on a record, X's *Los Angeles*, to cover the sound of their bickering.

Burn down the old heroes. Make way for the new! My father and his Porsche are foolish to me, as hopeless as the kid who arrives at the beach with a brand-new surfboard but no ability. He's gone Middle Age Crazy! I, on the other hand, have figured things out. I stare up at the blank walls, the naked screen of my own adolescence, the totems of teenaged sophistication—*Naked Lunch* and *Another Green World*, *Raw Power*, and *I Lost It at the Movies*—that have sprouted around my room. Make way for the new! Step aside for the Hollywood of tomorrow, whose hour has arrived today.

★ ★ ★

"HEY KID, RUN this over to Rosalie's office, will you?"

History runs in circles. One day I will understand this, that it never repeats but it does almost rhyme. Here I am in the summer of 1981, a quarter-century after my father's turn at MCA, pushing a mailcart through the halls of a building in Century City, pretending my dad is not among the agents whose offices I pass— summer of nepotism, summer of nightmares—at my first job.

"Where'd you hear that? That's bullshit! Bullshit!" Tony Ludwig, with his trim, gray beard and manicured fingernails, telephone cupped to his ear, takes a drag off his cigarette as I go trundling past his office. "He would never fucking say that."

This place is a hive of information, a place where a cadre of Rumplestiltskins, furry little men who look like Jewish hobbits and tall ones with New York swag, spin gossip into gold. I push my trolley with my eyes wide open (here's Marty Baum, the living legend, famous for once having sold a director on a client who was, in fact, dead), my silk tie dangling to my waist (here's Paula Wagner, as sultry and glamorous to me as Sophia Loren), my palms sweaty with the heat of midsummer (Rick Nicita, with his Paul Newman mustache and dark-haired good looks) as I enter the machine myself.

"Can I have one of those?"

On a July afternoon I stand outside, slouching in the shadow of the office tower on Century Park East, taking five minutes for myself. It's like working for a casino, or in the boiler room of a ship. I arrive each morning at eight, taking the bus to get in ahead of my dad, then leave each night at seven-thirty. An air of hilarity spills into the halls, the sound of agents and executives needling each other, but also a trace of fear. If Ron Meyer still rambles around in raggedy blue jeans, as cool as my high school's most easygoing stoner, he is the exception that proves the rule. If this

agency began as five guys in a tiny suite on Wilshire Boulevard—
with card tables for desks, their own wives for secretaries—it has
grown into a real engine, with the pressure to match. Earn or die.
I slouch outside, leaning against the hot glass front of the building
at 1888 Century Park East, groping in my pocket for a cigarette to
offer the man who has materialized at my shoulder.

"Sure." I hand over a Marlboro and a match, then realize I
know him. Not personally—he is an actor, one of Ovitz's clients
who's been doing some casting in a spare office—but his face is as
familiar to me as my own.

"You shouldn't have these," he says, speaking around the cigarette as he lights it, cupping the match against the wind. "You're
too young."

"You think?"

Dustin Hoffman is my height, a little shorter; dark-haired and
slight.

"Yes." He shakes out the match, holds his cigarette a little awk-
wardly, like a nonsmoker indulging a chaotic whim. "Bad for your
health."

"Bad for my health," I say. I've seen him in *The Graduate* and in
All the President's Men. I've seen him in *Kramer vs. Kramer*, playing America's divorcing dad. "What isn't?"

He grins. Light falls against the brown steel of the building
behind us, its tempered glass windows, dark as a pair of aviator
glasses, reaching up into the void. This neighborhood, Century
City, is a business district: eight square blocks that are like a
normal city's downtown in miniature, which seem to house only
agencies, entertainment firms, and television networks.

"You're kind of a smart-ass," he says. "I like that."

"Thanks." The names of these firms are tattooed on my heart,
the hours I spend running envelopes over to Ziffren, Brittenham,
Gullen & Ingber; to Armstrong, Hendler & Hirsch.

"I'm Dustin."

I introduce myself back, smoking and squinting into the afternoon sun. After a moment I flick my Marlboro over to the curb.

"You work here?" he says. It's like a stage set, this place: after
eight-thirty p.m. these streets will be deserted, the buildings as
impenetrably dark as obsidian.

"Yeah, why?"

He laughs. "That's bad for your health, too."

Is it? This is what I will never understand. Are the movies bad
for me—so much dreaming—or are they life itself? Are these encounters with the people who make them, the hundreds or thousands I will have over the course of a lifetime, valuable, or are
they just detours? I'll never know. I'll spend the rest of my life
brushing up against those people who haunt other people, crowding the margins of their dreams. That summer, Hoffman may be
America's divorcing dad but now he is mine by proxy, acting out
things—even though I will never see him again after this summer,
these few weeks in which we are smoking buddies, office mates,
in which I am his minor mascot—that are about to happen to
me, also. He is my delegate, or vice versa. I'll never know what it
means to have the movies at my mercy, to be Hollywood's biggest
star, but I'll also never know what it's like to be without them, now
that they have colonized my imagination like a swarm of bees.

"Hey, Matthew." Here comes my father ambling down the hall.
"You need a ride home later?"

"Yeah, if I can get off in time."

"They'll let you out." He pats my arm as he glides past. "Six-thirty.
I'll give you a lift."

In mid-afternoon this office takes on an almost languid cast.
A golden light honeycombs the halls, mellow sun spilling through
the glass walls in the post-lunch lull. The agents' offices are empty,
with their doors flung open. The assistants hunch over their desks
updating their call sheets, picking at salads, at sandwiches, orders
of French onion soup from the Hamburger Hamlet on the corner.

A momentary quiet prevails. The phones are silent. In the reception area, Paul Newman slouches alone on the couch, absorbed in his *Daily Variety*, waiting for Ovitz to return.

"You ready to go, sport?"

Six-thirty arrives almost too soon. I love this place, especially in its quiet hours, love it as both theater and enigma, a place where I am almost, if not quite, an adult. My father is its trusted soldier and will work here for the rest of his life, and so its questions enter me to the core.

"Yeah, sure." I follow him out to the lobby. "Let's bail."

These questions proliferate. Is it possible to work here and be a complete human being? Who is Michael Ovitz, the fearsome man in his corner office, monster in a glass box? I see him chugging around the halls, blond and inscrutable in his tan suit. Does the Agency belong to the agents, or to the artists themselves?

"What are you doing?" my father says, as we step into the elevator and I start box breathing, exhaling loudly through my mouth.

"Darth Ovitz."

"Come on," he says, laughing. "Really?"

This place is my Death Star, and my Tatooine. Ovitz's voice rarely seems to rise above a whisper, he is occupied but never unfriendly when he passes, and still, I am aware that at the center of everything there is fear, and that my father is not immune to it. We fold into his car and pull out of the building's underground garage, the silver frames of the ABC Towers gleaming in the day's late light above.

"You OK?"

"Yeah," I say. He seems uncommonly solicitous, weirdly concerned. "Why?"

We drive west into a bank of fog, the thick wall of gloom that rolls in off the Pacific every evening at this time of year. By the time we hit Westwood Boulevard we are deep inside a white opacity.

"No reason."

When I am older, I will understand what he is about to do. I will understand the trouble that clutches at his heart, just as it does now at mine. For the moment all I can see is that he is anxious about something, drumming his hands on the steering wheel, singing along with the stereo's cassette, Talking Heads' 77, that is turned up a little too loud.

"That's not what he says," I snap. "It isn't 'smartest God in town.' That doesn't even make sense."

His nervousness makes me irritable. By the time we arrive back in Santa Monica, we have lapsed into sullen silence.

"Dad, what are you doing?"

We're idling at the curb, exactly where he might usually park, but now, he just sits like a cabbie letting out a fare.

"You live here, remember?" The cold fog is wet on my face, so close to rain. "Mom's inside, making dinner?"

The car seems to shudder a little as we sit, top down, in the damp.

"I'm not coming in," he says. "I'm sorry."

It strikes me, as my father thus flicks the axe that will demolish our family, that he has no idea what he is doing. For himself, he knows—he is jettisoning weight, making his move—but the fallout will be greater than he anticipates.

"Ah," I say, not quite understanding yet, thinking he is just on his way to meet a client. "I'll catch you a little later."

I'm halfway out of the car when the penny drops: he has decided to change his life. In a moment I will walk inside to find my mother sobbing at the kitchen table, wailing into cupped palms, but this has long since been worked out. His closet is already half-empty.

"I'm sorry, son," he says. "I'm sorry."

I jog up the front walk, Warren Zevon now drifting tinnily out of the car behind me as I step inside. I can hear my mother weeping. The animalistic sounds she is making are more than a little frightening, but after I peek in at her I turn around and trot upstairs. I don't know where my sister is. The house is dark. My mother is alone in the gloom with the lights out, a glass of wine glinting yellow at her side like a dim signal from an underwater world.

Upstairs, I shut my door, reach inside my desk for a thumb-sized envelope taped above one of the drawers. I undo its origami folds and carve out two long lines of cocaine, chopping them into shape with an expired Visa card from my father's desk in the den. It will take me a while to forgive him, and when I do, I will understand that he has no choice, that what impels him out the door now is far more complicated than it appears. I stoop and inhale the two lines through a rolled twenty, then tuck the envelope back in my desk. I'm good at this: drugs, duplicity. As far as I know, my parents remain in the dark.

I tip my head and close my eyes, the better to feel that sweet sinal burn, that rush of numb invulnerability, the cocaine aggression that spikes my heart toward the sky. My pulse races, jaws clench, and my face feels invisible, my teeth locked shut. Suddenly, I am ecstatic, punching my fists in the air like a boxer, like a killer, like—I open my eyes so the world seems to flash toward me, and I can see for miles, everything shining gold and white—like a goddamn motherfucking *king*.

5. NEVER GET OUT OF THE BOAT

——

1981–1984

"MAYBE YOU SHOULD WRITE a script."

My father takes a thoughtful sip of wine. He stares at my mother across the dining table, fork resting sideways across a plate of angel hair that appears to have been licked almost clean. "What do you have to lose? It'll give you something to do while you're sending out stories."

"Do you think?" She swipes her tongue to dislodge a fleck of basil. "What do I know about writing a script?"

"What does anyone know?" my father says. "You think the writers my office represents all started out as experts?"

As in the movies sometimes, life can happen out of order. Cause and effect, action and consequence. Six months before my father leaves, he offers a solution to a problem that doesn't yet exist, throwing a life preserver to a woman standing on dry land.

"What about rewriting a script?" he says. "How would you feel about that?"

I believe my father is acting in good faith. My mother is an artist. She has been in her secret heart for years. Why wouldn't he encourage that?

"You're a writer," he says. Irrespective of any discontent that may be boiling up inside him, this is an act of support. "You're as talented as anyone I know. Why not see if you can get paid a little money for it?"

Let's look at her: a woman of forty-five, still young as these things go, still beautiful and funny. Her once-blond roots have darkened, her complexion has grown a little ruddy—too many hours in the sun, and perhaps the influence of something else—but she remains at the height of her abilities and appeal.

"I suppose I could give that a whirl," she says, with a little dash of the devil-may-care confidence that hides somewhere deep, deep inside her. "You got a particular script in mind?"

"You know that project we were talking about with Larry Peerce the other night?"

"The prison drama?"

"Yeah," my father says. "The one with Laddie." He takes another small sip of wine. "They could use some help with that."

Ah. Knowing what I will come to know—that after he leaves, my father will worry about her, wracked by the pain he is causing—I know he is paving the way for his escape, but he is also trying to do the right thing. She has gifts. Shouldn't she use them?

"I'll have a look," my mother says, shaking a cigarette from her pack. (What kind of person would he be, after all, if he didn't support her dreams?) "Is there a copy upstairs?"

★ ★ ★

MY MOTHER WANTS to be a novelist. In her heart, I know, this is her deepest wish. This wish she will pass along to me, but in the morning when she rises—it is the summer, now, of 1981, and she is able to take a few months off work—she is just a dedicated amateur. Perhaps it might be better to remain thus. "Why not get paid?" says the businessman, unable to imagine an alternate path to validation for an artist, or to understand that money can hinder as well as help, and so each day she wakes up and walks out to the cabana behind the house, carrying her coffee out past the pool and into the room with the clammy brick floors and glass doors, there at last to reckon with her fate. A screenplay is not a novel, perhaps, but it is no small thing to be invited to write one (but is she "invited," formally, I mean? We shall come to that), and, whatever the medium, no small thing to tell a story in words.

"Mom?"

She goes for it. She doesn't want to be a screenwriter—the movies are just commerce, where literature is art—but she gives it everything she's got. The existing script does not have a name. It is based on a segment that aired on *Sixty Minutes* about a woman named Terry Jean Moore who got caught up in an armed robbery in Florida. The script, written by a woman named Deena Gold-stone, is good, my mother thinks—the rub is that Terry goes to prison, where she gets knocked up by a guard—but allegedly the studio is not happy with it. Alan Ladd Jr., who now runs a pro-duction entity called The Ladd Company, is not happy, and Larry Peerce, my father's client who is onboard to direct, is not happy, and so she goes for it, rewriting the script from top to bottom. It's crazy, really, that they still make movies like this—movies about everyday people, rather than space operas, action dramas, thrillers with high-concept loglines—but they do. Just this year there is *On Golden Pond* and *My Dinner with Andre*.

"Mom?"

There has been *Kramer vs. Kramer* and *Ordinary People*, *Norma Rae* and *The China Syndrome*, all recent films that—

"Mom!"

She looks up from her typewriter. "What is it, honey?"

These movies are about human beings, rather than villainous caricatures and heroic cartoons. So is this one, which is why she is happy to write it. And so here she is out in her cold cabana during the summer of '81, alone with the French doors open, with her desk and the skylight and the tiny refrigerator. She wears gray sweats and a T-shirt still damp with sweat from a dance class she'd attended earlier. Her hands hover over her Selectric's keys like hummingbirds as I snap her out of her trance.

"Do we have anything to eat? The pantry's empty."

Saturday afternoon, hence, I am not at my job. She peers at me as if through a long telescope.

"Ask your father."

"He's not home," I say.

"All right," she says. "I'll be in in just a few minutes."

"OK."

She lowers her hands and begins to type, the electric carriage making a gunfire sound as the keys strike their mark: *rattattat . . . tat*. She glances up a moment later, astonished that I am still here.

"Go," she says. "I told you. I'm working."

★ ★ ★

BUT WHERE IS my father on these weekend afternoons? Surely my mother has noticed that he is often not at home.

"Wait—hey, wait!"

Maybe she hasn't noticed. After all, she is occupied, and maybe he is just out knocking down errands, dropping off dry-cleaning, trying on new suits at Alandales in Westwood, where his measurements are on file, or maybe—

"Wait up!"

Maybe he is running on San Vicente, chasing down a woman he has seen before, one who has caught his eye for—how easily we deceive ourselves sometimes—no particular reason that he is aware of.

"You do this every day," he says. "You run right past me. You look at me like you know me. You always smile when you pass. What's that about?"

She shifts from foot to foot, jogging softly in place. "What do you think it's about?"

"I don't know what it's about, but you can't just be out here lapping me every day like it's the Indy 500. There are rules."

"There are rules?"

"Yes." He grins. "At least, that's what I've heard."

You ever been in a dead marriage? My father isn't looking for trouble, but as he stands under one of the coral trees that line the boulevard's meridian strip one morning in the spring of 1981, trouble has found him, nevertheless.

"You're fast," he says.

"Fast." She is long and tall, this woman, with dark curly hair, which is more his style. A turn toward his Jewish roots, you might say. "I am fast."

Every word an innuendo. But it's not intended to be, it just happens.

"I guess you'd better watch where you're going." Maybe he is looking, but he has not sought it out. "You could hurt somebody, going that fast."

"I could hurt somebody." She laughs: a brash, urban cackle. "Who am I gonna hurt?"

Her accent is New York, outer borough. She is younger than my mother, of course, but not some kid. She's in her mid-thirties.

"I dunno," my father says. He isn't a cheater, a Hollywood philanderer, but now—he leaps. "We should have a drink sometime to discuss it."

"I don't drink."

"Then we should have an espresso," he says. "We should go for a run."

He digs in his nylon pocket for a business card.

"Fred Specktor," she says, turning it between her fingers. (Even here, he carries one. You never know.) "You're at Creative Artists."

"Yep." The agency's name carries weight now.

"I'm Pamela. I'm in executive search."

"Ah. You're a headhunter."

"Yes."

Cars whiz by on either side of the meridian, morning traffic heating up. She shifts from foot to foot, holding his gaze for a decisive moment before loping off, vanishing ahead into the mist.

He is not a person who does this sort of thing—there are others in his office, friends, who step out on their wives all the time, who use the job to generate opportunity ("Are you an actress? I feel like I've seen you before . . ."), but he does not—and yet here he is. He stares down the meridian after her, then turns and jogs back to the house. Morning fog sparkles, prismatic, as the sun burns through above. By the time he is home, this fog is gone, the day ceded over to California's changeless spring. By the time he is home his marriage is over. All that will be left is the execution, the detonation of the bomb that is ticking, now, in his heart.

★ ★ ★

AND THEN—IT IS fall. My mother is holed up in her cabana. Summer is over, school has resumed, and my father is long gone. Hobbled by piercing migraines—one comes on in September and then seems merely to ebb and flow for months, to remain always with me—I take refuge in my room. No one will disturb me here.

But there is one thing I notice, as my right eye throbs and I unfold a copy of *Daily Variety*, having taken to reading the trades now myself. My mother is not just rewriting a script. The situation is a little more complicated than that. My mother is a screenwriter, sure, but she is also—

"A scab." She thwacks her own copy down on the butcher's block in the kitchen, the December 7, 1981, issue in which she is front-page news. "They're saying I scabbed."

My mother and I have been spending a lot of time together lately. It isn't to be helped: most nights, we're alone in the house. Whatever informal custody arrangement my parents have made while the lawyers are grinding away involves my sister being with my dad much of the time and me remaining here with her.

"Is that what they say?" I watch her carefully. "That you crossed the picket line?"

"Yes." She leans forward, a little unsteady on her stool. "That's what they say."

Some part of me will always be here, alone in this room with my mother in cold twilight, seated on opposite sides of this table like a couple of barflies, two cigarettes burning in the ashtray between us.

"Do you think it's true?" she says. A bottle of vodka sits by her elbow. "Am I a scab?"

"No, Mom." I listen to her slurry consonants and decide not to poke this bear. "I do not think it is true."

Alas, however, I know it to be true—even as my mother insists, to me and to herself, that she is just fooling around, that nobody other than my father had invited her to work on the script, so how can she be scabbing? But on April 11, 1981, the Writers Guild of America went on strike. Their dispute with the studios was over residual payments for VHS and Betamax cassettes, the home video market that is just now developing. The strike had lasted for three months, which happened to be the very months in which my mother, a nonunion writer, had rewritten her still-untitled screenplay.

"You want another glass, honey?"

"Sure."

I'm no labor lawyer, I'm a high school sophomore, but as I watch my mother slop vodka onto the table, the bottle as lazy in her hand as a garden hose, it seems to me this is the very definition of scabbing. The strike is why the studio had not been able to hire a professional writer to rewrite the script that is just now entering production in Florida. It is why they hadn't hired Deena Goldstone to rewrite it herself.

"You got a light?" She pats herself down for a match, despite the fact she's not wearing pockets. "I need a light."

I'm no labor lawyer, but this is how it is. My father had a client, Larry Peerce, a director whose movie needed a rewrite or else it would lose its green light in the fall; my mother was an aspiring writer, an amateur who needed something to do, and my father was a man having an affair, trying to figure out how to leave his wife. These are the facts of the case.

"I'm not a fucking scab," she snaps. "I'm not."

The movies will show you who you are. Who you are and who you cannot help becoming. My mother the leftist and the strikebreaker, the screenwriter and the drunk, whose intake has sharply accelerated. This fall, she will take me to see Warren Beatty's *Reds*, his movie about John Reed; she will give me John Dos Passos's *The Big Money* and Clifford Odets's *Waiting for Lefty* to read. Her politics haven't changed. Only her perspective has.

"You wanna go down to the Yellow House?" she says, pushing up from her barstool. "Get some steamed clams?"

Her perspective, which is the problem with Hollywood to begin with. Everyone thinks they're the hero, even when there are no heroes really. She stands up—no heroes, and not always clear-cut villains either—wobbling on her feet like a boxer awaiting the bell in the late rounds.

"Sure thing," I say. "Only—let's take a cab."

"A cab?" She slurs, her words coming out in an unbroken string. "Why would we take a cab?"

"It's just down the hill," I say. "Let's take a cab."

Everyone thinks they're the hero, which is a problem not just with the movies but with America, which has no other culture besides its celebrity culture anyway. I've been spending a lot of time with my mother, not that I have a choice. But even at fifteen, I understand what she is going through, that she is caught between untenable alternatives—parent, artist, jilted spouse—that bind her into a set of contradictions she cannot possibly resolve.

"Tell me about English. What are you reading?"

Over dinner, she sharpens. In a restaurant she loves at the bottom of Santa Monica Canyon, she alternates ice water and Soave Bolla, leaning over a bowl of steamed shellfish to interrogate me.

"Hardy."

"Which one?"

"*Tess of the d'Urbervilles.*"

Wandering out of her drunkenness like a pedestrian caught in intermittent rain. For a moment she is sharp as ever: "*Far from the Madding Crowd* is better. What else?"

"*Heart of Darkness.*"

"Good," she says. "By the way, did you steal my copy of *Four Quartets*?"

It's impossible to explain, really, what this is like. My mother is my best—and for a few months perhaps my only—friend. In the grips of a full-blown dependency, a dependency she keeps hidden much of the time, so it will be many years before I understand the extent of the problem, she is both a wonderful parent and a terrible, Medean nightmare.

"How's your father?"

"Good."

"Oh really? How's his," she blows smoke, "girlfriend?"

"Good. She's good." I choose my words carefully. "She's—OK, I guess."

My mother is a wonderful parent, adept at every part of it except actual parenting. The caretaker in our relationship is me. But it hardly matters, as there are lessons I can absorb all the same.

"Your father's just a salesman," my mother pronounces. "He's Willy Loman with a Rolodex instead of a briefcase." She picks up her wine bottle and tops off my glass. "He'll never understand people like you and me."

The lesson is gaslighting, a kind of conscription. The lesson is that artists are not, somehow, ordinary people, a lesson I will later learn to be false. But I see my father on weekends, at the house he's rented in Westwood, a house like a suite at the Holiday Inn: empty cupboards, empty closets, a refrigerator that holds nothing but a bottle of Ramlösa and a carton of rotting Chinese food.

"Do you wanna go on Sunday to see *Rebel Without a Cause?*" she says. My father doesn't live in that place, really. He lives with his girlfriend in an apartment on Fourteenth Street. "It's playing at the Fox Venice."

"Sure."

"Have you seen it?"

"You took me last summer, remember?"

We are outside now, waiting for our return cab. In the elaborate hall of mirrors, the cinematic funhouse of my own adolescence, I have no idea what my mother remembers. We stand in the quiet of West Channel Road, two hundred yards from the Pacific. The restaurant lights flick off behind us.

"Nicholas Ray . . . is a genius," she murmurs dreamily.

By the time we are home, three minutes later, she is asleep, and

I must hoist her out and drag her unconscious, yet somehow still animated, body up the stairs.

"There you go, Mom." She moves like a marionette, shambling and spindly, as I lug her down to her room. "Bed for you."

I set her down, brush ash off my sweater. My sister will carry some of this, but for the next few years, she will be mostly mine to look after. I step into the hall, following a trail of moonlight to my room.

I already know I am leaving. I will run from Los Angeles in a few years as if my very life depends on it, because it does. I undress, then smoke a last cigarette by the window, dreaming of a world beyond Hollywood. Outside it begins to drizzle. I crush my cig against the sill then flick it down into the wet flowerbed. It is raining in Santa Monica Canyon, where they are locking up the Yellow House and the Golden Bull across the street, raining now upon West Channel Road, which stands silent and deserted, upon the beach and out over the Pacific, a rain falling faintly and faintly falling, but some part of me will remain, today and for the rest of my life, trapped inside that indoor weather, forever alone in that room with my mother.

★ ★ ★

"*NEVER GET OUT of the boat . . .*"

I have arrived at the movies. On a Tuesday night I board a bus and come to the Nuart Theatre in West LA, slipping out of the house while my mother is comatose, sliding five bucks to the ticket taker and finding a seat in a revival house that is largely empty at ten p.m. I have timed my arrival perfectly. The LSD hits the moment I step inside, synapses starting to spark and fry as I settle into my chair and the crimson room begins to pulsate in the dark. I lean back into my seat, jam my hands into the pockets of my thrift store overcoat, and then—I am catapulted into a wall of fire.

"Fuck!" I shriek, in the grips of full-blown hallucination as napalm seems to ooze from the screen. My voice is drowned out by the mechanical clatter of helicopter blades, the Doors fading up over Martin Sheen's face superimposed upside-down beneath the turning of a ceiling fan. The whole room seems to shake—"*Saigon. Shit*..."—and then...

Two and a half hours later I am shuffling along Santa Monica Boulevard. The film itself is a blur, the hours I have just spent in a Philippine jungle with Sheen, Marlon Brando, and Dennis Hopper ongoing, still clinging to my imagination like a petrochemical substance itself.

"Never get out of the boat!" Thankfully, it's late, as I am shouting at the top of my lungs. The street is empty, the shops shuttered. The light of a service station guides me down the block, glowing like a holy oasis. "Never get out of the boat!"

A rugged night. Of it I will retain only the most impressionistic memories, for obvious reasons, but when I return three nights later to watch *Apocalypse Now* stone sober, the movie will overwhelm me again. When it runs on Theta Cable's Z Channel, the proto-HBO that had launched in Los Angeles in the mid-1970s, I will tape it on my mother's Betamax so I can watch it at will, the better to memorize it chapter and verse.

"Never get out of the boat." The words spoken by Martin Sheen's Captain Willard are like scripture, words to be repeated between my friends. We have all gotten out of the boat, tumbling into the murky swamp of Los Angeles adolescence. Where this will lead it is too soon to tell, but we are determined to go all the way.

The movies will tell you who you are. That's true for everyone who looks at them long enough, but it's especially true for those who grow up inside the cradle of their making. Marlon Brando, who will eventually become my father's client, plays Colonel Walter Kurtz; Sheen, whose daughter is one of my emerging friends at Crossroads, plays the officer dispatched up the Nung

River to retrieve him, in a story based on Conrad's *Heart of Darkness*. The Nung River is fictional—all of this is fictional when you get down to it—but try telling me that. This is the dream that swallows reality. It is, in some sense, the only reality I will ever know.

Never get out of the boat. There is no boat, there's only fucking water. There is only fifteen-year-old me shuffling along Santa Monica Boulevard at two in the morning, high on LSD and screaming. There is only the blue bus that pulls up like a submarine, a little bubble of nightmares and light, here at last to ferry me home.

By the time I get home it is almost dawn, and I am coming down. The contrails I have been chasing all night are reduced to a gentle glow. When my mother comes downstairs, I am sitting in the kitchen spooning up a bowl of cornflakes swamped in sugar. I will need all the energy I can get if I am going to stay awake through the day's classes.

"Morning," she says. "You want some coffee?"

"Yes, please."

The sun is shining. Birds are twittering. Everything seems to burn a little brighter on this warm morning, but otherwise my household's ordinary disorder has been restored.

"Who's the commanding officer here?" I say.

"What?"

My mother turns around from the sink.

"Who's the commanding officer?"

She squints at me. "Did you go see *Apocalypse Now* last night?"

"Yeah."

"Isn't it great? I told you it was great." She crosses to the stove to light her cigarette. "You didn't stay out late, did you? Don't you have a test today?"

My mother can do a fair impersonation of a responsible parent when she wants to. That's because she is a responsible parent, in a way. Responsible to the wrong things, to the bitter imperatives of her own troubled heart, but responsible nevertheless.

"Who's the commanding officer here?" I say, putting my spoon back down. There's so much sugar in my bowl it's like white sand, like a tropical beach. I stare at my mother like I would like an honest answer, because I would, but she just stares right back.

"Ain't you?" she says, smiling from ear to ear. She's going to make an artist out of her child if it kills her. "Ain't you?"

★ ★ ★

"WHAT DO YOU think, kid?"

My father is moving up. One afternoon he drives me out to Malibu, and we walk through an empty house, a glass-walled palace overlooking the Pacific.

"D'you like it?"

"Yeah," I say. "I do."

Our footsteps echo on the pale oak floors. The windows are open, French doors swinging onto a brick patio wreathed with bougainvillea. The ocean sparkles, far, far below.

"Bedrooms are down the hall. You can take your pick."

The story of the movies is a story of real estate, of the dream's moguls shifting around their parcels of land both big and small. Ron Meyer, my father's colleague, has bought a house farther out past the Colony and so has sold this one to my dad.

"One is for you or Johanna," he says, "depending on which nights you're here. The other one is for Allison."

"Ah." He means Pamela's daughter, who is my age. "I'll take the one at the far end."

It doesn't matter. I won't spend much time here. Over the next few years, my father and I will see each other only occasionally, during which time he will affect his biggest transformation. Next year, he will remarry. A few years after that, this house, on Rambla Orienta, will burn down to embers, and in that time—my father will have moved back to Santa Monica before it does—he will assume his place among the masters of the universe.

"Nice digs, Dad." The sarcasm that creeps into my voice as we walk through the empty museum of his present isn't persuasive. He deserves this.

"Thanks, sport."

He deserves it, certainly, if anyone does. But who has he become? And who am I becoming now that I have fed myself into the machine? I'm working in the mailroom, still, after school, spending my weekends reading scripts. I may have only recently learned to drive, but I am old enough to say "this story has no second act." I am old enough to write in my readers' reports that "this seems perfect for Pacino, but the box office prospects here are a little cloudy, unless we can cast Meryl Streep in the opposite lead." I may be just a teenager, but I sink into my father's world like a professional. Already I know I'm no agent—I lack the temperament, the blood hunger for the deal—but I like working here. There is a discipline, an orderliness that is lacking at home as I arrive each afternoon at three-fifteen, gunning the beat-up Toyota I have bought with my saved-up mailroom money into the garage and then racing upstairs to join my colleagues at a job that is fast-paced, but also—fun.

"You wanna get high?"

"Fuck yeah." I look up from the pneumatic *tunk-tunk-tunk* of the Xerox machine to see my friend Jay Moloney has sidled up next to me. "Are you holding?"

"Am I 'holding'?" He looks back at me over the tops of his John Lennon–style glasses. "What is this, *Panic in Needle Park*? 'Am I holding'? Jesus, you're sixteen."

"You asked."

"I meant do you want to go smoke a joint downstairs."

"Oh."

Two paths are available to me, and this is one. Jay Moloney is nineteen, barely three years older than I am, and already—he is a student at USC, working part-time just like me—he is the golden child. It's easy to see why.

"Am I holding." He grins. "OK, Scarface. You moving weight now? You want that yayo, Tony Montana?"

He is as charming as he is good-looking, with his sandy hair and boyish freckles. He has taken me under his wing exactly like an older brother. Perhaps he sees this is something I could use.

"Ease up," I say. "If I wanted a hard time, I'd go hang out in my dad's office."

Perhaps it's something he could use, also. His father, Jim, was once an agent also. Two paths are available, and Jay will follow in his father's footsteps to become an agent himself. By the time this year is over he will have dropped out of USC to work first as my dad's second assistant, then for Ovitz directly.

"Who takes care of you?" he croaks. Down in my car, buried deep in the garage, we pass a joint back and forth. "Not your dad."

"Not my dad," I admit, and then study him. "Who takes care of you?"

He gazes back, light glinting off his glasses, then cracks a big smile.

"Touché."

Two paths, each pernicious. We stub out our joint and trundle back toward the lobby, passing the long row of cars with their vanity plates—Ovitz's brown Jaguar in pole position, next to Meyer's red Testarossa—on our way back in.

"I can't believe you thought I was gonna ask you to do drugs. Jesus. Stay in school."

"Yessir."

The day's almost over. We ride the elevator in silence, bearing stoned and glassy smiles. This place, it is on its way to dominance, to greater power inside the film industry than anyone can imagine, but right now it is still human-shaped and human-sized. It can still accommodate a pair of lightly baked teenagers, just as the movies themselves can.

"You fellas had something important to attend to?" Richard Lovett, who runs the mailroom, smirks as we come back in. "Some . . . burning engagement?"

"Shut up." Visine leaks from Jay's eyes, but he reeks of smoke just as I do. "It's six-thirty anyway."

"Someone's gotta go to Malibu," Lovett says. He's young like us, fresh out of the University of Wisconsin. Like Jay, he is smooth: clean-shaven, good-looking, sweet as a pediatrician. There is something different about these two, different from the agents of my father's generation, and of Lew Wasserman's. They lack their predecessors' rough edges. He holds up a rectangular envelope and shakes it at us. "Stallone needs this ASAP."

"Shit," Jay says. "I gotta go out past the Colony?"

"You'll go to the moon if Ron Meyer needs you to."

"Fuck," he says. "That's two and a half hours in traffic."

"I'll do it," I say.

"No." Richard hands the envelope to Jay, gives me an avuncular pat on the arm. "You go home and study. He'll take it."

They are smooth, where the elders were coarse. But in a few short years, almost before I have completed my education, these two will have leapfrogged everybody, leapfrogged even my father, to be running Hollywood themselves. We stand in the fluorescent overhead glow of the mailroom, steeped in the smell of toner and the copy machine's metronomic pulse, and I have no idea that the world they preside over will be nothing like the movie colony of my youth. I know only that these two are my brothers, that we are passengers on the same slow-turning, seemingly unsinkable, ship, and that as goes their fate, so will ultimately go mine.

★ ★ ★

MY MOTHER'S MOVIE flops. In the fall of 1982, *Love Child* receives its title and is loosed into theaters, only to vanish a few weeks later. But my mother by now has other problems.

"Fuck Alvin Sargent," she snarls, drunk out of her mind once again. "This is all his fault."

"Maybe you shouldn't have scabbed, Mom." Here we are in the kitchen again, leaning over that butcher's block to which we may as well be chained. "I'm not sure Alvin Sargent is the problem."

"Are you siding against me?"

My mother has been denied membership in the WGA. A senior member, the writer of *Ordinary People* who is also the mentor of the person my mother rewrote, has led a charge to blackball her.

"Not taking sides," I say. If I lit a match, her breath would catch flame like a circus act's. "But I think—"

She slaps me, putting her shoulder into it, her arm rigid and jerky like a garden sprinkler.

"Mom—"

I'm so shocked I can only laugh, sinking back onto my stool. She buries her face in her hands and sobs.

"I'm not a writer," she wails. "I'm not a writer!"

This, I think, is the core of it. My mother is haunted by a quote that appeared while her case was being litigated in public. "It's a moral and ego thing," an anonymous member of the Guild's disciplinary committee had told *Daily Variety* on December 17, 1981. "You're not a writer if you're not in the Guild." Thus, it is a matter of self-definition. If she is not recognized as a writer, if she is no longer a teacher or an administrator, an activist, or a spouse, then who is she now? What position does she occupy on the grand stage of life?

"I'm not a writer!" She sobs sloppily into her palms while I rub my raw cheek. "I'm not anything at all!"

The movie isn't bad. Amy Madigan plays Terry Jean Moore, the Florida hitchhiker who gets sent up for a ten-year stretch when her friend pulls a gun in the car. Beau Bridges plays the prison guard who knocks her up, Mackenzie Phillips her lesbian best friend on the yard. *Love Child* is decent. It is certainly no embarrassment. The *Hollywood Reporter* thought it was worthy of awards—and Madigan picks one up, a Golden Globe for Most Promising Newcomer—while the *Los Angeles Times* found it solid but perhaps better suited for television. The reviews were favorable—"Powerful," "unsentimental," "sincere"—but that's not what this is about.

"Mom."

This is about self-definition, about who she is allowed to be. Strangely, being blackballed hasn't stopped her from working. Studios and networks aren't supposed to hire nonunion writers, but CBS has just signed her on to write a television movie called *Princess Grace*. The Writers Guild is forced to offer her every protection they do to members, including pension and health insurance. But around town, at screenings and restaurants, she receives angry glares. *It's a moral and ego thing.*

"What is it?"

Morality and ego, those twin forces that drive the action not just on the Hollywood stage, but on the national one as well. My father, the businessman, is thriving. It's a good time to be a capitalist in America. My mother, the strikebreaker, the artist? It is not such a good time for her.

"Dad's getting married."

She picks up her glass and throws it at me. It whistles past my ear and explodes against the wall, showering me in vodka and ice.

"Get the fuck out," she says.

I stare at her a moment, dripping vodka.

"Get out!"

She's made her own bed, but perhaps no time has ever been a good time for my mother. And there is no betrayal like self-betrayal, that I now know. My parents are regular people, the kind you still see in the movies, as well as the kind who make them. But after my mom has ranted and raved about how my dad betrayed her ("That philanderer! That cheat!"), what is left? Whatever became of the woman who sang "Joe Hill" to me in my crib, the Weavers-loving leftist whose close friend when my sister and I were children was the folk-singer Judy Collins? She sang "Guantanamera," she sang "Deportee," she sang "Coal Tattoo," a union song if ever there was one. In the living room with her friends she sang from the bottom of her heart even as Ronald Reagan's political career was only just beginning to take wing.

Who, really, betrayed that person? Who? Who? Who?

★ ★ ★

A MAN ARRIVES. He sweeps into my mother's life with a sudden velocity. Stanton Korey, from New York, pulls up at our door in his maroon Mercedes sedan and moves right in. He is like an emissary from a distant civilization, and it isn't too much to say he saves my life. His own children, a son my age and a daughter a few years older, are back in Manhattan, so it's just Stanton and his dog, a dumb and lovely Golden Retriever named Barney.

"You like that picture?"

With his outer borough accent, his wiry hair and round, craggy face, he peers down at me over the tops of his half-moon spectacles. He looks like a Jewish professor from CCNY, not a producer, but indeed the latter is what he is.

"I do." I'm sprawled on the floor of the den watching one of my mother's favorites, *Annie Hall*, on the Betamax. "I like *Stardust Memories* better."

"What about *Interiors*?"

What he is, or what he claims to be, for it is never quite clear what movies, if any, he has produced. Years later, I will search IMDb and find credits for only an unaired television pilot and a softcore porn flick, *Young Lady Chatterley II*. He smiles down, genial and paunchy in his tweed jacket and sneakers. Barney sprawls next to me, gnawing a malodorous tennis ball. I shrug.

"See *Interiors*. Woody told me it was his favorite."

Still, I love him. He is an intellect—his books crowd in along-side my mother's on the downstairs shelves: Stanley Elkin, Paula Fox, Philip Roth—and a gentle presence, infinitely more relaxed than my dad. The source of his income may be unknown, but he steadies my mother, takes her by the elbow and guides her closer to sobriety. Her drinking doesn't stop, but it tapers. Champagne brunches at Charmer's Market, dinner and two glasses of wine at Spago. She takes on a healthy glow, resumes her regular dance classes. She sells her divorce car—a gray Mazda two-seater, vanity plate EXSPECT—and starts driving a four-door Mercedes herself. Above all, she is working, digging into an original script called *Not Always Greener*, which she sells to Warner Brothers. The script is a comedy about dueling ad executives, a former couple who can't seem to stop sleeping together long after their marriage has ended.

When Stanton moves in, everything settles down. My mother regains control. Her riotous outbursts, like the night she dragged the dregs of my father's wardrobe into her car and then drove to Pamela's apartment complex to unload them, raging, on the lawn, are a distant memory. In July of 1984, the summer after I graduate from high school, she and Stanton will be married at Ma Maison, and my mother, now Katherine Korey, will begin her new life.

★ ★ ★

I, TOO, HAVE begun a new life. Unburdened of my mother's sod-den weight, I feel a hundred pounds lighter. In the spring of 1984, I ramble through Crossroads' revamped and expanded campus after school when a man approaches me in the hall. He looks like Bobby Kennedy, he looks like Pretty Boy Floyd, he looks like Charlie Starkweather. He looks like these people because he has played them all in the movies.

"Hey, you seen Renee?"

"Sure thing, Mr. Sheen." He looks like Captain Willard, my

psychedelic commander, because he is Captain Willard in the flesh, and also, now, the father of one of my friends. "She's in the drama building."

"Thanks," he says, patting my arm as he sails off toward the quad. "I'll see you out at the house this weekend."

The empty hallway is lined with lockers; its concrete floor is lined with a blue industrial runner like the baize of a billiard table. I turn to watch my buddy's parent go, suburban-dad-like in a peach-colored polo shirt and khaki pants—more dad-like than my actual dad—as he steps out into the afternoon sun and wanders off across the alley's hazy expanse. Crossroads has gotten bigger: the campus now takes up most of the block. Enrollment has quadrupled, and there is a dedicated music building, a theater building, a basketball court. Still, the place retains its ramshackle charm and its intimacy: anyone's parents seem like everyone's parents, Martin Sheen included.

"Never get out of the boat." It seems as if I have finally made dry land. The movies are going to let me off the hook. Inside of a few years, I will be drug-free myself. I will watch a college friend chop out a line of flake and I will find this lame and unsophisticated. *Cocaine? What are you, twelve?* But most of my friends, now, are clean. We're high on coffee and Marlboros, or on watery Henry Weinhard beer; we're fucked-up on punk rock: the Meat Puppets, the Minutemen, the Gun Club, and Black Flag. We're out of our minds on cinema: on *Taxi Driver*, *Breathless*, *The Discreet Charm of the Bourgeoisie*. Jim Hosney, our film studies teacher, has done us right. This place is a laboratory for baby artists. These may be the Reagan eighties, but on the day the president was shot a ripple of excitement had echoed across campus like it was Christmas Eve.

I grab my messenger bag and slam my locker shut. I light a cigarette and step out toward the quad, past all the classrooms named after novelists and poets—the Brontë Room, the Dante

Room, Jane Austen—to emerge into the sun. I'm messed up on art, too stupid to think about my economic future. I'm just like my peers: like that shy girl in her pink polo shirt, Gillian Welch, who strides by me, dragging her cello down the alley in its case like a pool shark lugging his cue; like that boy Jack Black, sitting over on the smoking area's wooden bench reading, scowling under heavy eyebrows; like my friend Dana Spiotta, the future novelist, who sits next to me in English, her face as coolly inscrutable as a Quattrocento painting. Like Michael Bay, and Maya Rudolph, also, all the other waterlogged animals who roam this campus with me, each of us filled with our artistic dreams and with the breath of life, traveling one by one, traveling two by two.

★ ★ ★

"DON'T MOVE." A gun's hammer cocks right behind my ear, as fearsome a sound as I've heard in my young life. "Don't you fucking move, or I'll blow your brains all over the floor."

If you were in a movie, you'd know how dream-like things can become in an instant. And if you've ever had a gun pressed to your nape, to that soft spot between the top of your spine and your skull, you understand how slowly time can go. Every second feels as expansive as if it is passing underwater.

"Stay there." My assailant lifts his knee off my back. "Stay."

I'm face down on the floor. My friends, Adam and Renee, are too, the three of us fanned out around a living room in Malibu. Two men with guns and balaclavas have broken in and forced us to lie with our hands laced behind our heads.

"All right," the other one says. "Come on!"

It is just like the movies, only weirder, because this house, Renee's house, is so full of the movies already. Renee's brothers, Emilio and Charlie, are actors. So is her dad, and so are her brothers' friends—their names are Tom Cruise, Rob Lowe, Sean Penn, Demi Moore—who congregate at the house regularly, wandering in and

out like stray cats. These people are not stars yet—the term "Brat
Pack" lurks in the future—but they are all performers, who come
to this house for the same reason I do, because Renee's parents
are warm and down-to-earth, and are allergic to Hollywood
nonsense.

"Move!" one of the gunmen says. "Move!"

From outside, there is the calming sound of a fountain, a small
rock waterfall cascading into a swimming pool, but otherwise this
house is no stately Malibu manor. A Ranch-style box with glass
walls, it feels like almost any suburban home in almost any suburban enclave, familial, but not spectacular. We're way out past
the Colony, past Pepperdine, on a residential road that winds away
from the Pacific Coast Highway. Before the men entered, we were
crowded around the VCR jockeying over what to watch, playing
music, occasionally stepping outside onto the patio for a cigarette.
Adam, who looks like a young actor himself with his cropped
sleeves and biceps, his look part–Sex Pistol, part-pretty-boy pinup,
had decided on *Rude Boy*, a semi-documentary about The Clash,
to follow *Taxi Driver*. We'd just settled into the milky light of the
TV, hypnotized by our beloved punk icons, when—boom.

"Hurry up! Hurry up!"

It's quiet out here, and this far off the PCH it is uncommonly
dark. Renee's parents are out. Her brothers are God-knows-where—
presumably, they have better things to do than hang around the
house on a Friday night—and so we are alone.

"C'mon, hurry!"

The robbers move through the room with weird assurance, almost like they know the lay of the land already. From down the
hall there comes a rustling sound, a flurry of footsteps galloping
toward us, bare soles slapping on wood. Then there is the mechanical clack—*Shk-k*—of a pump-action shotgun.

"Why don't you guys drop those and get the fuck out of here."

Emilio's voice. In the vacuum of silence that follows—I guess we are not alone after all—I lift my head just enough to see Renee's older brother standing in the doorway in his underwear. He's cradling the shotgun, aiming it as coolly as he might in a movie.

"Why don't you two put those guns down," he repeats. "Just put 'em on the floor real slow."

He sounds like John Wayne, but he's just a young man in his boxer briefs. One with five movies under his belt, but he's no Rambo. He's barely old enough to drink.

"Real slow. Now, on your knees before I put a hole in your chest."

So quiet. I can hear the crickets shrilling outside, the soft gush of the waterfall, the quiet lapping of the pool. It glows with a vivid superreality beyond the living room's glass wall, as bright as a tropical lagoon.

"On your knees, you—" Emilio's voice cracks. "I'm sorry, line? Line?"

Laughter erupts around the room. It takes me a moment to piece it together, as I lift my head to see he has lowered the shotgun, the intruders have dropped their prop pistols and are peeling away their masks. Renee is already sitting up.

"Goddamn it," she says, breaking into an embarrassed smile. She looks like her dad: the same blue-eyed, half-Irish face. "Charlie!"

The one standing nearer to her, the youngest of her three brothers, smirks.

"We had you," he says. "This guy"—he nods at me—"was so scared he was gonna piss his pants."

"No I wasn't."

"Yeah." He grins. "You know you were."

The other one, closer to the door, just shakes his head and lobs his balaclava over onto the couch. Sean Penn is a little further on in his Hollywood career than either brother—his hair is long still, in the style he wore in the last movie he was in, *Bad Boys*—but he just smiles at Emilio.

"Fuckin' awesome, dude. We had 'em."

"You had 'em."

"No, you did! With the twelve-gauge? I was dying."

The three of them straggle away toward the kitchen. The masks are off and we, the junior victims of their prank, fade away: my friends and I are extras in their movie, in the lives they are leading way above our heads.

"What d'you guys wanna do?" Penn's voice drifts down the hall, garbled by a mouth full of food. "You wanna go get something to eat?"

"Aren't we eating right now?" Charlie says.

"Oh, right." More raucous laughter. "I guess we are."

"Put some pants on, dude," Charlie says to his brother. "You look ridiculous."

I get up. Adam is already up, squatting by the TV. Renee shakes her head with the bemused patience of a youngest sibling who is used to these things.

"Did you buy that?" I say.

"What?"

"Did you buy it? Did that seem real to you?"

The TV set flickers. The Clash are playing "Safe European Home," Joe Strummer spasming up against the mic like he is being electrocuted.

"No," she says. "I knew it was them."

"Bullshit."

"No, totally," she says. "I did."

We're right back to where we were: three bored teenagers adrift in the suburbs on a weekend night. I haven't had too many friends in high school: Adam, with whom I played Little League in grade school, is closest; Renee, my pal, will soon double as my prom date. But in the fall, I will leave this place, and wait now on my college acceptances. I cannot get free soon enough.

"It's all real," Adam says, smiling. "It's all a little too real, if you know what I mean."

I do. I know exactly what he means. I reach into my shirt pocket for Marlboros, open the pack and shake one out, holding it toward him. "Gic?" It's what we call cigarettes. "You want one?"

Adam takes it and the two of us walk out onto the patio, facing the pool.

"Too real," I say, lighting up. "Too fucking real."

"Exactly."

When he leaves home, he will go to NYU and become a musician, forming a band called Jawbreaker with our friend Blake. When I do, I will become what I already am—a writer, who spends most of his free time jotting down dialogue and ideas—but I have no way yet to express how much I hate it here, how tired I am of LA's distortions.

"Someday a real rain will come," I say, "and wash all the scum off the streets."

"Exactly." Adam blows smoke toward the sky. "Exactly, dude."

The rock waterfall babbles. In daylight hours we swim out to the middle of the pool and dive from it. At the far end of the property, a wall of palms stretches into inky darkness.

"All the animals come out at night," Adam says. "Whores, skunk pussies, buggers."

"Yes," I say. I know my upbringing is golden, but I also know it is eating me alive, and what happens if I stay will not be pretty. "Dude, yes."

Trapped between the radical unrealities of the movie business and the intolerable banalities of the world, between my mother's alcohol-fueled derangement and my father's opacity, I do not know what to do. I am like a fly snared between two windowpanes. My friend and I might quote *Taxi Driver* chapter and verse, might recite the whole fucking movie to each other like the holy American scripture we correctly understand it to be, but it isn't going to help me escape.

"You talkin' to me?" Adam says. "Are you talking to me?"

I must be because there isn't anybody else here. I glance up at the sky and catch some tragically secular flash, airplane or meteor, then lower my eyes again to the godless world. The Clash blares in the living room. Renee's brothers are laughing it up in the kitchen. But out here it's just the two of us alone with the shrilling of crickets, the splashing fountain, the ghost-shimmer of moonlight on water, the stars.

WRITER, DENIED MEMBERSHIP BY WG, DENIES 'SCAB' ALLEGATIONS

By DAVE KAUFMAN

Writers Guild has denied membership to a writer on grounds she rewrote the script of a motion picture for a struck producer during last summer's strike, but the writer involved denied it, and the producer — Alan Ladd Jr. — emphatically declared he did not commission the script involved.

Katherine Specktor is the writer who was notified last Friday by the Guild that her application for membership has been denied, following a hearing by the Guild strike disciplinary committee. A Guild spokesman commented this is the first time in the history of the Guild, established in 1933, that it has identified a "scab."

Specktor said that she was "absolutely astonished and appalled" at the Guild's action, adding "as I explained to the disciplinary committee and board, I do not believe that I rendered a service to a struck producer. It was my understanding that this was a dead script."

Ladd, head of The Ladd Co., which now has before the cameras "Love Child," the vehicle involved in the Guild imbroglio, supported Specktor, asserting "I don't think she is guilty of anything." He said what actually oc-

CBS Group Buys RCA Transponder Space

Washington, Dec. 6 — The CBS Broadcast Group says it has purchased a pair of transponders aboard the RCA Satcom 4 satellite, due to be launched in January.

The purchase price for the transponders was not revealed and web officials declined to say specifically what will be carried

III

THE COLONY

6. WHITE DANCING

1985

"In order for a person to bear his life, he needs a valid re-creation of that life."

He wrote those words a decade ago, but sitting now on a trans-atlantic 747 on its way from Côte d'Azur to Newark, New Jersey, in the fall of 1985, staring ahead at a blank screen as the cabin lights flicker, he can't help but think of them again. After all, aren't the movies supposed to offer such a re-creation, just like the novel and the stage do? He's loved the pictures all his life—he can remember seeing Ronald Colman and Elizabeth Allen in *A Tale of Two Cities* like it was yesterday, Bill Miller taking him to the Lincoln Theater in Harlem fifty years ago so, for the first time, he could sit with an audience that looked like him—but mostly what they've offered is just disappointment.

"Sir, would you like another drink?"

The stewardess peers down at him and he nods, holding up two fingers to indicate what he wants. Around him people have begun to pull down their window shades and so it's too dark for him to read anyway, the unopened book in his lap now useless. She pours him a Seagram's 7, rocks, and sets it down in front of him.

"Thank you, baby."

The movies have disappointed him because they've never been

able to accommodate him in full, because Hollywood has never been very convincing when it comes to Black people anyway. Even when he was a boy there were exceptions, like Canada Lee and Paul Robeson, sometimes unlikely ones like Sylvia Sidney or Henry Fonda (what white man ever walked like that?); directors like Fritz Lang, but they were rare, and still are.

"Would you like a blanket or a pillow? The show's going to start soon."

He shakes his head. He pulls on his scotch—what he really wants is a cigarette, but his throat's been bothering him—then stares back at the screen, because sitting here in an elongated twilight roaring over the Atlantic he knows it all might have been different, that the movies had at least offered him a small avenue of escape. He could have been a preacher—he *was* a preacher, at Fireside Pentecostal Assembly, while he was still at Clinton High—but he knew his mind and in the end he understood that if he didn't get out of his father's church and out of Harlem he was damned as sure as anyone he could have ever dreamed of saving. So, he left, first to New Jersey, where he'd almost gotten killed after he threw a glass at a white waitress who'd refused to serve him, and then to Greenwich Village, and then finally—in '48—to France. But not until he made it to Europe did he come face-to-face with what he'd have to call reality.

"Ladies and gentlemen, this is your captain speaking. In just a few minutes we'll be beginning our in-flight entertainment . . ."

Reality. He caresses the book in his lap—the one he's about to teach, *The Princess Casamassima*—because this one, Henry James, understands it better than anybody: understands how Americans even now refuse to see themselves, will do almost anything to avoid doing so, since doing so means you have to pay the price. When he was young, he latched on to certain writers with a kind of frenzy—Dickens, Dostoevsky—because they knew what it was to pay the price. But James, so American, is the one who'd really shown him, who'd understood what most Americans still can't: the devastating power of anyone's good intentions. When he'd arrived in Paris in 1948, he barely even knew he was American, but he'd learned quickly the night he was arrested at the Grand Hotel du Bac for possessing a stolen bedsheet. The sheet wasn't his—it belonged to a friend—but he'd learned then about the presumption of innocence, which no Black person really had at home, but no European had either. He was an American, and he was a Black American, but there in France where he's lived ever since he found he could be both but also neither; he could be everybody, any open face that revealed itself to him in the street, but also nobody. No one at all.

The cabin lights dim. He's gone back and forth now for forty years—crossing the Atlantic for him is like taking the subway is for other people—and this is the time he most enjoys: alone up here where he can read, where no one bothers him with questions about race or fame or what well-intentioned white people should do, questions they would be more likely to understand if they were to read his books carefully. The dim glow of the cabin; the warm, soft spread of scotch; the cold ice cubes on his tongue and against the back of his teeth; the sleek, turbine roar of the engine: these things together do for him what he wants, and when he closes his eyes for a moment, it's like he really is no one: just consciousness hovering alone in space, floating in the air between Europe and America.

America. He can see what it is, or, at least, what it thinks it is, from what comes up now onscreen. Legs. Just a bunch of legs and feet dancing, or trying to dance, in tennis and ballet shoes, high heels and espadrilles. No headphones for him—on his last flight, he got stuck with some nonsense about a bunch of white teenagers stuck in high school detention, so he'll choose silence for this one—but they're all moving in that herky-jerky, sunny-side-of-the-street way of white people. It's optimism, he thinks.

All that "morning in America" shit that Reagan pushes, also, the same destructive innocence Henry James was on to a century ago. White people want to believe that it's never gonna get dark, literally and figuratively. He stares up at the screen, the little rectangle at the front of the cabin that has none of the grace—"that movement which is something like the heaving and swelling of the sea," he'd described it once—of the movies you see in a theater, but he can't look away either.

He can't look away because he's wanted Hollywood his entire life. In 1954 he'd set out to write a movie about the Holy Rollers in Harlem, but instead he went to MacDowell and wrote a stage adaptation of *Giovanni's Room* for the Actors Studio, where he'd met Elia Kazan. Kazan was the one who invited him in, encouraged him to write *Blues for Mr. Charlie*. Before that, he hadn't really believed in the theater either, because it didn't seem to believe in him: there weren't many more Black people onstage than there were in the movies. But he wanted performance, and wants it still, because writing is all in your head. He wants communion, wants to see these dreams of his, the word, made flesh.

He wants a cigarette, too. And so, he finally gives in. This thing with his throat comes and goes, and he thinks it's reflux instead of what it really is: a symptom of the esophageal cancer that will kill him inside two years. He lights up, stares at the screen, which dissolves from all those stuttering feet to—what else?—a church: the clapboard kind, painted white, that sits out in the middle of America, where it is like no church he could ever believe in. White feet, white preaching: the actor who plays the minister, John Lithgow, reminds him of someone, but he's not sure who. He tugs on his cigarette and stares forward, past the rows of heads all tilted either asleep or in attention. The stewardesses have disappeared, but he'd like another drink, also.

He's written scripts and it usually ends in disaster. Hollywood can insult you in ways you've never dreamed. It came sniffing around his door the moment he got famous, as Kazan wanted to adapt *Another Country* for a while, and after that he'd met them all: Charlie Chaplin, Tony Richardson, Joe Losey, Warren Beatty. But the real fiasco happened in '68, when a producer named Marvin Worth hired him to write a picture about Malcolm X. They flew him out to LA, put him up at the Beverly Hills hotel. The whole thing was like being shoved into a glass terrarium: people looking at him like they wanted to shake every answer he had out of his pockets. When he spoke there in public with Stokely Carmichael, *Daily Variety* was quick to write an article explaining that he didn't agree with Carmichael or his "methods," but that's what Hollywood does: steals the value of everything you say or do, then does its best to render those things anodyne. He'd fought with Columbia Pictures over his script's tone and over casting—he wanted Billy Dee Williams to play Malcolm where the studio had wanted James Earl Jones or Sidney Poitier or even, God help them, Charlton Heston in makeup—until the studio had hired a minder ("co-writer," but he knew a minder when he saw one), and finally he'd had to take the script away so he could work on it again by himself.

"Methods." That's what *Variety* had said, in trying to separate him from what it called "the racial extremists," in wanting to make sure Hollywood wasn't scared off by his friendship with Carmichael, whose politics they saw as too radical, so they'd insisted his own preferred "methods" might be different. But the word makes him think, also, of Marlon, and of that bullshit Conrad adaptation, *Apocalypse Now*. He loves Marlon, and loves Joseph Conrad, with reservations, but that film was awful. What did the officer say about Kurtz in that film, words that are in the novella as well? "His methods became . . . unsound." As if it was just "methods" that were unsound and not the entire white imagination; as if the tragedy was one man going up the river and a handful of Americans dying, instead of the untold and mostly invisible slaughter of an entire populace. He loves Marlon, they've been close ever since they met in a class at the New School in '44, back when he thought he might become a playwright or even an actor himself, but—

Fading now, and fast. He drops his cigarette in the remains of his ice—man, there is nothing like a bad movie to put you out quickly—closes his eyes, and nods off.

★ ★ ★

"SIR?"

He wakes up on the ground, the stewardess tapping him on the wrist. He grabs his satchel, and shuffles drowsily off the plane. It's early morning here in America, everyone scuttling through the Newark International terminal with their coffee and pastries. He's slept maybe five hours, but it's enough. He has to teach this afternoon, and he's done it on less. He's missed the semester's first two weeks, but now he's here and he imagines the children will be happy to see him. Well, he'll be happy to see them, too. Teaching at a small college in Western Massachusetts is a strange post for him, all those lovely young faces, and all those ruined white ones in the surrounding towns, but he's used to it, and the children are beautiful, as children usually are.

He walks through the terminal on short legs, passing through its artificial dawn. He knows that people stare not just because he's famous—perhaps, in this increasingly illiterate country, not even for that reason at all—but because a five-foot-six Black man in a silk ascot and a herringbone jacket is a sight. Even if he were not famous, they'd stare. Sunglasses as dark as limousine windows, overcoat draped over his shoulders. No wonder they do. But as he moves through Newark Airport terminal B (Styron! That's who Lithgow, in that crappy movie, reminded him of: Bill Styron), he can't help but think anyway that fame is a prison: that it traps you inside other people's perceptions until you can't help believing in them yourself, until your own lonely effort to be a human being, to be nobody, is extinguished. You become everybody, and that's where the trouble starts.

You become everybody. That's Marlon's problem, Marlon who'd been blown up into the kind of monument few people in even Hollywood ever become, but it's also his own problem, even if no silver screen has ever come calling for him: only television, a bunch of magazine covers, and a thousand podiums that feel like pulpits. But, of course, Marlon will never carry what he has to carry, and in the end, he hasn't been able to stand it either: even without the movies, fame has worn upon him, so much so that he'd had to write *Tell Me How Long the Train's Been Gone.* Leo Proud-hammer, the actor in that book, is him. "The day came when I wished to break my silence and found I could not speak: the actor could no longer be distinguished from his role." He wrote those words closing on twenty years ago, and some days, like right now, he feels them all the way to his bones.

He quickens his step, on his way through customs—his connection to Hartford is tight, but he'll make it: still forty-five minutes to boarding—stopping only to buy a newspaper. "The actor could no longer be distinguished from his role?" Well, no, because you have to maintain that small sliver of separation when you write, but yes, because you also have to commit to it. Without a role you're not just nobody, you're nothing, which is a whole different bag entirely. This is why he can't live without the novel: he can write essays and exhortations, but inside the novel he is both himself and other people, and, without that freedom, he cannot live.

That is why people need the movies, why they are as necessary as sunlight and air. It is why he can never quite leave Hollywood alone. When Martin died, that's where he was: in Palm Springs with Billy Dee, by the swimming pool when the telephone rang. Hollywood has always been a foolish place, but it's also a real one, more revealing of life and of human nature than anybody gives it credit for. Because it is everywhere on this earth, even in the south of France, even here in Newark Airport terminal B, where he accelerates toward the gate: even here, it is Hollywood all over the world.

★ ★ ★

NOW HE SHOULDERS his satchel and walks up the path toward Skinner Hall, the *New York Times* he'd been reading on the connecting flight tucked under his arm. "Schultz Foresees Apartheid's Doom, Asks Compromise," reads the headline, because white people always want to "compromise," but on what? When William Faulkner had written in *Life* magazine in 1956 that integrationists needed to go slow, he'd written his own rebuttal: "There is never time in the future in which we will work out our salvation. The challenge is in the moment, the time is always now."

Always now. Maybe that's also why he likes the movies: because it is always now inside them, because there is no prevaricating or kicking the can. You work out your salvation in dream, which is the only way to do it, and the American story inscribes itself right in front of your eyes. He climbs the steps of the hall, the quad's green splendor unfurled behind him, New England with its clapboard houses and church steeples, its abandoned asylums and industrial blight. All this is the American grain, right here: James and Hawthorne and Melville, that obsession with whiteness, and concealment of weakness, which runs all the way to the root.

He enters the atrium and makes his way up the stairs, another one of those buildings that looks almost like a Gothic church itself, with its imposing brick facade and its roundel window, a Calvinist monument to which he's been called, once more, to testify. The students at Mount Holyoke College are all women, but his class is co-ed, drawn from the other four colleges in the consortium. There's a boy outside the classroom at the end of the hall, shifting anxiously from foot to foot. He's early, he realizes. The classroom must be locked. The boy looks like one of those children from the movie he saw on the plane, with his skinny jeans and too-big motorcycle boots, with his pale, bony face, long blond hair falling around his jaw. Framed against the window he looks like a photographic negative: a black silhouette against a solarized backdrop as he pulls out a pack of cigarettes and shakes one loose. This poor child seems nervous. They always are when they see him coming.

He walks over and takes the boy's wrist, guiding his match over to light his own cigarette, holding it gently between his fingers like a doctor, like he is checking the boy's pulse. As he guides the flame to the tip of his cigarette, he thinks of Marlow lighting his pipe in *Heart of Darkness* ("worn, hollow . . . with an aspect of concentrated attention"), while the light flares across the boy's face and the tobacco ignites with a sound as fragile as a kiss.

"Hello," he says, still holding the boy's wrist, which is my own wrist, and so I will never forget that touch, his voice, his kind, patient, and reproachful face. "I'm—"

7. THE MAP AND THE TERRITORY

——

1985–1988

"Mr. Baldwin."

We call him this, the fifteen of us who take his fiction workshop in the fall of 1985. I am here because I am lucky, chosen by lottery, not because I am worthy. I am here to bathe in this man's interrogative light.

"You do understand this story is beautiful. Beautiful." He fixes me with a skeptical, quizzical look—it is like being X-rayed in public, those inescapable eyes flaying me of every pretention—eyebrows lifted. "The question is whether beauty is enough."

I am here to get an education in something larger than the movies, an education that is also a moral education, as writing and literature, the things I am here to study, turn out to be so much more than just an arrangement of attractive sentences.

"This is not a good story." His gaze doesn't waver. He sits with a copper-colored silk scarf around his neck, its folds creasing its iridescence with pockets of shadow, and the short stub of a cigarette burning between his fingers. His elbow rests on a long table arranged with two others into a U-shape, a short stack of books in front of him alongside a spiral notebook and a pile of student pages. "It's not quite a bad story, because you are somewhat talented." He smiles faintly, almost imperceptibly, as if to say *and?* "But it is not a good story because you do not yet know what to do."

Sunlight slants through the window to my left: a rich, New England strain of it that reminds me I am far, so far from Los Angeles. I have come all this way, matriculating at Hampshire College in Amherst, to get away from it, away from my parents, away, at long last, from the movies, which I find fake and embarrassing. I have come all this distance, in other words, to reinvent myself—I already know I want to be a writer, even if I have no idea yet how to do it—but I find I am stuck upon a series of shallow gestures. I change my wardrobe, chop off all my hair, and then decide to grow it long; I fall in love with a girl from Ohio whose milk-fed Midwestern-ness—both of her parents are English expats, academics—presents to me as enviably regular. I subsist on coffee, oranges, and a Dutch housemate's Indonesian favorite, nasi goreng; in that month of October, I shrink down to 127 pounds. I can barely stand without having a fainting fit; when my girlfriend and I have sex we leave bruises just above the waist from the force of our bony hips slamming together. At night I lie in my narrow bed beneath a poster of Morrissey, smoking, delirious. Out of this, I can hardly make sense, let alone art, and yet here I am being catechized by one of America's greatest writers.

"You'll learn," he says, finally, after a silence long enough for me to feel the weight of my inexperience. (What is it, exactly, that I "do not yet know how to do?") "You will learn." He smiles, a drop of encouragement before he delivers the truth. "But this story fails because—"

It isn't right to say I am "rapt" exactly—I am as defensive as any other young writer whose work is being torn to pieces—but I am attentive; I might not even really know who I am listening to, having read only *Giovanni's Room*, but I know the truth when I hear it. I have arrived in this class drawn by Baldwin's fame, and so I don't really deserve to be here, but what he says sinks in even so. It is only through him I am finally able to understand that writing is not some glamour profession, a gin and tonic and a cigarette as you slouch over your typewriter, bitching about the studio's notes, but a moral one, in which you are tasked with failing again and again and again.

"You see?" Another day he stands before us with a paperback clutched in each hand, balancing them like the pans of a scale. "Conrad can be wonderful. But when he says the function of writing is to make you see, what is it that he does not see himself? When he describes the woman as 'like the wilderness, with an air of brooding over an inscrutable purpose,' what is it Conrad does not apprehend?"

He is chipping away at my adolescent tastes: at Hunter Thompson and William Burroughs, at Hemingway and F. Scott Fitzgerald. I've read *Heart of Darkness* in high school, where it was presented to me as a masterpiece, but he attacks it, questioning a dubious set of assumptions. He uses Conrad, often, as a negative example, hammering hard at *Lord Jim* and at *An Outcast of the Islands*, and Henry James, always, as the antidote.

"Now, James." He pauses, lifting the book in his opposite hand and wagging it at us. "James misses nothing. Nothing. Young Hyacinth Robinson here is an innocent, but he's not a fool . . ."

The *Princess Casamassima* is beyond me. But I read it, just as I do *Roderick Hudson*, *The Ambassadors*, and *The Portrait of a Lady*. I am able to grasp, eventually, one thing he is telling me: that it is not enough merely for something to have happened. After it has, if it has, one must reimagine it to bring it alive on the page. And in this pliable space between imagination and experience— this is what I do not yet know how to "do"—lies the only world any one of us will ever apprehend as true.

★ ★ ★

"HOW WAS JB?"

My housemate Marc flags me down once I return to campus, the boxy, condominium-like apartment we share with three of our friends on the green fringes of Hampshire College.

"Eh. He beat the shit out of my story yet again."

"Do better," Marc smirks. He is a lily-pale kid from Columbus, Ohio, with a long fringe of ink-black hair that dangles in front of his face. "Ever tried? Ever failed? No matter—"

"Shut the fuck up," I say, laughing. "Don't go all Sammy Beckett on me, man."

"Why not?" He's oddly delicate, Nordic and frail, with a voice so soft you have to lean in to hear it. "His Holiness would tell you the same thing."

"Touché."

Outside, the campus is swaddled in autumn fog. This peculiar outpost of twelve hundred students in Massachusetts's Pioneer Valley has an odd, institutional feel, a bucolic drug farm checkered with gray, Brutalist architecture.

"What are you reading?" I reach for the book on the table in front of him. "*Simulacra and Simulation*?"

"Yep," he says. "Baudrillard."

"What is it?"

"Read it yourself, Hoss." He smirks. "It's about the map and the territory."

"What?"

"It's about the real. The desert of the real. Read it yourself."

I will, without making much of it. The desert is where I'm from: the desert of image, cinema, and vanity. The real is where I've arrived: this green kingdom of seasons, cigarettes, and sex. But naturally, I am mistaken. The real, it eludes me still. The real, and my confrontation with it, will come soon enough.

★ ★ ★

COME CHRISTMAS, I go home to see my mother, who has bought a house on Twenty-Fifth Street, a few blocks from our previous one. The new house is smaller but sits on a larger lot. A small field of lemon and avocado trees separates my mother's rustic little office from the main unit, where Stanton likes to sit in the den and make deals. What kind of deals? It's never clear. I overhear him sometimes talking of start dates and greenlights, how its "costs are going to be cheaper in Copenhagen." But then—

"Where's Stanton?"

"Huh?"

December 1986. In the middle of my junior year, I step off a plane from Hartford and arrive in baggage to find my mother standing alone. Before now there has always been a welcome wagon, Stanton and the dog rolling up in his maroon Mercedes, Dave Brubeck blaring. Not today.

"Your husband," I say. "You know?"

It is the first time I have noticed her aging. In the wan light of LAX, her crow's-feet crinkle like paper. Her face, sun-polished and ruddy, looks drawn, as she lets out a soft sigh.

"Ex-husband?"

"He's moved out," she says. "We tried."

I study her. She seems to be managing well enough. Standing there at the carousel, she looks like any other mellow Westside parent, slouching in her dove-gray T-shirt and sweats, her Capezio jazz slippers.

"What happened?"

We step out into the humid night—LA feels like Miami after the sharp, brittle cold of an Amherst December—and my mother lights a cigarette.

"One day I looked at him and everything was different. I felt like I had married Daffy Duck."

"Daffy Duck?"

"You know," she says. "That voice of his."

I don't hear it, but I know what she means. You look at anyone long enough through the lens of extinguished desire and they begin to bend toward caricature.

"You should quit," I say, watching her tug again on her cigarette as we climb into her car. The diesel sedan reeks of stale smoke. Flakes of ash cling to its leather upholstery.

"I should quit?" She glares. "You should quit! Physician, heal thyself."

She pulls out of the airport garage and pilots us away from LAX onto Lincoln Boulevard. Earlier this year she turned fifty. If her life as a screenwriter hasn't quite taken off, achieved the lift she must have hoped for when she wrote *Love Child*, she is nevertheless working. Many places won't hire her because she is not a WGA member—most of them won't—but there are a few, either friends or producers who are not WGA signatories, who do.

"What are you writing?" I say.

"*Rough Strife*."

"Still?"

"It's a tough adaptation."

"I'm sure."

"You'll see," she says. We are referring to a novel by Lynne Sharon Schwartz she has been grappling with for the past many months, struggling to crack it. "You'll see."

"I'll never see," I say. "I'll never be a screenwriter."

"You'll see." She takes one more drag off her cigarette, then cracks her window and drops it onto the rain-swept corridor of Lincoln Boulevard, its neon path of liquor stores and taquerias. "One day, you'll see."

Doubtful. But what I do see, as I glance at my mother in noble profile—she seems practically regal, somehow, behind the wheel of this sleek, heavy German automobile—is someone who seems at last to be keeping her head above water. Who has finally arrived at her desired station in life.

★ ★ ★

LET'S LOOK IN on my father, while we are on the subject of my parents. When did he become the man who has everything, as he sits in the remodeled kitchen of his sprawling house in Santa Monica, talking on the phone?

"Don't insult me." He sits in the breakfast nook beneath a painting of a pink pig in violet clover. A playful, ironic touch, as this is him now, tugging on a cigar as he rakes some executive over the coals. "If you want Bob, you're going to have to do better."

His shoes gleam, tips angled against the terra-cotta floor. His suit is Armani. His hair is long and slicked back, his beard is cropped, fifty-fifty salt-and-pepper. He looks like Gordon Gekko, in his pink shirt and suspenders.

"How much better? I won't insult *you*." He studies his cigar—a Cohiba, perhaps, or a Cuban Punch Punch—dispassionately, checking the burn. "I'll be in my office in an hour. Call me back with a real offer then."

He hangs up. It is like a magic trick somehow, the speed with which he has become who he is, this bountiful creature of the Reagan eighties.

"Good morning, sport." He looks up as I enter, setting the cigar down on a saucer next to his espresso cup. "What's on your docket this morning?"

I shrug. He and I remain in a difficult period. I do not trust this life that has sprung up around him, its surfaces as smooth and bright as a museum's. I lean against the marble countertop, pulling the silver levers of his La Marzocco to fix myself a double.

"Dunno yet." It's Christmas vacation still, and I am spending a few days with him. "No plans."

No plans. When he was my age, my father was a Marine. He doesn't understand my dream-prone personality, the reverie that must look, to him, like inertia.

"Can I borrow the car?"

Of course, it is thanks to him I can afford any reverie, that I am not yet in a state of panic about what I will do after I graduate.

"Which one?"

"The Jetta." It is to my father's credit: he does not indulge me either. The Porsche, the Land Rover, the BMW. All of these are not for me. "Johanna's."

"You'll have to ask her." He shrugs. "See what she says when she gets up."

My sister still lives at home, a senior, now, in high school. She and I are no longer close, riven, also, by our parents' divorce. Warily, my father and I circle each other. What is to be done about this clumsy détente, this conflict between the successful businessman and the aspiring, if hypocritical, artist? My father wants what all parents want: a successful future for his children. He wants what all capitalists want: more. But how much more?

"Well." He pushes up from the table. "Be of good cheer, son. We have a reservation at the Ivy tonight at eight."

He sails out the courtyard door, lifting a hand by way of farewell, footsteps clacking against the pale flagstones as he makes his way out to the drive.

How much more? My father is a disciplined man, one who has always been able to recognize his limits. Lew Wasserman he is not. But what are his limits?

I listen to his Porsche's roar split the morning, then slide into the warm booth where he was sitting a moment ago. The house is quiet. My stepmother has gone to work already; my stepsister, Allison, is in New York, already back at NYU. I am alone with the spoils of my father's life in the movies, the Roseville pottery, the Picasso plates. A small David Hockney drawing hangs in the vestibule around the corner. Is this it for him? It's more, really, than anyone needs or should own. And while my father's clients are heavy hitters now, and he is happy to reap his rewards, I know what moves him is not merely money. I flick open his newspaper. (It is not predominantly money, perhaps. But then, what is it?) I nurse my espresso and I think on how Los Angeles defeats me, how trying to gain emotional purchase here is like trying to climb a wall of glass. I sink into a mood of depression. I am twenty, and my father is fifty-three. If not the movies, then what? For what else has my life and education prepared me?

I can't think here. I can't write. I can only bask like a lizard in the winter sun. I look around because I smell something acrid, something foul, and then see it: the smoldering end of my father's cigar, still resting on the saucer where he left it, filling the air with the sweet, the difficult, the *awful* smell of his success.

★ ★ ★

HOW DID HE get here? How did he become the man who tells the studio what to do, instead of vice versa?

Gunning his Porsche into his office's underground garage, my father doesn't wonder. For him it is simply a matter of hard work. He would be the last to deny there might also be some luck involved, but he has worked his way to the uppermost echelons of the middle. Perhaps even a little higher than that, given that he is in a business where real power concentrates itself in the hands of a dozen people at most. No longer an ordinary soldier, he has arrived at the premium end of his profession. He parks his white Turbo Carrera, wedging it between Rick Nicita's coffee-colored Jaguar and Steve Roth's black Ferrari, trots across the garage with his keys jangling in his hand. He won't be here long: Ovitz has already commissioned I.M. Pei, the legendary architect, to design a new corporate headquarters, as the agency has outgrown this one. He has approached Roy Lichtenstein about painting a mural that will dominate this new building's enormous lobby. He is making a statement, approaching Lichtenstein, commissioning Pei, who is busy right now completing the Louvre Pyramid in Paris, the Bank of China Tower in Hong Kong, saying something about how his agency, and Hollywood itself, is bigger than just the movies. In three short years, they will occupy their new fortress of travertine stone on the corner of Wilshire and Little Santa Monica

Boulevards, a building that will feel like a regional pyramid, an imperial structure meant to stand for a thousand years. But how is it CAA's ragtag gang of misfits—a decade ago, they couldn't afford to pay secretaries—has become so great and terrible? How are they now the most powerful force in Hollywood since MCA?

"Anyone call, Richard?"

Richard Lovett, my friend from the mailroom who is now my father's assistant, looks up. "DeVito."

"Who else?"

"Duvall."

"OK." My father doesn't quite know how the agency has amassed so much power either. He only knows that working here is nothing like working at MCA, like being under the thumb of an autocrat, but rather like being a member of a championship basketball team. The fluid cohesion on the floor is incredible. "Anyone else?"

"Glenn Close."

"OK." He walks into his office and sits. Century City, the pale artery of Olympic Boulevard, spreads behind him, the house in which he grew up visible out his window, the site of his father's inflexible reign as puny as a shoebox. "Let's try her first."

Lovett picks up the phone at the assistant's station. He is so young, so fresh-faced still, but he will not be on my dad's desk for long. In a few months, he will be promoted to become an agent himself, but— "Anyone else?" Yes. Yes, indeed. Now my father represents Jeremy Irons. He has Gene Hackman. Soon, he will have Barbra Streisand. His client list has undergone a makeover. No longer must he lug an unwanted Jack Nicholson around to meetings like a sack of potatoes. He's a heavy hitter himself now.

"Glennie! I'm glad I caught you. How's New York?"

How did all this happen? How has he come to be so central to the success of the team? He loves working here, as it is the most fun he's had in his professional life. If William Morris was a dull, horizonless bureaucracy, and MCA was a gladiatorial hellscape where the agents were pitted against each other all day long, CAA is like being a member of the Showtime Lakers. If Ovitz is Kareem, and Ron Meyer is Magic, my father is like James Worthy, or Byron Scott. He steps on the court, and he is ready to play.

"Great, great. Adrian's terrific, isn't he? I gotta tell you, I think this picture's going to be a huge hit."

He's always been ready. But now it is time. The lights are on in the arena. You play to win. You play for your life. You play— and my father knows this, deep down: it's what makes him more like his clients than he thinks—for a pure and absolute love of the game.

★ ★ ★

"SO, WHAT'S HE like?"

"What do you mean 'what's he like'?" Michael Ovitz looks back at my father, the two men crunching down an alley at high noon. "He's an actor. You know what that's like."

"No, I mean—what *does* he like?"

They are behind La Cienega Boulevard, their cars parked around the corner on the street. There has always been an element of secrecy to their profession and together they are indulging it, walking down a corridor that glitters with broken glass so they can enter a restaurant from the rear.

"He likes art."

"Right, his dad's a painter," my father says. "Abstract expressionist."

"Not always abstract. Gesturalist. Almost Fauvist in ways."

Let it be said that Ovitz is a man who does his homework. The person they are going to meet is an actor, and as with everyone Ovitz encounters—potential client, business leader, gallery owner—he's already sussed out his prey's relevant history and personality, his interests and dislikes, to a degree that strikes some as extreme. Perhaps this is why he's tapped my father for this assign-

ment: to balance against the part of himself that can seem a little
clinical.

"You're good for it, Fred. He's gonna like you." (He's not clinical.
He's curious, in that way that propels many moguls in their begin-
nings.) "You're the guy for him, I know."

And so, they bang up a metal staircase and slip into an
unprepossessing-looking building from the rear, heading for a private dining room on the restaurant's second floor. Ovitz greets the
hostess in Japanese, letting her lead them back to the room where
their prospective client is already waiting. There are things about
my father I do not know, and things about Ovitz, that Sphinx who
will soon loom much larger in this story, I do not know either, but
this, I believe, is how it happens.

"Bob? This is my associate, Fred Specktor."

Robert De Niro shakes my father's hand, sizes him up cautiously as they sit now on tatami mats at one end of a low, rectangular table. The room is windowless, quiet. There are clients who
prefer a dog and pony show, to be courted out on Main, paraded
in a booth at Spago. When Ron Meyer signed Sylvester Stallone,
he'd flown to Hawaii to ambush him in a hotel lobby, popping out
from behind a potted palm and pretending it was all just coinci-
dence. ("Sly? Gosh, what are the odds? No, no, I'm just here with
my family.") This is not like that, for De Niro is a deeply private
man. Ovitz has been courting him for a while, after the actor was
referred by his friend, Martin Scorsese. Ovitz has brought my father, now, to close.

"I thought you two would enjoy each other," Ovitz says. "Fred
and I were just talking on the way over about how much he admires
your work."

"It's true," my father says. One advantage he has is a long mem-
ory, and a history of being ahead of the curve. "I saw you do *The
Great American Refrigerator* off-Broadway in '72. I saw you in
Billy Bailey, too."

"You saw those?" The actor squints. "A couple of the first things I did."

"I saw them both. They were excellent."

A fine line between flattering and appreciation. De Niro is sharp, self-critical. He will not be gulled by the former the way some will. It must be noted he is an artist, a real one, inured to Hollywood bullshit, but also that he is given to hesitation and bouts of occasional uncertainty. His career is at its peak, with two Oscars under his belt already, but lately things have been coming up a little short.

"That picture you did last year with Meryl was good," my father says. "The performance wasn't a problem. But the studio didn't market it right. You aren't being positioned correctly."

What can we do that others can't? This is the question that is being answered and asked, but obliquely. They eat tuna—fatty toro dangling limply between their chopsticks—and the subtext of even this excellent meal is *We'll get you the best. We make things happen.*

"Good stuff, right?" Ovitz tweezes a piece of Hamachi. "The chef, Nobu, is a friend of mine. But it's not just him, it's the fish, it's the supplier . . ."

When he was a teenager, Michael Ovitz led tours on the lot at Universal Studios in the Valley. He was just a kid from Encino, his father a liquor salesman for Seagram's Inc. Younger than my dad, and solidly middle class, he knew who Lew Wasserman was without anyone stepping in to explain it to him—he was a good student even then, had already soaked up the whole history—and so he'd dreamed of being a boss mogul like Wasserman himself one day. But even Wasserman had never managed to inject such an insinuative, intimate touch in the pursuit of his clients, as if he could not just part the Red Sea but had created all the little fishies, too.

"You need movie star parts," Ovitz says, knowing that the actor's last few movies, *True Confessions* and *The King of Comedy*, have been flops, knowing that the actor certainly knows this, also. "But you also need something else. You need control."

"Control," the actor says. (As ever, Ovitz has put his finger on it, the one thing an artist wants and almost never has.) He tilts his head and looks back in a way that says I'm listening.

"Fred and I were talking about this on the way over. We'd like to find a way for you to produce some of the movies you appear in. That way, you'll have a stronger grip on the entire process. You'll also get a bigger piece."

My father leans forward. It is this, really, for which he has come. He has plenty of clients he's signed all by himself—he was on Danny DeVito back in the mid-seventies, when the actor had directed a short film called *Minestrone*—but this is what he loves about CAA: the teamwork, the camaraderie, the way Ovitz has set him up perfectly to sink a buzzer-beater from half-court.

"Mike's right," he says. He'll be the one who handles De Niro from here. "Allow me to make the following recommendation—"

A fresh feather for his cap. Another movie star in his pocket. He knows before the words are out of his mouth, they're going to sign this man, whose talent he so deeply admires, because of the way they've set it up. Ovitz is the floor captain, the man with the indomitable skyhook. But my father has the ball now, and he's taking it to the hoop. It doesn't matter what he recommends, which could be almost anything. What matters is the game, the players, and the outcome. What matters is the gross, the points, the score, and the net.

★ ★ ★

"SÍ, SÍ." MY mother stands in her living room, talking with her housekeeper. "Está bien que vayas a casa de la Señora Didion mañana. ¿Puedes venir el jueves en su lugar?"

"Sí."

"OK," she says. Her Spanish is a little rusty, now that she has given up teaching and speaks it only occasionally with her employee. "Would you like me to call her? Sí?"

Maria nods, her dark bob jostling. She has worked for my mother now for almost a decade, since my sister and I were in junior high, and on the days she doesn't come here she works for another couple who live close by. My mother goes to the telephone in the kitchen, and she cradles the receiver to her ear.

"Joan? It's Katherine Korey." She stands beneath the dangling copper pots, in a room that is cramped like a ship's galley, smoking as she stares out onto San Vicente Boulevard. "Maria has a doctor's appointment on Wednesday, so we're trying to move things around. Can she come to you tomorrow?"

From here she can see where it all went wrong, the site of my father's treachery, the runners still vaulting along the boulevard's tree-lined meridian. But she speaks, now, to her dream doppelgänger, the person she would be if her life had broken differently, perhaps. She and this woman are connected by geography, privilege, and vocation, by habits and mutual friends, and by a woman who shuttles between their households all week long. But my mother will never be Joan Didion, not now or ever.

"Wonderful. Thank you," she says, then pauses. "It's going OK, yeah." In the next room, Maria dusts the spines of my mother's books—of *The White Album* and *Slouching Towards Bethlehem*—but no inversion of this gesture occurs at the Didion-Dunnes'. "Just waiting on notes from Laddie. You know how that goes."

They are divided by talent, and perhaps by luck, whatever it is that has prevented my mother from accessing herself more completely. They are connected by regional manners, Le Creuset pots, and the maître d' of Chasen's on speed dial. But they are severed, irreparably, by fate.

"Yes, exactly." My mother laughs, a little bitterly. "Yep."

It is the summer her mother falls sick. In June of 1987, she and my grandmother are back in touch, and she is bracing for the worst. As she hangs up the phone, she feels another bolt of anxiety. Helen McGaffey is living up in the Pacific Northwest now, having spent the late years of her life in an Airstream, a traveling aluminum box that smells like porta-pottys and stale chemicals. She'd parked it in Barstow, parked it in Victorville, orbiting my mother like a distant star before arriving at last near Seattle, where my aunt and uncle live. She is dying of cancer but, Christian Scientist to the end, has refused to treat it.

My mother is hardly a monster. She was raised by a cold and broken person who happens to be the only parent she has left. Her father was gone too early. Her sister and cousins are constellated around Washington state, and her children, too, have flown the coop. She is almost all alone now, left with an industry that mostly refuses her. She walks outside and crosses the long lawn on her double lot, moving between the citrus trees on her way back to her office. Her dog, a black Lab puppy she has named Irish, frisks along behind her. Lemons glow in the sun. She was Katherine McGaffey and then Katherine Specktor and now Katherine Korey, although now that the man is gone, she will drop the name soon and revert to her original. She is fifty-one. Perhaps there is another marriage in front of her, perhaps not. She is not looking for a husband. She still drinks, but everything's under control. She sits down at her desk, picks up the coffee cup she had intended to refill, takes a swig of its cold contents, and grimaces, then turns her attention down to her typewriter.

The script she is working on—it is the last one she will ever be hired to write—is about a newscaster who died, a woman named Jessica Savitch. Irony of ironies, it is her neighbor and hero, the one she was just on the phone with, who will co-write the successful version of this story some years from now, when it will be directed by my father's friend Jon Avnet. By the time *Up Close and Personal* is released in 1996 my mother will be living another life entirely. But now she sits with her wrists resting against the Selectric's cool, blue metal; its quiet electrical hum the only sound audible as she reaches over to take another slug of cold coffee, to light another cigarette before—

★ ★ ★

DID SHE THINK she was prepared? I sprint out into the kitchen to answer a ringing telephone, a call I know can only bring bad news, for it is two a.m. here in Columbus, where I am spending the summer with Alice, my girlfriend.

"Mom?"

I stand in my boxers, sweating in the August heat. Her clotted sobs are so violent I can barely decipher a word she is saying.

"Mom? Mom, slow down . . ."

It's hot, so hot, even in the darkness of the small hours. I open the refrigerator, hoping its freon chill will shake me out of this nightmare into which I seem to have fallen.

"Mom?"

She is drunk in a way I have not encountered for years. Her voice is like a bear's, a furry warble of grief and unreason. I lean on the fridge, eyes closed, forehead against the freezer door.

"My—my mommy's dead!" She sounds like she's downed a quart of vodka. I can practically smell the liquor through the phone.

"Get some water. Mom, why don't you drink some water?"

What can I say to her? What can I do besides listen to her spew her grief, her despair: her mother is dead. That Helen was neither loved nor loving makes no difference. She is alone now. All alone.

"I'm sorry," I say. "Mom, I'm sorry."

It's so late. Over on the kitchen table there are ashtrays, ciga-rette butts, empty bottles of Rolling Rock glinting green in the dark. There is a copy of *Under the Volcano*, which Alice and I have been reading together. I peel my forehead off the freezer's tacky linoleum surface, carry the telephone over to sit down. The pile carpeting is gritty beneath my feet.

"Slow down. Would you, please?"

She can't. It's like the lock has been knocked off a hydrant: years of unhappiness shooting out of her from all sides. I can't get a word in. I set the receiver down, reach for a cigarette. My mother's voice sizzles on the table like a bee inside a jar.

"—Korotkin," she is saying, when I pick back up, ranting now about her last husband. "His name was Stanley Korotkin, not Korey! And I bought it! I fell for his bullshit like—"

I set the phone down again. There's nothing I can do to console her. I sit, smoking, in my underwear, my mother's voice tinny and distant. It must be a hundred degrees in here. After a moment I walk out onto the rear porch, which juts out from our building's second floor over an alley, but it's just as bad outside. The moon hangs, useless, over a landscape of rickety wooden tenement buildings. I flick my cigarette down to the concrete below. Indianola Avenue, that humming thoroughfare at the end of the street, is silent at this hour. Even the High Street drunks have stumbled home. I go inside, understanding even before I pick up the phone that I cannot hide, and my mother's mania will find me wherever I go. But that doesn't mean I have to sit still for it.

"—just hates my script. I know he hates it, and if Laddie can't hire me anymore and Marvin Worth won't either then I'm really up a—"

God. It's like sitting inside an oven. In the front room, where we sleep, Alice is splayed on our futon on the floor, a fan blasting across her body. My mother talks, rants, weeps. It no longer matters if I am listening, as it's possible she doesn't even know I'm here.

I set the phone down. I will see her when I graduate, but then after next summer, not for many years. You have only one mother, but mine is beginning a descent I cannot follow. Her life in the movies is over. A time of heavy, heavy drinking has begun. Gently, as if I am defusing a bomb, I pick up the receiver. I hold my breath, I make no sound, careful not to disturb her as I lay the handset back down in its cradle.

★ ★ ★

"BABY WANTS TO fuuuck!"

Dennis Hopper straps on his tank of nitrous oxide. I am not the only one with Oedipal questions, it seems. I sit in the balcony of the Calvin Theater in Northampton, Massachusetts, trying to make sense of my mother, trying to make sense of—anything, really. It is the spring of 1988, not so long until I graduate, and I am front and center, perched in this otherwise empty room. My friend Dana is the projectionist—occasionally, I turn around and see her coppery hair, dyed almost pumpkin-colored, flashing in the yellow booth—but otherwise I am alone.

"Mommy loves you."

"Don't you fuckin' look at me."

Alone, except for the ghosts on the wall, the sacred traces of Hopper and Isabella Rossellini, playing out a sadomasochistic psychodrama that feels as old as time.

"Stay alive, baby. Do it for Van Gogh . . ."

Have you ever had the feeling movies were coterminous with your life? That the map they offer and the territory they describe are the same? I have—I do, as Laura Dern, my childhood playmate, arrives in this one as the embodiment of all goodness, fair witch to Isabella's dark—but this isn't what I mean. I don't mean in the sense that the people are familiar, that you have crossed paths with them in what we erroneously refer to as "real life," but rather the opposite: that their uncanniness is something you can neither do without nor escape, even if you happen to be the sort of person who isn't wild about the movies at all. Who would you be without a fantasy arena to create you? Without a magic mirror to show you, even when you aren't looking, who you are?

Blue Velvet plays at the Calvin for weeks. This place is a former opera house, built in 1929. Down beneath it are catacombs, abandoned dressing rooms, a cobwebbed darkness of velveteen furniture and shattered glass, and movies tend to remain here long after their original run. This one, directed by my own preadolescent oracle, the man in the crooked strawberry slacks, I see ten or twelve times. In this room I've seen *Heartburn*, Nora Ephron's sour drama about her divorce from Carl Bernstein, and will soon see *Fatal Attraction*, that commercial triumph featuring Glenn Close, my father's client, but it is *Blue Velvet* to which I return over and over, trying to make sense of my life. Dean Stockwell blazes up in front of me in pale makeup, to sing the song about a candy-colored clown, about the Sandman, Roy Orbison's "In Dreams," and I find I cannot do it. The film's meaning eludes me. Its mood clings, though, like flaming chemicals. I walk home later still encased in it, tormented, burning.

The streets are empty. It is late. The town—I am living in an off-campus apartment now, on the fringes of Northampton—feels like a variant of Lynch's Lumberton itself. I walk down King, across Main. Not a single window is illuminated. In a few hours, these frigid streets will be populated by the inmates of the local psychiatric hospitals who come out just before dawn to sweep them: slow-moving, apparitional scarecrows pushing their brooms across the vacant intersections in semi-darkness until the day cracks open above them like an egg.

I climb the narrow stairs of a tenement building on Michelman Avenue, all the way up to its third floor. I crawl into bed and pick up my copy of James Baldwin's *The Devil Finds Work*. In it, he writes, "To encounter oneself is to encounter the other: and this is love." He writes that evil, the Devil, is "that moment when no other human being is real to you, nor are you real to yourself." I already know that I am failing at this, that I will spend the rest of my life trying to render myself and others more real, but I also know that I am young. There will be time for me to fail at it again, over and over.

In the morning, Northampton is bucolic and green. The professors gather to have their poppyseed waffles at Curtis & Schwartz; the students loiter at Main Street Records, Bonducci's, Broadside Books. I come from a place that is nothing like this, that strikes most of my compatriots as exotic, peculiar, fantastical. "What was it like growing up in LA?" they ask, as if I have any point of comparison, let alone the vocabulary with which to tell them. But I am certain by now that I will never go home, that this university oasis surrounded by factory towns, the ruins of the last century's once-thriving manufacturing culture, better reflects who I am. Alas, I am mistaken. Northampton is exactly like home, and I am exactly like it: blighted, doomed, and inescapably American. The sun rises and I walk into it, certain that its light is inextinguishable, that I, too, exist inside the panorama of an everlasting day.

IV

‑TRANSNATIONAL‑

8. NEMAWASHI

1989–1992

MICHAEL OVITZ STANDS IN the first-class cabin, shoving his bag in the overhead bin, looking like any other vacationer—khaki pants, canvas shoes, sunglasses dangling from the neck of his Breton T-shirt—headed for Honolulu to unwind. But anyone who knows Ovitz knows that he doesn't unwind, not like other people. He slides into his seat, still feeling like the weight of the world rests upon his shoulders, because, here on the cusp of a new decade, indeed it does.

"It's gonna be fine." His seatmate glances over at him, a moon-faced man named Sandy Climan. "You worry too much."

"I worry just enough, down to the decimal point," Ovitz says, grinning because this is his attempt at a joke: if anyone could hope to titrate even his own anxiety with scientific precision it would be him. But Climan just shakes his head.

"It'll be fine."

Another funny pair, or, rather, quartet, since the two men in the seats behind them—their names are Ray Kurtzman and Bob Goldman—belong to the same party. If the phrase "talent agent" even still conjures up an image of warty cocaine cowboys, these guys ain't it. They look like middle management figures at a St. Louis accounting firm: Climan in his blue-blazer, Kurtzman with his neatly parted silver hair. So what are they doing on this flight?

"Hey, Ray," Ovitz turns in his seat. "Hand me my copy of *Not by Bread Alone*, will you?"

These are the people Ovitz has chosen to go with him, the calmest ones in his circle. My father is somewhere far away, dependable, a steady earner so far as Ovitz is concerned, but even he is too emotive for an operation that requires professional poker players, men with slow, slow pulses and faces as ungiving as clocks. Kurtzman reaches into his bag and hands a book forward.

"Thanks."

This flight, it will change my father's life. It will change many other lives as well, not least my own. But as Ovitz leans back and cracks open the book, which is already dog-eared and well-underlined, not a beach read but a business treatise by one Kōnosuke Matsushita, you'd be forgiven for not seeing what is hiding in plain sight. Around them are actual holiday travelers—it is mid-November—on their way to soak up some sun, the adults hunching over their paperbacks by Tom Clancy and Michael Crichton, writers who, like almost everything else that flows through Hollywood now, have already made Ovitz and his partners a tremendous amount of money. But money is not all they are after in this instance, as the plane begins its movement down the runway, a Hawaiian Air Lockheed L-1011 beginning its voyage. Only Ovitz knows where they are going for sure. He closes his eyes as the cabin fills with the hiss of pressurization, as Climan studies his newspaper, a *New York Times* he has grabbed out of the seat pocket in front of him, its front page showing East Germans pouring through the Brandenberg Gate. Even his colleagues are half in the dark, but Ovitz knows they are en route to swallow the world.

★ ★ ★

IT'S GOOD TO be King, but wouldn't it be better to be Emperor?

Like Lew Wasserman a generation before him, Ovitz is tired of the client service business. His freedom is curtailed insofar as everything he does depends upon the whims of his clients, so many of whom are—artists, be they ever thus—capricious personalities indeed. But where Wasserman was the purest pragmatist, no more interested in art than a bumblebee is in an automobile tire, Ovitz lives for it. Not for no reason does his T-shirt bear the blue-and-white fisherman's stripes of which Picasso, a hero of his, was so fond. If he does not seem to others a passionate person—a rational approach coupled with tempered aggression is the secret of his success—he is nevertheless exhilarated in art's presence when he sits down to watch Scorsese's latest opus, or stands in front of the paintings he collects. He loves art and he loves artists, which is why he got into the agency business to begin with. But it is also why he is now, after twenty-one years of doing it, so restless, and so bored.

Boredom has always seemed to him a feeling for other people, dreamy or indecisive people. He rarely slows down enough to feel it. The stories that are told about him in these years—next spring, when *Premiere* magazine debuts its first annual power list of Hollywood moguls, it will place him in the top slot, with Wasserman, the aging lion who retains his perch as the head of MCA, at number two—all paint Michael Ovitz as a wizard, a powerful man who holds the business on a string. The ones they will tell in just a few years will paint him as a Machiavellian threat, a man so drunk on power he cannot help but commit a string of fatal mistakes. But none of this is correct. Power? Sure, he likes it. He likes to swing it around a little—there was that unfortunate incident a few months ago with the writer Joe Esterhaz, who told the press that Ovitz had threatened him, insisting that if he left the agency CAA's "foot soldiers" would "blow his fucking brains out"—but people who think Michael Ovitz, the reigning king of Hollywood, is driven by power? Those people don't understand him at all.

Leaning back in his seat, the engine roaring as he nurses his club soda (Ovitz's own recollection differs. Whatever he had said to Esterhaz, not that exactly, the remark was made with irony), he has no interest in the exercise of force. He doesn't even care about fear, which he is aware he inspires not just in those teenage hires who dart into his office to refill his glass bowl of Hershey's Kisses and who pretend he's Darth Vader, but also in his colleagues and competitors. It is not these things themselves, but rather the perception of these things—how he appears to be one way, but is, in fact, another—is what delights him. "Foot soldiers?" All that says is that Esterhaz has a hackneyed imagination—no surprise, really, from the man who will make his bones writing over-the-top blockbusters like *Showgirls*—because he is no monster, no crude general, no thug. All that is just a trick of the light. But it's this trick, precisely, that drives him forever toward the horizon.

Perception. There's no art without an audience, no painting that exists free of its perceiver. When he was a young man, he'd walked into La Scala restaurant one day and ripped a hundred-dollar bill in half. He handed part of it to the maître d', promising him the other after he ate. A hundred dollars was not a sum he could easily afford to lose in those days, and he didn't really care about the table, but the public perception of him as someone who could torch a C-note without a care? That was priceless. These days he can afford to burn bales of money, but what interests him beyond the ten percent he can squeeze out of every deal—not that he doesn't enjoy that; he's a capitalist, not a saint—are the things he can't buy: the strands of art, architecture, and culture that manage to elude capture no matter whose name is on the deed to them. When he crosses the lobby of that I.M. Pei–designed temple at 9830 Wilshire Boulevard, glancing up at Roy Lichtenstein's twenty-six-foot-high Bauhaus Stairway, which dominates the atrium like a stained-glass window, he doesn't think, merely, "I own that," but rather, "how did he do it?" How does Lichtenstein create the things he does?

It is a question that might drive anyone who isn't an artist a little crazy. When Ovitz writes his memoir, three decades from now, he will note, ruefully, that "as agents, [CAA] didn't create anything." He will call himself a "frustrated artist," one without any discernible aptitude, who fell into agenting to support those creative people he so admired, and whose chosen profession is, in this way, an act of love. Those are the words, in the memoir's chaotic storm of record-correcting, self-justification, tale-telling, and occasional introspection, I will find most revealing. Only—I think Ovitz underrates himself. I think Ovitz is a successful artist, one with a larger canvas than even he might imagine.

★ ★ ★

THE ECONOMIC MIRACLE. It takes something to lift Ovitz up in the air, to move him counterclockwise around the globe on a journey in which Hawaii is, after all, only a midpoint. He reaches over to grab a section of Climan's paper and sees it right there. "Japan Buys the Center of New York." A headline on the Opinion page explains everything. Is the transfer of American assets to Japanese ownership something to worry about? For some people, Ovitz knows, it is. The recent sale of Rockefeller Center to Mitsubishi Estate Co. is just one more salvo in a tug-of-war that's been going on for a decade. Textiles, semiconductors, automobiles, appliances. Japan's been kicking America's ass in almost every aspect of its manufacturing economy, so why wouldn't they come after the movies? Some Americans see this as a threat (the movies: America's greatest remaining export, perhaps the only one that matters, in a way), but Ovitz? He knows it's an opportunity. When Sony Corporation went shopping last year for a US movie studio—after losing its format wars around their videocassette player, the Betamax, to their rival Matsushita, the Japanese electronics company was determined to prevent that kind of humiliation from ever happening again—Ovitz stepped in to broker the deal. Why wouldn't he? New ownership meant new capital for the studio, the better to drive up prices for his own clients. He'd spent hours with Sony chairman Akio Morita—what better way to avoid future humiliation than by owning the software as well as the hardware, was Morita's reasoning—smoothing out all the edges between him and a CBS Records executive named Walter Yetnikoff, who'd hoped to become the studio's new boss. It didn't work out, because Yetnikoff was the sort of boorish American who didn't understand Japanese manners at all, but Ovitz? Ovitz has spent decades mastering these, not just through his daily Aikido sessions but through his close study of Asian business cultures as well. Long before it will become a cliché to cite Sun Tzu, Ovitz has absorbed every word of *The Art of War*, as he has Morita's two books and those of Edwin Reischauer, everything he can find that might enlarge his own ways of thinking. He admires the Japanese practice of *nemawashi*, which involves decision-making from the ground up. Hollywood has always been a top-down culture—Lew Wasserman certainly never looked to his subordinates to tell him what do—but Ovitz approaches things differently. He likes to build consensus first, just like Japanese executives do. That way, his underlings will never question his decisions.

He'd helped Sony choose its target. His first thought was Universal, but Wasserman wasn't selling—they'll have to pry that studio from his dead hands, probably—and so he'd settled upon

Columbia Pictures. Coca-Cola, who'd bought the studio just four years earlier, was already looking to get out—making movies had turned out to be a hairier proposition than making soda pop— and after Ovitz had brokered the sale, CAA had walked away with a fee of $11 million, a larger commission than the agency has ever received for even its biggest star clients. Some thought Ovitz would jump ship to run the newly owned studio himself, that this had been his whole game all along, but those people don't get it either. Sony's bureaucracy would have killed him. ("Even the most ingratiating American would wind up needing a food taster" is how he will put it in his memoir one day.) So he'd bent over back-ward not to take the job when Morita came calling, asking for a compensation package so lavish some took it as evidence of his greed when it was really just a Japanese courtesy, a face-saving way to make Sony look elsewhere and spare them the embarrass-ment of his saying no.

His colleagues back home might find all this esoteric, or even irrelevant. My father might think that none of this will ever make much difference to him, and if he does, he's wrong. Still, why shouldn't CAA expand its portfolio? Why should "talent" confine itself to the motion picture industry? Why not act more like a global consulting firm, like McKinsey? Talent is talent, whether it's a corporation or a person, and Ovitz's job is to advise it. As his plane begins its descent into Honolulu, Ovitz is ready to go again, because it turns out that the Sony deal was just a palate-opener. He and Climan have spent months arranging the meeting that is about to take place, an elaborate cat and mouse that began with the baiting of a salaryman named Henry Ishii. "No means Yes." "Stop means Go." Ovitz knew that approaching Ishii would lead him to an executive named Masahiko Hirata, who happens to be the number three at Matsushita Electronics. According to the principles of *nemawashi*, Hirata, and not the company's top dog, is who he needs to see. After months of due diligence and heavy secrecy—they are meeting in Hawaii because if anyone spotted him on a flight all the way to Tokyo the rumors of his itchy feet would begin all over again—they are set to make it happen. Another American studio is about to come under Japanese control. But those rumors, the ones that persist about how he is ready to leave CAA? Those rumors are untrue. He'd negotiated the deal for Sony not just because it was lucrative and interesting, but because it would be good for both his agency and his own profile. The Japanese company had paid a whopping $3.1 billion for Columbia Pictures, roughly five times what Coca-Cola had paid only a few years ago. There's money to be made here, and a chance for CAA's empire, which has already begun to push out into music and other avenues anyway, to exist on a global scale. As the plane taxis through the humid Honolulu afternoon, he knows the process he is instigating now will be delicate. In the months ahead, he will travel to Tokyo so many times he will begin to dream in Japanese; he will wake up some mornings without even knowing where he is, will maintain an elaborate subterfuge—routing himself via San Francisco, returning phone calls in the middle of the night so even his colleagues don't know he's out of the country, filling his luggage with gifts that will make even his wife and children think he has been to London instead of Japan—the better to keep his eyes on the prize.

"Remember." He stands up, as the cabin lights flicker on and then the stewardess unlatches the passenger door, the balmy island air drifting through to greet him. "No talk about business."

"None?" Ray Kurtzman tucks the Matsushita electronics catalog he's been studying back in his bag. "What on earth are we gonna talk about? The weather?"

"Anything." Ovitz smiles. He remains, with Climan, the only one who really understands how the people they are meeting work. *Yes means No. Stop means Go.* It would drive his more impatient colleagues, like my father, insane. "We'll talk about anything other than what we're actually here to do."

★ ★ ★

"WHAT'S UP, BOY?" My friend Jim walks over to headbutt me gently, as I stand at the curb outside the LAX arrival terminal. "Safe flight?"

"Yo." I sling my carry-on into the trunk of his battered Honda Civic, red paint scraped away on the passenger side to reveal gunmetal drab beneath. "Why so dressed up? You coming from a bar mitzvah?"

"A job. I've joined the ranks of the gainfully employed."

"A job? The kind where they give you health insurance and shit?"

"The kind where I get fired if I don't come correct," my friend says, smoothing the lapel of his cashmere blazer. "So, yeah."

Nemawashi. The word means, literally, "digging around the roots," but for my friends and me, it means nothing. Michael Ovitz flies to Japan to make a deal that will change the course of America's corporate history, but for people like us, wannabe writers, actors, and layabouts, line cooks and temp workers with head shots in our crappy cars, half-written screenplays that are already too long, the business is just an environment, occasionally a means to an end.

"Where are you working?" I slide into the front seat.

"Sony."

"Sony?" I say. "The electronics company?"

"No, you idiot, the movie studio." Vin Scully's voice crackles over the radio as Jim pulls away from the curb. "Columbia-TriStar. Ain't you paying attention?"

I am not at all paying attention. I am living in San Francisco, having fled after graduation so that I might keep away from the movies. I spend my days trying to write fiction, turning on my boxy laptop and pecking at it a while before giving up in despair, and working temp jobs: a law firm, a clothing company, a toy manufacturing outfit, where I answer complaint letters.

"What's it like?"

"Treacherous." He accelerates onto Lincoln Boulevard, punching the gas as we race under a corridor of tall palms. "Any minute someone's going to walk into my office and stab me in the goddamn chest."

Corporations are viper pits. We may be all of twenty-three, but even we know this. A studio is a hellish pyramid in which people must step all over their neighbors in a futile race to the top. In his other life, Jim is a screenwriter. His job at TriStar isn't meant to last—he is a creative executive, the lowest rung on a studio's ladder, there just to pay the bills—but he knows more about movies than anyone I've ever met. They are in his blood. His father, Henry Gibson, is a character actor, known for his key parts in Altman's *Nashville* and *The Long Goodbye*. His mother is a successful television writer. His future seems unlimited, favorable outcomes assured.

"When are you gonna get a car that works?" I say. "Now that you're making 30K you can probably afford a muffler."

"Tape deck works," he says, grinning. "Not sure what else I need."

We pull up at a light. A wire dinosaur squats atop the roof of a Mexican restaurant across the street. I'm just visiting, here for the weekend to see my dad, but I am falling in love with Los Angeles against my will. The Pacific air is chill and damp, Lincoln Boulevard is the eternal mélange of Googie-style buildings and supermarket lots it has always been, a weirdly appealing seam between the city and the beach, and the night is dense with possibility. Dream as I might of resisting this place, I don't stand a chance.

"Where are we going?"

"Wanna hit Dominick's?" he says. "We could do that first."

On a different night, he might say Small's, the Olive, Boardner's, the Dresden; he could say Jabberjaw, the Burgundy Room, Jumbo's Clown Room, Al's Bar. In a sense these places are one and the same.

"Yes," I say. "Dom's."

Jim's car shudders like a dying animal. He works the clutch, until the engine jerks back from the edge of extinction and we squeal out into the intersection.

★ ★ ★

"DUDE, IS THAT James Toback?"

"Where?"

"It is! It's totally Toback! He's with Warren Beatty!"

Nights of one's twenties are endless, Homeric. They happen over and over. In a room like a camera obscura—windowless and dark, pale limbs and faces floating in a haze of smoke—we crash the door, coming in off the street lit silver of Beverly Boulevard, blinking as our eyes adjust.

"Dude, that's not James Toback," Jim snorts. "And it's definitely not Beatty."

Some other aging pretty boy, then, in an Armani suit; some other gargoyle gangster with a face like a raisin in a roomful of people thirty years his junior.

"I guess that's not Madonna over there in the corner booth either."

"No, that's—wait, that totally is Madonna. What the fuck?"

A Hollywood night out is a slot machine, the plastic tokens mixed with occasional pieces of gold. My friends and I are the supercilious little nobodies propped up against the bar: Nick (actor, blond, working); Tudor (actor, brunette, sous-chef at a restaurant in Venice), Jim; and myself. We look like guys who have the answers, or who think they do, at least.

"You read for Marty Brest?" Tudor stares at Nick, leaning against the bar, long hair sweeping down around his face. "Shit, I haven't even had a callback for weeks."

"That's because you suck."

Tudor tugs on his longneck, smiles. "Be nice."

Nick's career is lifting off. He's got a part in a forthcoming

Christian Slater movie called *Mobsters,* will soon book a part in *Scent of a Woman.* He rattles the ice in his glass, holds up two fingers to the bartender.

"We gonna stay here?"

He's from Minnesota. The lowest-key, least affected of us all. He surveys the room—his manner is warm, easy, like an animal that's been napping in the sun—then lifts a sharp eyebrow as his gaze settles upon me.

"Who's gonna hit on Madge?"

"What? No way, man."

"Come on." His face lights up, grinning as he baits me. "Live a little."

"No way."

"Do I have to do everything around here?" He leans along the bar to reach his near-empty martini. "Jesus Christ."

It's all one night, which seems it will go on forever.

"You dare me to do it?" he says.

"You won't."

"Watch."

The way it works is the way it has always worked. My father used to come here as a young man. Dominick's has been open since the fifties. In those days, it was Sinatra and Kim Novak crowding the booths, my father and his friends eyeing them wolf-ishly from across the room.

"I don't think that's really Madonna."

Jim smiles. "Man, who knows?"

The place looks the same. Spruced-up after a moribund stretch in the eighties, it remains louche and Rat Pack-y, with its maroon upholstery and moody lighting. The bartender—actor, if I had to guess—sets Nick's fresh martini down in the vacant space next to me.

"We staying here?"

"Yeah, yeah." Tudor sprawls, propping up his part of the bar like he owns the room, the block, the neighborhood. The place is crowded, all of us half-shouting to be heard above Digital Underground blaring on the house stereo. "We gotta see what happens."

What happens is our friend approaching a woman who is or is not Madonna, who is the spitting image of our time. What happens is this room, the generational tides that wash through it. What happens is Hollywood, which might grow older, but which, my friends and I know, can never die.

"Look, look!" We all know it. It will last forever, just like us. "He's getting her number! It's on!"

★ ★ ★

GREED IS NOT the driver.

As Michael Ovitz and his colleagues cross the lobby of the Kahala Hilton now, as they approach a conference room in which their quarry is waiting—Ovitz is spruced up after his flight, wearing a sportscoat but no tie, carrying, of all things, a plastic container filled with cookies—what crosses Ovitz's mind isn't the struggling young nonentities of Hollywood, but rather Walter Yetnikoff. He has to suppress a smile thinking of Yetnikoff, a creature of pure entertainment industry id, one even the Sony executives had referred to as "the Evil Dwarf," trying to negotiate with these people.

"Hirata-San." He bows from the waist, greeting the man from Matsushita (what would Walter do? Probably whip out his penis and start waving it around in rotary circles) with immaculate courtesy. Hirata bows back. He is a small man, five-three, and so even the modestly proportioned Ovitz looms over him. But a height advantage and all the politesse in the world cannot mask the fact that Hirata and his associates are killers.

"Please accept these," Ovitz places the Tupperware on the conference table. "A gift from my wife. They are delicious."

Not greed. Humility. As Hirata gestures for him to sit, as Ovitz and his compadres, who are salarymen, too, in a sense, the most loyal people he has, remove their jackets—everything according to protocol; the Matsushita men have brought gifts for them also—Ovitz knows it isn't just avarice that has brought him here. It is, rather, the thing that has driven him from the beginning, the feeling of freedom that derives from shaping a deal.

"Ah, so you prefer *Stray Dog* to *Drunken Angel*?"

Matsushita wanted it. Ovitz knew even before he met with Henry Ishii, the company's man in Los Angeles, that Sony's recent move was not going to go unanswered—not for no reason do the people in Japan refer to the company as *Maneshita*, meaning "copycat"—but as he walks across the golf course with Hirata later that same afternoon, he knows that some still question his motives.

"*Drunken Angel* is great," Ovitz says. Over and over, people seem to get him wrong. "But I prefer the later Kurosawa."

"Yes? *Throne of Blood*?"

"Yes, very good," Ovitz says, smiling. Do these people, too, think that he is Macbeth, driven to rule at any cost? "But *Rashomon* is my favorite."

Three days, across which everything remains in code. Small talk contains subtle pressure, but it is mostly about familiarity and respect. It is about *nemawashi*, which will allow them to reach a deal in perfect harmony, one none of them have even alluded to yet.

"Surely you agree that Sadaharu Oh is the greatest baseball player in our country. There is no contest."

"Certainly, yes." Ovitz lines up his shot, then turns to his caddy at the last minute to select a different club. "Although Kōji Yamamoto was very good in his time."

He can see his colleagues getting tired. They are here to negotiate, not to talk about baseball and Japanese film. But as they move from conference room to luncheon table, from golf course to hotel bar, Ovitz knows they are getting close. The movies are an American asset, always have been. Other countries have their own cinema, of course, but Hollywood is the crux of America's dominance. The people who worship the nation from abroad, and the ones who hate it, are drawn to its movies, to the power and glamour Hollywood creates, which is why the studios have remained, from their inception, under American control. The companies and industrialists that have bought out the studios in the past—Kinney National, Gulf + Western, TransAmerica, Marvin Davis, Kirk Kerkorian—were all American themselves. When there happened to be an exception, when the UK-based Decca Records bought Universal, the mistake was soon corrected by MCA's acquisition of Decca a few years later. This is why the Sony sale had caused such upset in the American press, and why Rupert Murdoch's purchase of Twentieth Century Fox just a few years earlier had done the same.

"Ovitz-Sama, we would like to request your assistance with something." Finally, on Sunday night, it comes. Hirata sets down his silver and glances at the bones of his chateaubriand like he is embarrassed to mention the reason he is actually here. "Matsushita would like to purchase a motion picture studio."

"I would be honored to help," Ovitz says as he picks up his glass of George Stagg whiskey to refill it, preparing for yet another toast. "All of us are at your service."

"What will it cost for you to help us?" Hirata speaks cautiously.

"Nothing."

"Nothing?"

They've been at this for hours, drinking to every person's spouse and to each of their individual children by name, starting with sake from the Hyogo Prefecture, and then moving on to the whiskey, which, too, Ovitz has brought as a gift. Like Lew Wasserman before him, Ovitz isn't much of a drinker. He likes a clear head. But he feels now as if he has just woken from a refreshing nap, like all the alcohol in the world can't touch him.

"No fee," he says. The newspapers can wring their hands over the Japanese acquisition of American assets all they like, because this country's xenophobic imagination never sleeps, but he feels a pure serenity. "It will cost nothing for us to consult. If you are unhappy with our services, we will ask only that you reimburse our expenses."

"And if we are not unhappy?"

Ovitz sits back. He is not here for the money, and he is not here to run a movie studio himself. He is here because the deal itself is his medium. But even granted the soul of an artist the capitalist imagination can only arrive at one place.

"If you find you are happy with how we perform our services, I would like you to fill a Brink's truck with gold and drive it to our office."

★ ★ ★

"HOW'S YOUR DAD?"

Outside Dominick's, I collide with Jay Moloney. He's on his way in, just as the four of us are leaving.

"You'd know better than I. Don't you see him every day?"

Beneath a streetlamp we embrace, my friend from the mailroom clamping my shoulders.

"I see him, but I don't really see him," he says. "I just pass him in the hall."

I see him, but I don't see him. Isn't this every talent agent's creed? *Stay out of the spotlight, it fades your suit.*

"Are you slumming?" I say. Moloney's suit is Armani, the sleek uniform of his profession. "Are you lost? Shouldn't you be at Helena's, or the Roxbury or something?"

"I could ask the same question." He smiles. "You should be home with milk and cookies. Nothing good can happen in a place like this."

He's an agent now, as is Richard Lovett, and not just any agent but, along with a handful of others our age—Bryan Lourd, Kevin

Huvane, David O'Connor—part of a group the media has dubbed the "Young Turks." Moloney, also, had worked for my father, and then for Ovitz, but now he is the hand of the king. His clients are Steven Spielberg, Martin Scorsese, Leonardo DiCaprio.

"Give my love to Pops when you see him," he says. "He's a legend."

"I will."

"And to you." He slides away into the club. "Love you, buddy."

Overnight it has happened: my father has attained an emeritus status, become iconic while my peers have moved into pole position. Soon, these young Turks will run things. Soon, my three pals and I—Gen X slackers, aspiring artists all—will get serious, and our real lives will begin.

"Was that Jay Moloney?" Jim says, tumbling out into the street behind me.

"Yeah." I look back. Jay looks strong and invulnerable, his shoulders as broad as an athlete's as he vanishes into the crowd.

"Dang," he says. "You know all the players."

So I do. But maybe the players don't know one another. Ovitz is off doing deals in Japan. His minions, my father and the Young Turks, carry on like it doesn't matter. Maybe they assume that as Hollywood is a global business, global money can only help. CAA has the movies, they have TV, they have book-to-film adaptation all sewn up, thanks to their partnership with Janklow & Nesbit literary agency in New York. They have a music department, and soon will establish one for "new media," a field many people, my friends and I included, might struggle just as yet to define. Still, analog, digital, business overseas. It's all one thing to them.

"Where should we go?"

The four of us stand, swaying, in the uneasy quiet of the street, the sounds of the bar muffling as the door swings shut behind us. Across the way, Cedars-Sinai Medical Center looms like the hull of an ocean liner.

"Boardner's?" Tudor says.

"We could do that," I say. "Or the Dresden."

The next time I lay eyes on Jay Moloney, a few years from now, things will be different. The next time I see him, he will be in a coffin, having taken his own life.

"Do we have time to get there?" Nick checks his watch.

"Oh, we have time, dude." Tudor lights a cigarette. "We have time."

A black BMW glides up in front of us, disgorging more people who want in at Dominick's. The hospital's windows glow opaquely, concealing from us the building's sick patients, its hurrying nurses, its light within that is neither night nor day.

"Let's hit it," I say, leading the walk back toward Jim's car, which sits alone by the curb in the shrill halo of a vacant ATM. "Last call's not for another hour or so."

Nemawashi is a process of forging toward consensus, as we have just done, but what sort of consensus is possible between artists and businessmen, or between one ambitious American abroad and his own crooked, contradictory heart? What kind, too, between a talent agent father and his wannabe writer son, who does not seem to know yet that life is not just for the wasting? Who is spending his days the way both nature and the movies may have also intended, letting the hours pour through him like water through a sieve.

★ ★ ★

WHO IS MICHAEL *Ovitz?*

When he writes his memoir, three decades hence, he will title it thus. Who is this man whose shadow falls across Hollywood, and whose job it is to wield his power—power that is real, as well as illusory—to bring his industry to the world and vice versa, to make the movies a multinational game?

He wakes up in darkness and slides out of bed. *Who Is Michael Ovitz?* This title is so like him, a feint at candor that is really a circular question. He walks downstairs, moving quietly so as

not to wake his wife and children. He has always been an early
riser, but right now all this flying to Japan—it is dinnertime there,
four a.m. here—has scrambled his sleep. He makes his way down
in bare feet, passing a Lichtenstein, a Picasso, a Brice Marden,
paintings he loves and is thrilled to own, but which do not, for
all their wonder and complexity, generate the same excitement as
the one he is heading for, his prize. When he'd first bought it, he'd
agreed as part of the terms of the sale not to display this prize to
anyone, not even to his family, and so for a year it sat in a locked
room at the back of his house, but now it hangs where no one can
miss it, smack dab in the center of his living room: Jasper Johns's
White Flag.

The canvas is large, six and a half feet by ten, and as he stands
in front of it now, even in the room's very darkness—the moon
outside is high over Rockingham Avenue—he feels something like
awe. This image reaches something in him nothing else can. Its
braided simplicity and complexity—it is, after all, an image even a
schoolchild knows by heart, but this one white-on-white encaus-
tic, so faded it is almost invisible within its many layers—are inexhaustible. He sees something new in it every time.

Who is Michael Ovitz? Is he just the sum of all this, the cold
stone floor, the nine-thousand-square-foot house that is filled with
modern art, this private sanctum that is, in fact, designed entirely for display? This, perhaps, is the difference between him
and other people. All his complexities are hidden right where you
can't miss them. His depths and surfaces are the same. Los Angeles is a shallow town filled with shallow people, but this is the
opposite of shallowness, a dazzling sophistication he wears like a
gown. Who is Michael Ovitz? He is exactly, exactly as he appears.

Forty-eight stars—the painting dates from 1955, before Alaska
and Hawaii were admitted to the union—and thirteen stripes,
the body of the canvas collaged with fabric and newsprint, layered with beeswax, then attacked with Jasper Johns's brush. You

have to see it. To look at a photo of it is one thing, but to stand in its presence is another. It has the scarred physicality of a weather-beaten barn, an enormity that extends beyond its physical dimensions, but also a feeling of intangibility. To stand in front of *White Flag* is to confront a history—your own, America's: it almost doesn't matter, as they become one and the same—and to feel pursued by it, exactly as you would be by a ghost, but it is also to feel liberated. At night, to see the image saturated in moonlight, it feels even more uncanny. Happiness may be impossible for people like Ovitz—it may be impossible for people like you and me—but when he stands before it now, he feels the purest exhilaration. He feels, for want of a better word, free.

I don't know what goes through his mind exactly, but I do know the joy of confronting a piece of art you love, which makes you feel like everybody and nobody at the same time. I know that the movies, which are a public commons, which have colonized the American imagination and also begun to destroy it, have been hijacked by people like this, artists without a medium, who forget that all art necessarily eludes capture, and can no more be owned than sunlight or air. But I also know that this man, who is the conduit through which Hollywood will enter its period of imperial decline, is just like me. He loves art with a ferocity few people can equal.

He stands in his bathrobe, arms slack at his sides. Through the French doors behind him, a black-bottomed pool is cold in the predawn, a mirror to the fading stars. The moon shines upon his yard just as it does on those of his neighbors, and the painting breathes upon him just as it does upon everyone, telling its long story of license, liberty, and infinite renewal, its circular and abiding nightmare about freedom and loss.

★ ★ ★

"TELL HIM I'M not fucking selling."

Lew Wasserman detests Michael Ovitz. The head of MCA Inc.

always has, and why wouldn't he? Agents and studio bosses have been at loggerheads since the days of Jack Warner. But in this case, the dislike is also personal. When Sid Sheinberg, his own number two, calls him up one day to let him know Ovitz is making overtures, Wasserman doesn't mince words.

"Tell him I'm not selling." He sits in his office, as spartan as ever, on the fifteenth floor of his vaunted tower in Universal City. "Not to him. And not to the fucking Japanese."

Below him sprawls the hazy gray plain of the San Fernando Valley. Selling MCA, his own company, whose holdings include Universal Studios among many other things, to Michael Ovitz would be like selling your dog to your worst enemy. It's not happening.

"Lew, maybe we should listen." Sheinberg keeps hounding him. He's been at Wasserman's side since the fifties, was part of the legal department that vetted MCA's original acquisition of the studio, and so he has the old man's ear. "These people have a whole lot of money to spend."

"Oh, I'm listening. I'd like to hear Ovitz grovel"—he leans back— "but I really don't plan to sell."

As he sees it, Ovitz is an arriviste, greedy, which only proves you can never count on a plutocrat to have a strong sense of irony, but even Wasserman must admire the meticulous perseverance of the man's approach. First, Ovitz works through Sheinberg, then through a mutual friend, Felix Rohatyn, the M&A wizard at Lazard Bank in Paris. In the spring of 1990—Wasserman does not know this, of course—Ovitz flies to Osaka fourteen times, sometimes just for the day, and always under the cover of strictest secrecy. If word of what is happening should get out, it might blow the whole negotiation process to smithereens. With the help of Herb Allen, another heavy-hitting investment banker, Ovitz conducts a comprehensive valuation of every movie, every television show, every recording artist currently under contract or part of Universal's library: seventy years of intellectual property precisely catalogued, so his friends in Japan will know to the penny the worth of what they hope to buy, why he has targeted this studio for Matsushita's acquisition. Then, and only then, does Ovitz call Wasserman directly, careful to make clear the most important part: that Wasserman and Sheinberg will remain in place as senior management.

"You'll make a killing," Ovitz says. "You won't even have to get out of your chairs. Matsushita wants to keep things just as they are. You just won't be the owner anymore."

"A hundred dollars a share," Wasserman barks.

How similar they are, and how different. When Ovitz was a young man running the tram tours on the Universal lot, Wasserman was like a god to him. He knows the old man's ask is outrageous—MCA's stock is trading in the thirties—but Wasserman is not going to give up on his life's work without a fight.

"They're not gonna go that high and you know it."

"Then I'm not selling."

But even as he hangs up, it also happens that Ovitz's timing is on point. Wasserman's not selling, he's not selling, he insists, but he's also creeping up on eighty years old. His remaining brother died six months ago, Jules Stein has been in the ground for a decade, and he and Edie recently purchased a plot in Hillside Cemetery. If not now, when? MCA's stock keeps falling—Saddam's invasion of Kuwait in the summer of 1990 really screws the market—and this might also be his best chance to get out with real value while at the same time keeping his hand on the tiller. So he decides to play the game. When Hirata comes calling, he greets the man politely at his home, showing off his koi pond; he flies to New York so he can meet the Matsushita brass for dinners at the 21 Club and at the Plaza Athénée. It's a deal he can walk away from, or so he tells himself—his whole life has been a series of such confrontations, and you can never lose if you're always ready to walk—but then word leaks to the press that a sale is underway.

Who does this? Ovitz insists that it's his rival, David Geffen, an MCA board member who's always eager to fuck him over. Matsushita believes it's MCA, hoping to boost its share price. And Wasserman thinks it's the Japanese, trying to crush his leverage and force his hand. In the end, it doesn't matter. Wasserman accepts an offer of $66 a share, plus an equity stake in one of Universal's flagship television stations. Factor in his new contract that will keep him in place as MCA's chairman for another half decade and a little fancy footwork to reduce his capital gains hit—he swaps his MCA stock for Matsushita's in lieu of taking cash—and he walks away with something in the neighborhood of $400 million. A canny deal for an aging man, who won't live long enough to spend it, and who's never given much thought as to who his successor will be. And just so, in November of 1990, the Music Corporation of America, Jules Stein's little band-booking business whose Midwestern roots are entwined with the story of Prohibition, whose expansive rise is, in some sense, the very story of the nation, is American no more.

★ ★ ★

WHAT OF MY father, who's just rolling in tonight after another fancy dinner with his friends? What does all of this have to do with him? By his own lights, not much. Ovitz isn't going anywhere, so what difference does it make if his boss wants to move a few corporations around on the side, help place Columbia or Universal Studios under new ownership? He's no protectionist. Who cares what Michael Ovitz does, particularly if it enhances their agency's dominance?

"Fred?"

Who cares what he does? It is the summer of 1991, and my father is trimming his salt-and-pepper mustache now, tidying his beard, studying his face as he gets ready for bed. What difference does it make if the owners are Japanese or Tanzanian? His clients are stars. So long as there's a market for Gene Hackman or Bobby Duvall, it doesn't matter who signs the checks.

"Fred? Come to bed."

Maybe in the big picture it does, just like it matters who runs Hollywood—Mike Ovitz is not Lew Wasserman, but an even newer brand of mogul—or who his wife is, but in the day to day, not so much. He scrutinizes his face's crags and angles. He is fifty-eight years old.

"I'll be out in a minute."

(Fifty-eight. Creeping up on thirty-five years since an afternoon in the car with Wasserman—it is the purest memory of the man he owns—back when he was the MCA chief's beleaguered assistant and driver. A baseball game was on the radio and he'd fucked up by saying that Ted Williams was "old." "What's that, kid?" Wasserman leaned forward from the backseat, and for a moment he'd thought his boss was going to rip his head clean off. "You think forty is old? What does that make me?" But then—Wasserman decided to let it pass. "You're right," he'd murmured. "This is a young man's business." Which was and still is true, and yet here he is, all these years later, still doing the job himself.)

"I'm turning out the light . . ."

His mother died a few months ago. He still feels the guilt that attacked him as he stood out in the sun at Forest Lawn, watching Stella Specktor's coffin go into the ground. He was a good son, dutiful and attentive, and she was always loving, never as tough as Ruby, but still there is guilt. There is guilt, also, over Kathy, whose drinking was never his fault, whose suffering—sure, he'd caused some of it: no illusions on that score—was beyond his control.

"I'm coming."

Kathy is out of the business now entirely. She's moved to Washington state. Whether she still drinks, he has no idea, but she might have had a career and she might have been happier, and the fact that she didn't, and wasn't, still makes him sick sometimes.

He twists the cold-water tap (he feels guilt, but what could he have done to save her from herself?) and splashes his face. When he looks up it is Ruby's face he sees looking back in the mirror.

His father's face. A few years back he'd shaved his beard, and Pamela, who'd never even met Ruby, was so upset it shocked her back into her old Queens accent. ("Fred! Yeww look like youwr fawwwther!") He'd grown it back, because she'd begged him to and this was all the incitement he needed, but—you cannot outrun who you are. He braces his hands on the wide, marble basin— the clawfoot tub visible in the background, the room itself an immaculate laboratory white, like winter snow—and he knows this absolutely. He makes more money every few weeks than Ruby ever did in a year, but he remains that troubled man's overcriticized son. Nothing will ever carry him away from that, really.

He snaps off the light. Nothing carries him away from that, and yet—everything does: who you are and who you used to be diverge even though you can never seem to outrun anything, which is the weirdest and most difficult paradox of living. He walks out past his closet—so many Italian suits in there he could wear a different one every day for six months—into the bedroom with its slate gray carpeting and the frosted, beveled glass windows. Pamela has already donned her sleep mask.

"You OK?"

"Yeah," he says. "I shouldn't have had that third glass of wine."

Or maybe it was that second glass of Fernet-Branca that did it. Who knows? Dinner with the DeVitos. With Mike and Patricia Medavoy. With Rick Nicita and Paula Wagner, or with Mike and Patti Marcus, his closest friends from the office. The nights run together for him, too, because life is like that as you age.

"I told you not to," she rolls onto her side, her voice hazy. She is already half asleep.

"Ah, yeah." He smiles. "You did."

Is he happy? Yes, essentially. Is he satisfied? Never. Is there some part of him that longs to wear the crown, like Ovitz? Yes, but also no. It's complicated. Success is a hair shirt. Anyone who looks at his life and sees only soft surfaces should try being him for twenty minutes, an anxious man in a heart attack profession. It is a dream, sure, but it is also a nightmare.

He slides into bed, reaches over to kill the light, then stops for a moment to take it all in. Anxious, perhaps, but—this works. His marriage works, he thinks. Kathy was too passive, where Pamela is driven like him. Her search business is booming. She loves art, theater, and books—she reads almost as much as Kathy did, but without the tangled impulse to be an artist herself—and he likes this. It challenges him, reminds him of what is actually real.

He kills the light. Outside, the street is silent. One of Pamela's green jadeite coffee cups shines dimly on his nightstand. Beside it is a book by that writer I am always going on to him about, Michael Ondaatje. He hasn't read it—not enough time to read for pleasure, much as he wishes otherwise—but he has flipped it open several times to note the epigraph, by John Berger. "Never again will a story be told as if it is the only one." He knows what this means: the story of his success, and of his failure, are entwined. The story of his own life, and of his father's; the story of his children, and of his friends. How does anyone get through this world thinking they are alone? And—how does anyone live with himself, he wonders, as he sits up sharply, bolting upright. Suddenly, he is wide awake. He'll be up for a while, no matter how easily his wife sleeps, because he is up now and wondering. Because everything you do somehow creates a problem for somebody else, and because his life in the movies has brought him this far and no further. Because one life, one life is never enough for everything he, too, had in mind.

★ ★ ★

"DUDE, DUDE, YOU can't be serious."

"I am serious."

"You can't possibly believe *Brewster McCloud* is better than *Three Women*."

"I didn't say better. I said underrated."

What is the problem, created by our forebears? The problem is the movies. The problem is success. We are jammed into a booth at Canter's Delicatessen, my friends and I, arguing about the only thing we know—we are not prepared for anything else, are too narrow in our purview even by the narrow standards of young people. We are the hatchlings of this room on Fairfax Avenue, of these booths where my father and his peers did the same thing thirty years ago.

"What about DePalma?" Nick says.

"Jesus, man, we can't get into that. We'll be here all night."

"Isn't that the idea? We're here all night already."

Our heads droop above two a.m. sandwiches. The stained-glass patterns of the ceiling, autumn leaves, shine atop the oily surfaces of our coffee cups. Real adulthood is coming, its riptide swirling around our ankles.

"Dude, I can't believe you got Madonna's phone number."

"I can't believe he *ate* Madonna's phone number," Tudor says.

"What else was I gonna do? You were grabbing for it!"

"You were supposed to call it!"

Adulthood is coming. There's only so long we can dine out on the same stories, things that happened weeks or months ago.

"I was never gonna do that," Nick says, grinning. "I have a girlfriend."

"Gab would've forgiven you."

"Nah." He hunches to take a bite of his sandwich. "Not my scene."

We are children of the movies, not fit for anything else. And if we are, by now, aware of the currents of power somewhere above us—our friends Zak Penn and Adam Leff, first-time screenwriters, have recently sold their first to Sony Pictures for half a million clams, a sum that would've made the previous generation's eyes bleed—it is not yet clear if we will all prove to be the beneficiaries of the industry's multinational churning.

"It's a good story."

"It's a great story."

"Dude." Tudor slaps the table. "I hate to say it, but I gotta jet. I'm working a brunch shift tomorrow."

History isn't written by the winners. It is written by the artists, who are usually the losers. The winners are too busy erasing their tracks to write anything at all. My friends and I don't know this yet, but we're happy to fight over the scraps.

"Anyone have ten bucks?" Nick says. "I'm tapped."

"Why don't you ask Mr. Sell Out Corporate Whore?" I say.

"Dude, I don't even work at Sony anymore. They pink-slipped me six months ago."

"Eh. You're still a corporate whore."

"Ten bucks." Tudor yawns and sets a twenty on the table. "Plus, a little extra, from me. I'm flush this week."

"You flush enough to cover me, Holmes?"

Tudor looks at me. "Sure thing. Whaddya need?"

He will be the first of us to fall. In a basement in Louisville, he will drink himself to death in the wake of a failed marriage, his career never fully off the ground, gone just two weeks after his forty-fifth birthday.

"Nah, I'm good, I'm good." I slap a tenner on the table. "I'm just teasing."

Outside the air is an aqueous gray, the color of not-quite morning. The traffic lights flash yellow; the grate is down over Damiano's Mr. Pizza across the street. On our greasy plates a spray of mustard, a limp green pickle, a swatch of pastrami as lurid as a severed tongue.

"Hold on a second. I gotta stop at the bakery counter."

"You're still hungry, Jimmy? I might not eat for a week."

"It's not for me, man, it's for my mom. I told her I'd bring her some rugelach."

Even our real lives have this cinematic, dream-like quality: the sticky, brick-brown tiles of the linoleum floor; the faintly aggrieved faces of the waitresses who flit from table to table; the famous disc jockey, Rodney Bingenheimer, who slouches in one of the orange booths with his Beatle bangs and his prematurely wizened face browning like an apple. It's as real as anything could possibly be, and it has, all of it, evaporated even as we step out onto the street.

"You need a lift, brother?" Jim turns as we stagger up the block toward his car, our farewells to our friends still echoing on the wind. The Silent Movie Theater—the last of its kind, opened in 1942—looms, shuttered, on our left. "C'mon, I'll drive you home."

★ ★ ★

MICHAEL OVITZ IS back in Japan. As my friend and I drive through the pinkening light of dawn, it is nighttime in Tokyo and he is wide awake, walking through Tsukiji Market, where the vendors are gone, and the stalls are shut, and the air still smells of fish even after the asphalt has been hosed black. He is a guest here, but as he moves down the street, still crowded with people even though it is close to midnight, he feels at home, watching the teenagers slide by in their American jeans and T-shirts with English-language slogans, gazing up at Arnold Schwarzenegger's face on a billboard advertising an energy drink called Alinamin V. His Japanese is mediocre, but it hardly matters. Everywhere he goes they speak the same language he does.

"G'night, homie." We pull up in front of my father's house on Fifteenth Street. "Give my love to your Pops, willya?"

"I will." My father loves Jim, his favorite among all my friends.

For a moment, in the seventies, he'd represented Jim's dad as an actor. "Same, please."

"Of course."

Halfway around the world, Ovitz makes his way toward Tsukijishijō Station. Up is down, stop means go, morning is night—he's jetlagged, but clear—and he remains at the very top of his ecosystem, just like my friends and I sit at its absolute bottom. He isn't thinking of us, doesn't know we exist, but he creates a new room temperature, through which my friends and I move like frogs swimming in slow-boiling water.

"Same thing tomorrow night?"

(The temperature ticks up one degree, two . . .)

"Of course."

Inside, the kitchen light is on. Out here, my dream of Michael Ovitz fades as my father is up early with the Saturday *New York Times*, fixing espresso.

"Go home and get some shut-eye, buddy. Love you."

"Love you, too."

The script my friend is writing, a comedy about an untalented magician, will never sell; the novel I am now sniffing around will remain just a bunch of loosely assembled notes on a hard drive; Nick will go back to Minnesota in a few years; Tudor will die alone. But just now our possible triumphs—any day now, any minute, we will break through—are as real as the dawn.

I turn and walk toward the house. Dawn paints its upper story, the shadows of the palms waving across pale stucco. Somewhere nearby, in Beverly Hills or Brentwood, my friend Jay Moloney sleeps, his face serene and beautiful, his wire-rimmed glasses folded on the nightstand. He looks almost seraphic, his own future as Hollywood's future king, Ovitz's golden boy, assured also.

"Hey, Matthew." My father hears me come in. "You want some coffee?"

"No thanks, Pop. I'm going to bed."

Heroin and cocaine will take Jay. With his ascent will come pressure, and with pressure will come temptation, and he will begin using for real.

"Late night?"

"Yeah," I say. "Remember those?"

He will lose his reputation. He will lose his job. He will be granted a second chance only to backslide; only to wind up in a rented house on Mulholland Drive, his prospects murky and uncertain.

"G'night, son."

He will walk into his bathroom and tie his belt around the shower nozzle, then loop the other end around his neck. He will pull the loop tight, and then tighter still, until—

But all that remains a few years in the future. Tonight, as I make my way back through my father's dining room, toward the guest cabana behind the house where I sleep when I visit, I wonder what it is I am running from, why it is I don't live here. Los Angeles is beautiful, after all. I walk down the terra-cotta steps to confront the gentle glow of the morning and then stop a moment to crouch down beside my father's pool, trailing my fingers in the water to find it is warm, so warm, and blue, so blue, so blue.

Happy Holidays
1995

Robert De Niro

9. YOUR VOICE, AMERICAN

1994–1996

DOWN SULLIVAN TO SIXTH, I walk against the breeze, across Canal, past Laight, York, and Lispenard, pulling my coat tight as I struggle up N. Moore toward the river. The air smells like manure from the stables on Varick, then pie from Bubby's on Hudson, before I step into the lobby of 375 Greenwich and wave to the security guard, flashing him my pass. Inside the elevator, a large man in a cashmere overcoat waits for the door to close.

"Morning." The city roars in my ears: wind, traffic, construction. The man's eyes, black and incurious, strafe me, then stare straight ahead. I study him: the rolls of fat beneath his chin, the acne-scarred cheeks. The elevator lurches toward the second floor—an IWC watch; a white linen shirt; hand-sewn shoes—where the doors open, and the man is swarmed.

"Harvey! Hey Harvey!"

I recognize the accouterments of power, but not yet the man. The doors close—MIRAMAX FILMS, reads the sign above the reception desk opposite—and I bask in power's corrosive, narcotic glow.

"More flowers this morning." The receptionist nods as I step off the elevator. "I put 'em in your office."

"Thanks."

Power is a drug. No matter that my new office is the size of a broom closet, or that my business card, which reads "Director of Literary Acquisitions," suggests an authority I don't actually possess. Powerful forces stand behind me. Michael Ovitz knows that perception is everything and now, at last, I do, too.

"Binky Urban, please." At my desk I stretch my legs, cradling the phone's receiver to my ear. The room overflows with congratulatory fruit baskets, flowers, envelopes, notes. Word of my appointment was front page in the trades last week. "I'm returning her call."

I reach blindly into the nearest basket on my desk, grab an apple, lean back in my chair.

"Listen, I don't think this manuscript you sent is quite right. The part's a little old for Bob."

I study the apple, fat and obscene. I've been on the job ten days and have sunk so deeply into the role you'd think I'd been doing it for years.

"OK, sure. What else have you got?"

Power is a drug. Especially when, it turns out, you don't even need to possess it to wield it. I breathe deep. I study the apple in my hand as if it's the very skull of Yorick. I listen to the woman, a literary agent, talking on the other end of the call. When I bite down, at last, the sweetness of the world explodes in my mouth.

★ ★ ★

BOB AND DANNY. Danny and Bob. Two actors, both clients of my father's, have partnered up to hire me, sending me here to New York. De Niro and DeVito—"Double Des Team to Hire Lit Honcho Specktor," reads the article I have torn from *Variety*—are the twin masters I serve. The arrangement is a little tricky, as their companies are technically competitors, with production deals at separate studios. But for cost-sharing purposes they have come to an agreement to hire me together.

"Right," I say. I'm on another call, talking this time to a friend who works as a book scout for foreign publishers. "Tell me about the Tom Wolfe. Has he delivered it yet?"

(I didn't ask for this, exactly. I wasn't looking. A few months ago, I was in Los Angeles, visiting, when I ran into a friend on the beach, a man I have known since I was a teenager.

"Are you still working for Francis Coppola?" This man, an agent named Jon Levin, for whom I used to read scripts, wanted to know. "There are some folks who are looking to hire. They need someone well-read, who can relocate . . ."

I stood on the sand at twilight, staring off at a barge that was poised to shoot fireworks as soon as it was dark, a Fourth of July party. Five feet away, Faye Dunaway sat on a blanket. Farther up the beach, Jack Nicholson was hanging out with my father, the two of them drinking margaritas. What would you do, confronted with this opportunity? If it were your world, your beach, your Hollywood summer—if you were two drinks deep, and Faye Dunaway smiled at you over the rim of her champagne glass under a shell-colored sky—what would you do?)

"Oh, what's—*American Tabloid*, it's called? Tell me about that."

Now it is December, and I am still drunk. Nepotism and luck have launched me clear across the country. I wasn't doing anything for Coppola except reading scripts, the same freelance job I'd been doing since high school, until Levin put two and two together and realized someone who'd been steeped in the industry since earliest adolescence might be set for a much bigger job.

"Great. You wanna bring me a copy later?"

It is a strange gig I have signed on for, a kind of industrial espionage. I spend my days shaking down literary agents, editors, and editorial assistants for books, plays, and magazine articles, those things that will one day be referred to as "IP." Just like the ten or twelve people who do this job for rival producers and studios, my friends and competitors, my job is to get to these things first, to strike to acquire film rights ahead of the curve.

"No conflict, no. Bob's deal is at TriStar, Danny's is at Columbia, so—yes, it's a little complicated, but they've agreed to partner up as producers if they want the same project."

A strange task, but I am built for it if anyone is. People in Hollywood speak one language, film, where I am at least as comfortable talking about books. If my bosses are ghosts—I rarely see them, even though De Niro's office is directly above my own, his footsteps sometimes audible overhead—I understand that the essence of the job is illusion. I'm no Michael Ovitz, but I know enough to manipulate the shadows, to pretend to an access and intimacy I don't have.

"Of course I'll introduce you to him. You wanna go to Nobu? Not that I know if he'll be there. Thursdays, you never know."

A strange task, but these are my days. I finger the corporate credit card that sits in my pocket.

"Great. Seven-thirty." What's more intoxicating than cocaine? Throwing around the money that belongs to a multinational corporation like Sony, as my expense reports pile up. "Bring a copy of the Ellroy. It sounds great for Bob."

The truth is, I'm not just more comfortable among these young literary agents and editors than I am among producers and studio executives, but I am happier as well. Even if I remain just a person in a windowless office, a boiler room, really, trafficking in information, a kind of shadow economy for the American motion picture business. Most of the manuscripts that cycle through my office will never be adapted, but it doesn't matter. The conflation of perceived with actual value, the millions upon millions of dollars spent on projects and ideas that go nowhere: these things are Hollywood, are capitalism at its finest.

★ ★ ★

RAYMOND COMES UP out of the subway, my friend, my secret sharer: the man who is better at this job than anyone. He climbs the stairs at Columbus Circle, feeling tired, looking almost like a ghost—tall and gaunt, his copper hair thinning—but also local, urban, with his messenger bag slung over his shoulder. In his black Levi's, black Converse, and leather jacket, he emerges from the fetid cave of the station, gazes up at the old Gulf + Western building, 15 Columbus Circle, then makes his way across the plaza. The building has just been sold—soon, it will be renamed Trump Tower, and his boss will move them down to Times Square—but he's here for another few weeks yet, huddling against the cold as he passes beneath the red marquee crawl of the theater showing *Forrest Gump*, the mothership studio's current and seemingly imperishable hit, six times a day. He strides beneath it and on into the lobby, moving with the resignation of a person forced to hurl himself into the flames.

Raymond Bongiovanni. He is my friend and these days also my mentor, but right now he is just another development executive being hassled by his boss. His pager goes off again—the fourth time this morning even though it is seven a.m.—as he crosses the lobby with its stale light, the security guard's hand popping up to greet him. This place feels hollowed out now that Gulf + Western has sold Paramount, its former subsidiary, to Viacom, but Raymond and his boss, Scott Rudin, remain here for now. He steps into the elevator, bobbing his head along with the music on his Walkman, Brian Eno's "The Big Ship." Recently, he turned forty. Some part of him had believed he was never going to live this long, had thought, when he first came to New York in the late seventies, that the city would take him the way it took everybody, but that was just the nihilism of youth. He leans back against the wall, catching sight of his reflection in the elevator's brass doors: so skinny, his complexion as pale as paper, his hair receding, lips lightly chapped. When he came here, he was stardust incarnate, his hair long and falling to the middle of his back, but now he is mild and middle-aged, clerical-looking behind his glasses' wire frames.

"Good morning!" The receptionist perks up, her whole body tensing and then going slack when she sees it's only him. "The coast is clear."

"I know," he says. "How many times has he called?"

"Three."

"The record is eight." This poor girl is a temp, holding down the fort until they find another receptionist. "Eight times before seven-thirty. But don't worry, his bark is worse than his bite."

"Is it?"

"No." She went home in tears on Friday night and all he wants is to help her keep it together, so he smiles. "But I thought it might make you feel better."

He walks down the hallway—poor kid: twenty-three years old, and she has lucked into a post working for one of the shortest tempers in Hollywood—past the kitchen, where the interns are scrambling to make sure the Snapple is cold and the cupboards are stocked with Oreos, cashews, and M&M's, those things Rudin demands. He steps into his office, past the doorplate that reads VICE PRESIDENT OF PRODUCTION, and his pager vibrates again, so he picks up the phone and dials.

"What's up?" Vice president of production. Some people don't last in his spot for six months, or even six weeks, but he has been here nearly two years, knows the secret of contending with the boss's legendary temper is equanimity. You never crack or fold. "Yes. Yes, I know. It's in your bag."

Rudin is the most powerful producer on the Paramount lot and is used to having his whims anticipated. Raymond listens evenly—after two years, he is used to anticipating those whims in turn, knows what Scott will demand well before it happens— staring down at the piles of manuscripts staggered across his desk.

"Nope, you have it. Both the book and the coverage. Check the other pocket."

Behind him, through a smoke-tinted window, spreads the long, green rectangle of the park. He bites his tongue, quashing an urge to say I told you so.

"I understand. Right. No, I— I couldn't. I was on the train."

What is it about the culture that creates such furious and pointlessly cruel people? Is it only the ballooning costs and profit margins—$100 million gross used to be a miracle that happened once or twice a year, now it is the bar you hope to clear every time—or is it something else, the fact that trafficking in illusion makes you begin to expect the impossible even in real life?

"OK," he says quietly. (But no, Hollywood has always been full of raging bullies. There's nothing new under the sun.) "I'll have a second copy on your desk when you get here."

He hangs up. He doesn't mind, not really. That girl at reception was so upset because she wasn't prepared. He is always prepared. His somatic baseline is like an astronaut's, his slow pulse and gentle temperament further insulated by a fathomless sense of irony. Scott can yell all he wants. When I ask him why he puts up with it, he will simply shrug. ("Do you know how hard it is to make a decent movie?")

He crosses the room, weaving between the moving boxes. Rudin may be impossible, this job a thinking man's bucking bronco, but he is also intelligent, well-read, often charming: the very antithesis of everything "Hollywood producer" usually signifies. He's one of the few who reliably makes good movies. This is why Raymond puts up with it. Because the boss's movies are good. He loads a CD into the portable stereo that rests along the opposite wall, then walks back to his desk. Shostakovich's Symphony No. 9 fills the room.

Shostakovich. Such a jagged, atonal composer for such a mild person to love, but he does. A few years ago, he'd brought in a manuscript called *The Firm*, by an unknown writer named John Grisham; he'd brought in Richard Russo's novel *Nobody's Fool*, the film of which just opened a week ago. Some portion of his boss's recent run of success is attributable to him, but unlike almost everyone inside a credit-hogging industry, he doesn't do it for that reason. He does it because he loves movies. To him, Paramount Pictures is Adolph Zukor; it is the Marx Brothers in *Duck Soup* and Lubitsch's *The Love Parade*—Viacom paid $10 billion for this place, and it might be a bargain for those things alone—but it is also *Naked Gun 33⅓* and *The Hunt for Red October*. He's no highbrow, just a person of unusual education and truly catholic, far-ranging, tastes who happens to work in the movies. He was born in Port Jefferson, grew up in Miami, went to Harvard, and then came here with his degree in Russian literature to reinvent himself, the way people still do. He worked for a literary agent named Elaine Markson, and then for a producer named Lee Rich, but it is here, working for a powerful man who famously treats people like dirt, he is free.

★ ★ ★

"HELLEYOOO . . ."

Every day, he is the first person I talk to. I step into the office to call my friend, whose voice comes humming down the line, wry and relaxed.

"How's the office today?"

"Quiet," he says. "Scooter's in LA. How are the Italians?"

Always the same ritual. Raymond and I are competitors, but we are also, and immediately, compatriots, brothers. He is the one who will teach me how to do this job, this strange and confounding hustle that involves endless triage among the dozens of manuscripts circulating each day, a game as intricate as poker.

"Also out of town. I've got the run of the house."

"You wanna play hooky?"

We are competitors, but he beats me every time. Whenever we are chasing the same piece of material—because our bosses are at separate studios, we are often forced to bid against each other—he is there first. But then, he has been at this from the beginning. The success of *The Firm* in 1993 had touched off a frenzy for adaptations, for films based on novels, articles, and plays. Original ideas still sell—the market for high-concept spec scripts is robust—but other producers have opened satellite offices in New York, hoping to emulate Scott Rudin and his production company's golden touch. One week before I arrived a colleague of my father's, an agent named Robert Bookman, had sold the film rights to an unwritten novel called *The Horse Whisperer* for $4 million. Its proposal consisted of a single page.

"Sure thing. Trattoria?"

"Yep. I'll book one-fifteen."

The market is irrational, like all markets—easily overexcited, just as easily spooked—but Raymond is not: he is methodical, as measured as an assassin. This is why we like one another. Each of us realizes the job we are doing is ridiculous, a frenzied response to hype cycles seldom justified, and so we take a more patient approach. Our bosses rarely know what they want, but respond to press, to reputation, to perceived currents of hunger—Sony wants a science-fiction drama; they want a vehicle for Cameron Diaz; Paramount wants an elevated horror drama; "the Kopelsons are already bidding against us over at Fox"—which they then chase, shoveling books and scripts at the studio like coal into a furnace.

"So?" At Trattoria Del'Arte, on Seventh Avenue and Fifty-Seventh, Raymond leans across the table, propping his elbows on the white cloth. "First things first. How many words this morning?"

"Seven hundred."

"Not bad. Graham Greene only managed five."

"Graham Greene didn't have my boss breathing down his neck looking for something Scott Frank might adapt."

"Oh yeah?" He cocks his head like he is measuring some distant tremor of the earth. "Is that what your people are looking for?"

Raymond is the only one who knows that I wake up every morning and work on a novel. My bosses don't know it, and neither do most of my other friends. It is a secret, and I prefer it that way. My life as an artist, and a conflict I will struggle over the next few years to resolve, happens underground.

"You know what they're looking for," I say, smiling. "They want a stylish psychodrama. *Rosemary's Baby*, but contemporary."

"Right." He sips his Diet Coke. "They want *Die Hard*, only set on a submarine."

"On a submarine? No, no, we already have a movie that's set on a boat. What about *Die Hard* in a library?"

"Perfect." He cackles. "John Woo to direct, or—Ringo Lam! I can see the one-sheet. *Quiet Storm*."

We laugh. Our job is so easy to make fun of, those rote repetitions and formulas—X meets Y—everyone in Hollywood uses, the way movies are now made with their posters conceived first. To step outside these repetitions is now risky, rare.

"I'm gonna get Scott to option *Wonder Boys*," he says. "I think it's a movie."

"You do?" I shake my head. "I tried to get my people into that one, but they didn't see it."

"Just watch." He reaches for the check even as I dig for my wallet.

"It's my turn. You always pay."

"Next time," he says. "Unless—you want another glass of wine?"

"No, no. Do you?"

He shakes his head. "Just Diet Coke for me. Doctor's orders."

In the bright yellow space of that Midtown room with its charcoal drawings of human anatomy above each scalloped booth, a small plate of olive oil, lambent and green, by my elbow, I drain the last of an espresso. Together we sit on this cloud, this pediment of money.

"Doctor's orders?"

"Liver trouble," he says. "I had Hep-A a few years ago."

"Hep-A?"

"Yep. Careful where you get your sushi."

We walk out into the mild coolness of early spring, passing underneath a scaffold, breathing in plaster dust, pretzels, and exhaust: the hopeful smell of New York rebuilding itself, the predatory economic perfume of Giuliani Time.

"*Wonder Boys*?" We pause on the corner for a moment. "You really think he'll go for it?"

"Just watch," he says. He does not belong in this job any more than I do. Neither a businessperson nor an artist, but a creature in-between. He smiles, shifting softly from foot to foot. "You'll see."

He turns and walks off uptown. I watch him go, so impossibly pale, his reddish hair flashing, his black jacket mantled in sunlight for a moment until he is lost, vanishing back into the crowd.

★ ★ ★

SOMETIMES, WHEN HIS boss loses his temper, Raymond soothes himself by remembering why he is here. He is here because Adolph Zukor came over from Hungary in 1899 in lieu of becoming a rabbi; because Zukor became an upholsterer, then a furrier, and then, in 1903, went in with his cousin to buy a nickelodeon on 125th Street.

"Are you fucking stupid? How did you miss this?"

(The pictures were just a distraction, but Zukor liked them because, as he told someone later, it's not like making shoes, or automobiles. Every picture is an enterprise by itself.)

"I didn't miss it." Raymond sits at his desk while Scott storms in waving a copy of *Variety*, shaking its headline—a manuscript has sold to one of their competitors on the lot—in his face. "I gave that to you last week."

"Then why didn't I fucking buy it?"

("There are certain ingredients you have to study, and certain ingredients where you have to say, I don't think I'll take that story. I don't think I'll make it," Zukor said, because he understood that the movies were a personal decision, and not just a response to what other people did.)

"I don't know."

"You don't know?" He's in one of those moods, mimicking and mean. "You total fucking moron. I pay you to know."

(Zukor understood that you practice a certain discernment, and out of this discernment had come Paramount Pictures.)

"I pay you to fucking know!" Rudin goes off now, this rubicund man with the neat, brown beard and the roly-poly physique, this person who is capable of an almost impossible charm—most people never even see the side he unleashes now—leaning over to get in Raymond's face. "'I don't know' isn't an acceptable answer, you idiot. You fucking imbecile."

Paramount was once the place you went for high European elegance—Josef von Sternberg, Marlene Dietrich, the Lubitsch touch—and now it is just a man yelling in an office in Times Square; it is potted plants strategically placed around the room to obscure holes he has kicked in the plasterboard walls in his rages; it is Viacom, NewsCorp, and Sony, all chasing the same thing.

"Find me something else!" The boss leans close, his breath like a blast from a convection oven, then straightens up abruptly and turns. "Today!"

My friend stands to brush himself off. He counts to five, and then reaches for the phone.

Why does he do it? As his boss rampages out into the hall-way, transferring his aggression onto his assistants—"Get me a fucking Snapple! Now!"—he wonders again if this is worth it. The movies are such an attenuated version of what they once were. Outside his office hangs a poster for a recent, superfluous remake of *Sabrina* starring Harrison Ford and Julia Ormond, which predictably flopped, and the same film had been perfect in 1954 anyway. So why do it?

Later, as he leaves—there is no answer to this question, of course: he does it because the worst job you can have in the movie business in New York is also the most prestigious and the best paying—he stops to help one of the assistants who is sweeping up the afternoon's wreckage in the hall.

"You OK?" He kneels to pick up the jagged fragment of a coffee cup.

"No." The kid looks over. He's wearing the cup's contents, his white shirt mottled brown. "He fired me."

"He does that." This kid is wholesome and blond, with the muscled solidity of a soldier and a calmness, as he kneels with his dustpan and brush. "Come back tomorrow and he won't remember."

"Won't he?"

Raymond studies him. This one might stick.

"Just come back."

He lays his hand on the kid's shoulder and stands, heading for the door. The one thing he's learned, what his time working in the movies has shown him, is that everyone is the mirror of everyone else. How you speak, how you act, how you think, even, is just the sum of what you see. Your own voice is just a slaw of other people's, your gestures, intonations, and ideas—everything that makes you who you are—are borrowed, brewed, and diluted from other people, spiked with whatever inviolable tincture your individual "self" is. When he was a teenager in Florida, when he'd worn his hair long, worn bell-bottoms and tight, patterned shirts, styling himself after an English glam musician the people around him—Italian kids, Latino kids, and Cubans—had never heard of, he'd felt like a freak, but he was true, thus, to his own personality. When he came to New York in 1979, he'd felt like an outsider then, also, but here you can do that and remain invisible. There are fundamental parts of himself he keeps hidden—half-hidden, even, from his own open awareness—but there is a gentleness of spirit that draws others to him, a sense that he might be rare.

On the train, heading downtown, he wears a rider's weary mask: hypnotized, intent. As he climbs the stairs of 347 East Nineteenth and unlocks the door to his apartment—he stoops to scratch the two cats that swarm around his ankles—he belongs to me, and he belongs to history. There are others who know him better, like his friend Mary Evans, a literary agent, and his friend Elisa Petrini, but I know him well enough to imagine him just so, crouching in the darkness before he stands to snap on a light and drop his heavy satchel, then sets the takeout bag from Veselka on a table. He is such a private person, the very definition of such a thing, in ways that will prevent me from ever knowing him better, but he is generous, vital, and exacting, brought to life by art more than by anything else. When something excites him—a film, a book, a piece of music—he is galvanized, becomes its soft-spoken but implacable advocate. That is living, after all. It is.

See him now, as I do, as he drops to his couch and exhales—he is tired all the time these days, achy and exhausted for reasons he knows, but cannot face—and then feels the gentle weight of the cat land in his lap, her paws kneading his thigh. Ever since he was in the hospital in 1991, shortly before he went to work at his current job, he has been out of sorts, his body not feeling like it should, his limbs and joints often weak or tender. But he doesn't act on this. There are things he'd rather manage by himself, things he hopes will sort themselves out somehow. He pets the cat, resting his other hand atop his abdomen a moment, then gets up to unbag his dinner.

"Oh, really?" He talks to the cats now. "You'd like a pierogi?" He speaks to them the way everyone does to their pets, their children when they are alone: an intimate intonation no one else hears or can quite imagine. "Be nice."

If you were watching from the street, you'd see only lamplight behind a curtain, and later the lunar glow of a television in the dark. This is the life you do not see, the life that is irreplaceable, which the movies used to show in glimpses, Elliott Gould waking up in the middle of the night to buy pet food in *The Long Goodbye*, and Steve McQueen ducking into a corner store for TV dinners in *Bullitt*, but which they no longer touch. Before bed, he smokes a joint and reads another manuscript, turns off the VCR and strips off his Converse, his black T-shirt, and jeans—at least, working for a producer, he doesn't have to dress like a suit—and slides between the covers. This is Hollywood, too: this unlikely man whose mind hums with eight different languages, who might speak to you in Russian, Italian, or French; who is the very antithesis of the industry's backstabbing culture; whose name will appear in the credits of a motion picture only once, at the very end. In the dark he can make out the shelves filled with books and CDs, things he loves that he knows he'll never finish, and his thoughts balloon with fear. But then the weed kicks in and his limbs get heavy, his jaw softens, and he begins to drift. . .

★ ★ ★

"—NOT A CHANCE!"

"I'll bet you a hundred bucks," I say. "He's leaving."

I'm on the phone with my father, crammed inside an office that is so jammed with manuscripts stacked atop my desk and along the walls I can barely swivel my chair. This serving two masters, effectively doing two jobs at once, has begun to wear on me. I stare down at the *New York Times* that sits open in my lap.

"It says right here in the paper of record. 'Will Ovitz go to MCA?'"

"That's your paper of record," he says, laughing. "Not mine."

"It sounds like he's got itchy feet."

"That's just 'cause you've got itchy feet, old sport."

True. I don't know it yet, but soon I will move uptown. One of my bosses, DeVito, is about to recapitalize his production deal by moving it from Sony to Universal, a move that will allow him to hire me away from De Niro and offer me a promotion. For Universal is on the block yet again. Matsushita, it turns out, had little stomach for the movie business, its wild swings from quarter to quarter, and has put the company back up for sale. Ovitz is at the center of things, once more brokering the deal.

"Where there's smoke there's fire, old man. Your guy is moving on."

My father, of course, cannot afford to believe this. What will become of his agency if the big man jumps ship?

"Bullshit. I'll put a hundred bucks on it. Mike's not going anywhere."

"Make it five." What the hell, I can afford to take a little risk. My days of living on rice-and-bean burritos, the lean years of San Francisco, are behind me. I'm living on Japanese money now, also. "Five hundred says Ovitz goes to run Universal."

"Deal."

Maybe I'm wrong. Everything is happening way over my head. Sony is wobbling, with its studio coming off a $510 million operating loss for 1994, MCA/Universal is about to be flush—Seagram's

Inc., the Canadian whiskey distillery, has offered $5.7 billion for eighty percent of the company—and I feel rich because I am earning a shade under six figures, still more money than I have ever made in my life. Coming off a pair of hits, *Pulp Fiction* and this fall's *Get Shorty*, DeVito's company is in the process of hiring me away from De Niro's, and can afford to pay me even better. Raymond, too, is on the move, having finally had enough and taken a job running an office for Fox 2000, a newly created feature division of Twentieth Century Fox.

What does he want? I wonder. What's my friend's endgame? What do *I* want? I took this job in the movie business on a lark, accepting an offer few sane people would have refused, but now that I have discovered I am good at it, good enough to play the game and get substantially promoted, I find myself on an elevator shooting skyward. What, too, does my father want, now that his agency is no longer an underdog but a leviathan? Is he going to ride that rocket until it, or he, explodes?

It is a hot summer, August of 1995. I have been in New York less than a year, and already it seems like I have been doing it forever. The movies this season are *Braveheart* and *Batman Forever*, *Clueless* and *Waterworld*, whose $172 million budget—more, once you factor in the marketing—and subsequent failure are what has spurred Matsushita to want to unload Universal to begin with. I think I understand the industry, but I don't know anything yet. As I hang up the phone—my dad and I talk often these days, but it is largely just industry talk—I imagine that I am right, and already five hundred dollars richer. But I am wrong, and not for the last time.

Nothing ever goes according to plan.

★ ★ ★

HAVE I GIVEN you the impression that CAA's success is all about Michael Ovitz, the man who, driven by hubris and ungodly ambition, has managed to redraw an entire industry in his own enigmatic image? Perhaps I have, but it isn't true. CAA had five partners, then it had seven. Now, after a few have cashed out— Mike Rosenfeld has retired, gone off to fly his prop planes up in Sonoma; Steve Roth, a latecomer, has gone back to being a producer—and a few new senior managers have been brought in, it remains a many-headed hydra. Ovitz may wear the crown, as the company's CEO, but it is Ron Meyer who manages its day-to-day, as president. In the beginning, the partners had agreed upon an even split, but when Ovitz began pulling the most weight and bringing in the most money, way back in 1979, he'd demanded a bigger piece. Meyer didn't like it, but he went along. He didn't complain because he loves being an agent, because the gregarious nature of the job, which might be a little uncomfortable for an introvert like Ovitz, still suits him to a T.

"Ten percent? Mike, that's a lot of money!"

It suits him because he likes being number two. He doesn't particularly want to run the world. But maybe, also, he retains something else, some wisdom or restraint his partner has misplaced, as he sits with Ovitz in the latter's office one afternoon in the spring of 1995.

"Five," Meyer says. "If we can get them to five, we should be happy."

"Five is OK. But let's start at ten."

"OK." Five percent of a company that is changing hands for $6.5 billion is itself an obscene amount of money. Michael Ovitz may be the best agent in Hollywood, but when he needs someone to negotiate on his own behalf, he turns to his best friend, the only one who may be his equal. "I'll push Edgar for ten, and we'll see what he comes back with."

What is it about an industry in which everyone wants to take sole credit for everything that demands alliances of opposites like this one? Ovitz's office is like the man himself: cold, a little geometrical, everything in its right place. Meyer slouches on the couch like a school truant.

"Five is the minimum." Ovitz stands up and stalks over to the window, gazing down on Little Santa Monica Boulevard. "The whole thing falls apart if we can't get him there."

What are they negotiating? Ovitz's departure. Not only is he going, but he plans to take the other partners with him: Meyer, Kurtzman, Climan, Bill Haber. It's time for him to get out. A five percent stake in MCA Inc. may be a big ask, but it's what it's going to take to replace the equity he's giving up in selling the company he built, and to dole out a few slivers of it that will ensure the colleagues who come along stay happy.

"You sure you want this?" Meyer scrutinizes him. He's seen Ovitz go back and forth on this and understands his friend—they are closer to each other than they are to their own spouses, almost—might also be having cold feet. "You sure?"

"Yeah." Sunlight filters through the blinds to paint tiger stripes across his suit. "Either we do this now or we wind up holding our dicks in five years, right? It really is now or never."

It turns out Ovitz is not Macbeth. He is Hamlet. He's gone back and forth—last year, he'd come within an eyelash of going over to run Disney—because it is not so easy to walk away from something you've spent two decades building. But he's tired of client service, stars and their twenty-four-hour egos, and the business is changing: studios are making fewer movies every year, costs are going up, and this in turn will reduce demand for what CAA has to sell. It's time to get out, and for Ovitz to effect his own radical transformation. Just like Lew Wasserman before him, he's ready to change from vendor to buyer, and to go run a studio himself.

"All right," Meyer says. "Then we'll get Edgar where we need him."

Is it time for him, also? He loves being an agent, two a.m. phone calls from Sylvester Stallone notwithstanding, but there's a certain restlessness that's been eating at him lately. And it makes

sense they should go together. If Ovitz is a student of human nature, a guy who works four times as hard as everyone else to wind
up eight times as prepared, then Meyer *is* human nature, a warm
barrel of contradiction so widely, and justly, beloved he almost
doesn't need to prepare for anything because people just surrender to him. If people have trouble with Mike, they call Ronnie.
That's why the partnership works.

"Set the meeting," Ovitz says. "Tell Edgar we'll meet him tomorrow morning at the Century Plaza."

What Ovitz wants is to have his cake and eat it, too: to repli-
cate the strength of a Golden Age Hollywood studio and yoke it
to all the resources he and his agency partners will bring with
them. To take Lew Wasserman's very job—the man is now into
his eighties, and Seagram's, unlike Matsushita, will have no use
for him—but to be stronger than Wasserman ever was, bestriding
the global corporate world like a colossus. Bringing his partners
with him will make it feel like he's not giving up anything. And
Meyer? What he wants is a little more complicated, perhaps, because he's not some Olympian world swallower, he's just a person
who wanted to be an agent more than anything—back when he
was fresh out of the Marine Corps, when he was selling shirts at
a men's boutique on the Sunset Strip, he'd read a novel called *The
Flesh Peddlers* and decided that was it—and who brings to the job
a certain firm integrity. Back when CAA was starving, in the very
beginning, he'd once turned down a five-thousand-dollar commission, money they desperately needed, because the script was
garbage, and he didn't want to hurt their client's career. That's the
kind of guy he is. Not without vices—Ovitz has stepped in a few
times to cover his gambling debts, and he's been known to have a
roving eye for the ladies—but he's decent to the bone.

"I'll make the call."

How that novel had sunk under his skin! To be a talent agent
seemed unimaginably glamorous, but also impossibly fun—all that

wheeling and dealing—and so he'd asked everybody he could find, his hairdresser, his dog walker, if they knew anybody in the motion picture business, just so he could get his foot in the door. First, he'd worked at Paul Kohner Associates, then at William Morris, and now here. He's making more money than he'd ever imagined, doing exactly what he'd always dreamed. Does he really want to give it all up? His clients are taxing—sometimes, he really does want to chuck this and find another gig—but are they really what he's tired of? Ovitz is out there trying to bring an NFL team to Los Angeles, throwing receptions for Bill Clinton in the company lobby, making deals for Coca-Cola and Crédit Lyonnais, advising a French bank on its debt portfolio and a soda pop company on its advertising strategy, instead of putting together movies. But isn't putting together movies what they signed on to do?

"There's something else." Ovitz turns to him the next morning, as they ride the elevator up at the Century Plaza. "One last thing I'm gonna need Edgar to agree to."

"What's that?"

Is Meyer tired of agenting, or is he tired of something else?

"I need him to pay all the taxes on this deal."

Jesus. Twenty years of partnership, of shared vacations, of talking on the phone two dozen times every day. This is his best friend. But as he looks at Ovitz now, he feels some hesitation. Perhaps it is not agenting Meyer is tired of, but the partnership itself.

"Don't blow this up, Mike," he says, as the elevator dings and they step out into the hall. "If we push too hard, he'll walk."

Even a good marriage can go on too long. But this time, things are different: the rumors are all over the papers, and neither man can really afford to stay. The Young Turks are ready for their close-up— they've already made their arrangements to buy Ovitz and the other partners out, in tandem with a couple of department heads who will also stick around—and so if they don't go, Ovitz and Meyer will be lame ducks. They'll need to hire a food taster themselves.

"He might. But I don't think Edgar is the one driving this deal anyway."

"Edgar" is the man they are negotiating against: Edgar Bronfman Jr., the scion of Seagram's. Ovitz believes it's Edgar's father and his uncle, both Seagram's board members, who are really in charge there. He's already wary of having to report to anyone higher up the corporate ladder—unlike Meyer, he's nobody's second-in-command—and so he especially doesn't want to wind up working for a man who isn't really flying the plane. Even after Ovitz has guided Bronfman, who has a reputation in the press of being a feckless young playboy, through the purchase from Matsushita—he'd needed to liquidate Seagram's holdings in DuPont Chemical to do it—even now he doesn't know how much juice Edgar Jr. really has.

"Mike. Ronnie." Bronfman greets them at the door of his suite, where his lawyers are waiting. "Shall we get started?"

Plenty of juice, it turns out. For as they sit down to their silver urns of coffee, their plates of strawberry and melon, it's possible Ovitz has underestimated his adversary just this once, or maybe just misunderstands the byzantine nature of public companies. Bronfman's in charge, he just needs someone to run the studio, MCA Universal, while he keeps his eye on the bigger picture at Seagram's. All along he's had his eye on Ovitz, for who could be better for the job than the reigning king of Hollywood? But now, as Ovitz starts up with another impossible set of adjustments—for indeed, he's about to blow up this deal—Bronfman can't help but wonder. Isn't there someone else he could hire? Someone who might be a little more reasonable than Michael Ovitz, and who might integrate more easily into the existing corporate hierarchy?

★ ★ ★

"MATTHEW?" MY ASSISTANT'S voice comes through the intercom. "Ron Meyer's calling for you."

What went through his mind? What really happened in those negotiations between Bronfman and Ovitz? I'll never know. But as I pick up the phone in my new office at 445 Park Avenue, a building that was once owned by Jules Stein and Lew Wasserman, then by Matsushita, and now by Seagram's, it happens that it is Ron Meyer—and not Michael Ovitz—who is now my boss.

"Congratulations, kid." My boss at many levels of remove, I suppose—my boss's boss's boss's boss—but his voice is as warm as a favorite uncle's. "I saw in the trades you're moving up in the world, so I thought I'd call."

"You can see me from all the way up there? Geez, Ronnie, I'm not the one who's moving up!"

What went through his mind? Because after Ovitz blew up the deal and Meyer flew to New York to beg Bronfman to reopen negotiations, it was there Edgar Jr. made his move. "You should take the job, Ronnie. I'd rather it was you." But I would imagine, as Meyer sat that prior morning watching Ovitz blow his chance in the hotel suite overlooking Century City, that strange cluster of skyscrapers and malls that squats in the center of Los Angeles's westside, a faded futurist's commercial dream, he could gaze out the window and remember how it was: ranch land, a plot of green acreage that had once belonged to Tom Mix, and then to Twentieth Century Fox, and then, after Fox had sold it off to Alcoa Chemicals in 1961 while he was still a teenager, became what it even still remains: opportunity. "A studio is a place where fiction is made." Yes, sure, but a studio is also a place where ideas become persuasive illusions and actualities; where real people are sculpted into presidents, and where land, that consummate blank screen, is shaped into money. He mustn't have been able to resist the lure of transformation in the end either.

"Listen, I'm so glad you called," I say, after kibitzing for a moment. "It's wonderful to hear your voice."

Can I resist it myself, now that I have also been sucked into the maw of MCA?

"Absolutely," I say, wrapping up. "Talk soon."

It makes sense that Bronfman would've chosen Meyer. "New MCA Head Hailed as Nice Guy by Friends, Foes," read the headline in the *Los Angeles Times* a few months ago, and this is the crux of it. When even your enemies won't talk trash about you, you're probably a decent fellow. Why hand the reins to the fearsome, enigmatic Ovitz when you can hand them to the man everybody loves instead?

"Matthew?" My assistant's voice comes over the intercom again. "Raymond's on line two."

What have I become? This building was MCA's New York hub, the headquarters of its music and theater departments. It still looks the way it did in Wasserman's day, with its walnut wainscoting and leather desk blotters, its carpet the color of camel hair, but the offices are half-empty, a ghost ship. We're a long way from the old Hollywood—Meyer's defection has set off shock waves and Ovitz, desperate, has jumped ship to join Michael Eisner at Disney instead—but, oddly, not much has changed. CAA retains every inch of its influence under its new management. Several of his friends may have scattered, but my father remains in place.

"Helleyooo. Listen, Matthew, I have something for you."

"What's that?"

What am I doing here? What's my endgame now that Hollywood has outgrown itself? The industry is too big now for one person to run; everyone is just a gear inside its global apparatus. Even Ovitz's transformation from agent to studio mogul won't last long. In a year and a half he'll be out, another meaningless turning of the wheel.

"A novel. Manuscript just sold to Norton. It's a dark comedy, perfect for you to produce. Someone like Danny Boyle could direct."

"Send it over."

Raymond and I are no longer competitors. He works for News Corp, whose newly minted subdivision of Twentieth Century Fox has a mandate to make movies targeted at an adult female audience. Some executive or consultant somewhere has determined this to be the most important of the four demographic quadrants. I work for Jersey Films, DeVito's production company that is housed at Universal, but free at least in theory to make movies elsewhere. My friend and I could team up.

Then again, perhaps not.

"Raymond." I call him back at the end of the day, having read the manuscript at my desk, where I stare now again at its first line. "Buddy, are you insane? *'Bob had bitch tits'*?"

"What's wrong with bitch tits?"

"Nothing. But this book isn't a movie. Not in a million years."

"Sure it is."

"No way," I say. "Listen, how do you pronounce this guy's name?"

"Palahniuk."

"You really think Rupert Murdoch is gonna fund Mr. Pollynook's little terrorist pamphlet here? You think forty-year-old women in Ohio wanna see a movie about dudes beating each other up in basements?"

"I do. I may have to twist the studio's arm, but I do."

"You're a person of faith," I say. "Good luck with that."

Raymond is persuasive, but it will surprise me even so when his company, Fox 2000, options the novel several months later. *Fight Club* seems unlikely, but then again Fox 2000 is also a furnace in need of fuel. A year and a half ago the division had launched with a clean slate, an entire studio without any movies, and so they are on a buying spree, snapping up rights to novels, short stories, and nonfiction books right and left. Some of their purchases, like Laura Zigman's *Animal Husbandry*, make sense, while others—Raymond had pounced on a nonfiction book called *Working on a Miracle*, about an experimental treatment regimen for HIV—leave me scratching my head. He is lucky to work for a buyer, where he can go direct to the purse. I'm working for a supplier, where I have to convince my bosses and they have to pitch the studio in turn. But it doesn't matter. In the end, I don't envy Raymond, because I already know my heart is not fully in this job I've been hired to do. I'm no producer, I'm a writer. I already know this, even as I embed myself into a life I only half-want, and so don't even, for all its privileges, truly deserve.

★ ★ ★

"YOU'RE GOING OUT of town for a month? Who's going to look after Bob and his bitch tits?"

It is April 1996, and I am on the phone once more with my friend. Raymond is going on vacation, an announcement that leaves me feeling bereft.

"I dunno. My staff will be here, but the studio's going to have to get by without me for a few weeks."

It's lonely, oddly lonely, to do a job you're not cut out for, and to spend each day pretending. I'm doing OK at it, well enough to reel in some interesting material—a few weeks ago, we optioned a novel by George Dawes Green called *The Caveman's Valentine*, which will ultimately be made into a movie directed by Kasi Lemmons—but I feel like a fraud. Every morning I wake up at five to work on a novel, writing for several hours before I come into the office. This, my secret life, is the one that feels real.

"Where are you gonna go?"

"Memphis for a few days, and then London, then Paris, then Berlin. I'm doing my grand European tour."

"What's in Memphis?"

"Mahlon Johnson."

"Ah." That's the author of *Working on a Miracle*. I still don't understand why Raymond was so hot for that book. "And you're going for a month?"

I feel like I'm missing something, like an essential piece of information is right in front of my face. I feel like life is slipping through my fingers, too. Who goes on vacation for a month?

"I had some time accrued, and Laura"—that's his boss—"is being very cool. Let's make a plan for when I return."

What am I missing? Besides that killer instinct that lets people like Michael Ovitz and Ron Meyer soar to the top of their profession, that lets someone like my father set himself up for the long haul, and someone like Raymond read a novel like *Fight Club*, which is nobody's idea of a commercial movie in 1996, and decide to push that boulder uphill? We make our plan—dinner in early June—and then hang up. After a moment, my fax machine rumbles to life on the far side of the room. I walk over and peel from its tray a single photocopied page: communique from Raymond.

> *The buildings of capital, hives of the killer bees,*
> *honey for the few.*
> *He served there. But in a dark tunnel he unfolded*
>   *his wings*
> *And flew when no one was looking. He had to live*
>   *his life again.*

He and I entertain ourselves sometimes by faxing each other poems, a way of remembering that our jobs, this trafficking in novels and stories as if they are stocks whose value depends on how easily they can be translated into film, are not the most important thing. I study this one, by Tomas Tranströmer, then cross over to pin it up on a bulletin board next to others by Constantine Cavafy, W. H. Auden, John Ash.

I stand for a moment, resting my hand on the cork. Outside, far below, traffic crawls along Park Avenue in silence. "He had to live his life again." Indeed, I do, and indeed I might, but the one I am enmeshed in just now happens once, only once.

★ ★ ★

"LET'S TAKE A cab."

"I'd rather walk."

"Raymond, c'mon." He's flushed, shaking like a nervous dog as we stand on the pavement on Second Avenue, caught in a summer rain. "You don't look too good. We should find a taxi."

"I'm OK. It's just jet lag."

Twilight. We stand in the gray light of an incoming storm trying to sort out where to go, what to eat, Raymond, myself, and our friend Elisa Petrini. He is just home from Paris, where he has picked up a cold. That's all this is, he insists. A cold. He hunches with his hands in his pocket, the rain soaking through his windbreaker.

"All right." I look to Elisa. *Does this seem right to you?* "Let's get out of this weather though."

We walk downtown into the East Village, the evening soupy and dank, the rain accelerating as darkness falls.

"Chinese?" Raymond says. "Here . . ."

I almost blew it. I'd forgotten, in fact, we had a plan until he phoned. Hungover, I was tempted to cancel, but now I turn to Elisa and mouth, "What's going on?" Discreetly, she clutches my wrist and squeezes.

What's going on? Why is my friend so ill?

As we pick at plates of mediocre lo mein, slurp tepid cups of hot and sour soup, it strikes me that the oddities have been piling up, that Raymond's extended vacation, his intermittent absences from the office—a day here, three there—and even his boss's willingness to option a manuscript, like *Fight Club*, that only he seems to believe in, as if she is granting him a special favor, all appear to point to the same thing.

"God, this food is lousy."

"It's not so bad," Raymond says, with a weak grin. "I guess Paris was a little better."

His hair is plastered against his forehead, still soaked. His complexion is yellow, but I can see that he is dripping sweat, clammy and fevered. Raymond is a private person, and even Elisa, who knows him much better, finds him opaque, but I know now what he has kept invisible, not just from his friends but possibly from himself: that he is very, very ill.

"Maybe we should just go home," I say. "It's Sunday night. Go rest up and we'll have lunch later this week."

"No, no, I want to see a movie. Let's walk over to the Village East."

How can I deny him? But also, how can I accept what I refuse, also, to understand, which is that he is not just sick—this seems like pneumonia—but dying?

"Come on." Later, after we have hailed a cab to send Elisa back uptown, I search to find another. "Let's get you back to your apartment."

"I'd rather walk."

"Raymond, you can hardly stand up."

"I'd rather."

Hepatitis. "Bad sushi." A trip to Memphis to visit the writer of that book. All of it begins to come together, a series of signs all pointing the same way. I finger the stub from our eight o'clock showing of *Spy Hard* in my pocket. For the rest of my life, I will wish we'd seen a better movie, eaten a better meal.

"All right."

StuyTown looms, massive and dark, on our right. The Sunday-night city feels at once frantic and sleepy: the stray taxis rippling

by, the traffic thinning as we cross Fourteenth, the solitary walk-
ers dipping in and out of shops to buy cigarettes and scratch-offs.
He's so weak! He sways on his feet like a balloon tied to a fraying
string.

"Hold on," he says. "I need cat food."

He ducks into a bodega. There's nothing I can do but stand on
this corner of Nineteenth and First, listening to the rain patter on
concrete, watching him walk down an aisle and then approach
the man at the counter, digging in his pockets for change, turning
in the room's grimy yellow light, fixed inside its sudden silence,
where he will remain, for me, forever.

★ ★ ★

HE SPEAKS IN your voice, American—

"Is he in?"

I call the next morning. I'm seated at my desk with a manuscript in front of me—I haven't slept, am anxious and bleary—
when his assistant, Kristen, picks up.

"He's not here yet." She's his friend, my friend, another one of
his beloved mentees who will go on to have a successful career,
one day, as a screenwriter. "Can I have him call you?"

"Sure. He hasn't checked in?"

"It's early."

"Right. I'll try him again in a bit."

*He speaks in your voice, American, and there's a shine in his
eye that's halfway hopeful—*

"You OK? You sound worried."

I am worried. In fact, I'm a wreck. My eyes keep sliding off
the page in front of me, but that's all right, as I have read this one
months ago, have pulled it from the shelves—fourteen hundred
loose-leaf sheets—because it is a favorite of mine, and of Raymond's. He and I have discussed it endlessly.

He speaks in your voice, American—

I give up. I set the manuscript, Don DeLillo's *Underworld*, aside. I go down to the street for a coffee and then come back upstairs, where I sit on the edge of my assistant's desk, waiting for the workday to begin. The halls of 445 Park Avenue are empty, silent in a way that feels disquieting, almost ominous. When the phone finally rings, I practically jump out of my skin.

"Hello?"

At the far end of the hall, past the long row of assistant's desks, a man appears. He, too, is ominous somehow: a pale rider.

"Hi." It's Kristen, calling me back. "Matthew, I . . ."

"What is it?"

I watch the man approach. Even from a distance I can see he is ancient, a Methuselah. His dark suit is immaculate. His thick hair is white. His square-framed glasses are tinted yellow.

"He's not coming in." Her voice cracks. "Mary Evans called and said he's in the hospital."

He approaches and I realize—I recognize him! I do. He is as familiar to me as my father, but this place no longer belongs to him. I watch as Lew Wasserman, the chairman emeritus of MCA's board, shuffles past me. He no longer controls anything. Inside a year, he will be ousted from his board seat, and thus from the industry forever. I study his profile, so sharp and severe, eyes fixed blindly on the horizon.

"Matthew, I don't think—I don't think he's going to make it."

Once upon a time, the movies were made by people, cold people, strange people, greedy ones it is impossible to sentimentalize, and still I feel a wild urge to fall at this man's feet and embrace him. Because they have also been made by kind ones, decent ones, people whose names might remain unknown, but who are just as responsible—or more responsible, even—for their being. And now they will be made by corporations and boards, by the migrations of capital itself.

"I know," I say, as I look down at the floor, listening to Kristen's quiet sobbing. She loves him just as I do. "I know."

I look up. My friend is gone. And Wasserman, the man who invented my father, has turned the corner and vanished now, also, disappeared down these camel-colored corridors into the desert of the future.

10. LOVING

———

1997–1999

"YOU WANNA TALK TO Ben Stiller?"

One year. One year is all it takes for everything to change, for me to find myself in yet another office, another elevated room with another view of Midtown, this one gazing down on the diamond merchants of Forty-Seventh Street.

"Sure." I lean over to talk into the intercom box on my desk. "Put him through."

Some days I can still feel Raymond's indentation in my chair, the faint shape of his lanky body pressed into inexpensive leather. His stereo, his Shostakovich and Roxy Music CDs, his manuscripts and books, DeLillo, Palahniuk, and Auden, all stacked on the shelves that were formerly his also. Each morning I emerge

from the subway, the B or the F, and wind my way up into this
tower of limestone and glass, what was once called the Celanese
Building but now belongs to Rupert Murdoch's News Corp.

"Ben?" Most days, I don't feel my friend's presence at all. I am
a cog, passing through the same office and the same job. Each
day, I grow a little more disappointed, even bored, never mind
how the money and the prestige have increased. "How's it going,
man?"

If you live long enough, you get to act every role. A friend of
mine likes to say this, but it's true. My turn to play the glib executive, Hollywood asshole. My turn to become everything I thought
I never would.

"Of course." My turn to betray myself absolutely, as I cup the
phone's receiver to my ear. "You want me to bring a copy to lunch?"

It's the same job I had before, only turned upside down. Fox
2000 has overhead deals with roughly two dozen producers, and
it is my task, as head of the studio's New York office, to feed them,
to try to match each one with material. My boss, who was Raymond's boss, is Kevin McCormick. Kevin reports to Laura Ziskin,
who is the head of the studio. Laura reports to Bill Mechanic, the
chairman of Fox Filmed Entertainment, who reports to Peter
Chernin, the COO of News Corp, who reports to Murdoch. The
people are not the problem—Kevin and Laura, Chernin and
Mechanic are all likable enough—but the machine, the machine
is what kills me.

"Jane?" I buzz my second-in-command, who has an office down
the hall. "You got a copy of *Civilwarland* in there?"

Jane Long is my lieutenant, and my friend. Recently she has
introduced me to a woman I have begun dating, and who will, in
a few years, become my wife. Jane is the person who should really have my job. She lacks my cynicism, and her matchmaker's
instincts, for the movies as for romance, are formidable.

"Is this for Ben Stiller?"

"How did you guess?"

My own instincts are questionable. I don't know, at this moment, what makes one book more adaptable than another, or what makes this particular studio tick. Fox 2000 is making *Fight Club*, a gothic western called *Ravenous*, and a nightmare crocodile movie called *Lake Placid*. None of these are precisely my style. But what is that style?

"Does he want the whole book?" Jane appears in my office doorway now. "Or just the title story?"

"Not sure. Gimme the whole book."

I study her: tall, willowy, bright. We've been friends since I worked for De Niro's company, where she was an intern. I'd helped her move over to Fox 2000 when Raymond's successor was looking for an assistant, and then, when I replaced him, her promotion was a condition of my own hire.

"Y'know," I say, "you really do look like—"

"Don't say it!"

"What?" I smile. "I was just gonna say Emma Woodhouse."

I like to tease her over a resemblance to Gwyneth Paltrow. She is younger than I am—twenty-six, where I am thirty-one—and she is sharper, quicker to handle the math of the movie business as it currently exists. She stands in the doorway of my office, the white-blond rope of her ponytail flopping. Behind her, the open floor of the office holds marketing people, business affairs, employees from each of the studio's three feature divisions.

"You're just saying that because you're in love." She grins. "Mr. Knightley."

"It's true."

"I'm happy to be your Cupid. You can name your firstborn after me."

"I think you're getting ahead of yourself. Hey, you busy?"

"No, why?"

"I've got that pitch. Rupe's nephew."

She groans. "You need me to come to that?"

"Yep. Love's gonna need an executioner. You can help me deliver the bad news gently."

Three divisions: there is Twentieth Century Fox proper, which is geared more and more toward expensive event movies like *Speed 2*, the Alien franchise, or *Titanic*; there is Fox Searchlight, which exists to make lower-budget, independent-style cinema. And then there is us, pitched squarely in the middle.

"I'll expect you to name an army of children after me for this."

"That's assuming I have an army of children, my friend."

"Just wait." She elbows me as we walk down the hall toward the offices of one of the big boss's relatives whose credits are unclear to me, and who appears to hold what is known in the trades as a "vanity deal," an arrangement that pays a plush salary and benefits to well-connected, but not always effective, producers, whether wannabes or stars. "They'll be here before you know it."

Thirty-one. I am thirty-one. Raymond was forty-one when he died. "The cause was a blood infection," read the obituary that ran in the *New York Times*, and while this is a euphemism—at long last, there are the drugs arriving on the market that might have kept him alive, protease inhibitors and antiretrovirals—it is just what such a private person would have preferred.

"I can't wait to meet little Jane 2: Jane Strikes Back and Jane 3: Jane vs Predator."

"Shut up," I say, as we round the corner so we are heading east, moving down a corridor flooded with morning sun. "You're getting way ahead of yourself."

★ ★ ★

MAYBE SHE IS, but I am in love. I spend my lunch hours browsing at the Gotham Book Mart on Forty-Seventh Street, ducking under the sign that reads "WISE MEN FISH HERE" to hunt for novels I'll give to the object of my besottedness. I write long, romantic emails, which I send from an AOL address. I stagger around in the blast furnace of Midtown, pounding iced coffee, seeing signs—meaning—in everything, the way you do when you are in that state, the one you are always so certain can never end.

"Hello?"

(I am in love! I am in love not just at home—as I race up the stairs on a Saturday afternoon to catch a ringing telephone I hope will be Lindsay, my girlfriend, calling—but at work, where I was hired at first sight. I met Laura Ziskin briefly at Raymond's memorial, then six months later, after she invited me for coffee, she'd offered me a job on the spot. There was no interview, no preparation: she just looked up from her desk as I walked into her office and said, "I want you to work for me.")

"Hello? Who is this?"

(However I feel about my job, I love my boss. Raymond had loved her, too, and it's easy to see why. Laura is warm, approachable, intuitive, bright. Everything a studio boss so often is not.)

"It's your mother."

"I— Mom?"

I stand in my vestibule on Mott Street, panting, having just run up three flights of stairs. I cup the receiver, leaning against the wall with a package under my arm and my keys still in my hand, on a humid summer Saturday. I stare out at the June haze hanging over the street.

"Did you get it yet? I sent you something."

"What—oh!" I study the package I had picked up downstairs. It is postmarked from Tacoma, Washington, my mother's spidery scrawl—I recognize that much—across the front, although the return address denotes her as "K. Howe," a stranger. Which, I suppose, she is. "So you did."

Ten years. I have not spoken with her for almost a decade—our last exchanges had been temperamental and ugly, as when I begged her to quit drinking, she'd scoured me with enough verbal abuse that it ultimately seemed better to cease contact indefinitely—and so I find myself at a loss. I tear open the package, a book, of course, and study what she has sent: an older hardcover.

"I figured it was time for me to make amends."

"Is that what this is?"

"Well, no, not nearly," she says. "But I thought it might be a start."

Shirley Hazzard. *The Transit of Venus*. Both the author and title are unknown to me, but I turn the book around in my hands—slate blue, a first edition, kept in a mylar sleeve—studying it for clues. Why this, after ten years?

"I'm glad you did," I say. "But what's up with your voice?"

"What do you mean?" She's dropped almost an octave. She sounds like Lauren Bacall. But I'm happy to hear her sober.

"Never mind," I say. "Who is 'Howe'? Are you in witness protection?"

"I got married again." On the other end of the line, I hear the sharp flare of a match, the inhalation as she pulls on a cigarette. "Tom Howe is my husband."

"Uncle Tom? Tom Howe, who used to be married to Aunt Marge? Isn't that a little *Hannah and Her Sisters*?"

"Long time ago, honey." She exhales. "Marge is actually the one who set us up."

Long time. Long enough to become someone else, to marry her older sister's ex-husband—Marge and Tom split up ages ago, shortly before I was born—and to sound reasonable, even wise. Whether she will stay that way, I don't know, but I am glad she called.

"Honey, I have to go." After we've spoken for about fifteen minutes, she breaks in. "I have to get to a meeting."

She's been asking about my girlfriend, and about the intricacies of my life in New York ("A studio executive? You??"), which I take as a good sign. Even before she became a blackout drinker, her talk was mostly self-focused. But not today.

"You haven't even told me about—"

"We'll talk again. Soon, if you like. I'll call you."

She hangs up, jumping off the phone so quickly I am left to wonder what just happened. Who, exactly, is the woman who just called? Mott Street is quiet—she never told me what she does now, if she still writes or even goes to the movies—and I lean out over the fire escape to stare down at the Italian men clustered in front of the social club next door, the green canopy of linden trees rising opposite in front of the Elizabeth Street Sculpture Garden. I set the book down on my desk, where I will forget about it for a few weeks. I'm too besotted these days even to write. But even in the midst of gentrification—this block was once Little Italy but is now becoming something else—this city feels imperishable, beyond the hand of alteration. It will never be anything other than it is. So what makes me imagine a person, really, can change?

★ ★ ★

"AND YOUR FATHER?" Another zesty exhalation of smoke. "How's he?"

My mother calls again a few weeks later. This time, she asks after my dad, phrasing the question, which once would have been needling, passive aggressive, almost as an afterthought.

"Is he still agenting?"

"What do you mean? What else would he be doing?"

"I don't know. Now that you're a studio executive, anything seems possible."

"Not for him. The movies are the glue that holds him together."

"The movie business is. I don't know if the movies themselves do."

"Touché."

It's late. She has caught me at an odd hour, which is the only time I'm ever home. Lindsay is out with her roommates, so I'm alone, reading in bed. Rain spatters down the airshaft abutting my bedroom. Thunder rumbles overhead.

"You didn't answer my question. How's he doing?"

"He's great."

"Is he?"

"I think so. Yes."

Is he? Late in life, she has returned to be close to her sister and nieces and cousins, the members of her family who were never John Birchers, and has shed herself of almost all her former connections. She hardly knows anyone in Los Angeles at all. But my father is embedded, still, inside the cocoon of his success. All that managerial changeover at CAA seems to have made no difference. His client list is mostly intact, and he's signed others—Jack Lemmon, Kirk Douglas, Marlon Brando—who were huge stars when he was a young man, actors whose names would've struck him with awe when he saw them on Lew Wasserman's call sheet. He's added Helen Mirren and Geoffrey Rush, taken on Sylvester Stallone. The movies have provided him with an identity, as well as a vocation. If an ownership stake in the company has passed him by—CAA remains firmly in the hands of the Young Turks—so has any turmoil. Many friends of his had gone off to run studios, signed production deals that, however lavish, are already expiring. One or two no longer have jobs at all.

"I'm glad to hear it."

"You don't sound glad."

Does my father regret not grabbing for the crown? This is the one question that nags at me. When the time came, could he have muscled his way in for a bigger piece? It's hard to say, but still I wonder.

"No, no, I'm not mad at your dad at all anymore. I just wanted to know."

All my life I will think of my mother, I suppose, as a failure, just as I will consider my dad a success. This is accurate enough, but it's also just—capitalism, a matter of both historical timing and luck. If my mother's movie had broken another way, if it had been a hit or if she'd chosen not to scab, would she appear otherwise?

"You really don't write anymore?"

"No, honey, I don't. Why?"

Or even if she'd just continued writing, would that have been enough?

"You can't just turn it off."

"*You* can't turn it off. You're a writer," she says. "I was a dilet-tante."

"You were a professional."

"There's not always a difference."

She lives off her residuals, and, much more substantially, off the chunk of money she was able to extract from selling her house in gentrified Santa Monica, which, too, is capitalism, historical timing, and luck. She owns a place now that sits on a lake, halfway down a cul-de-sac, an hour south of Seattle. It's a life I can't really picture, as I lie in the dark in lower Manhattan in an apartment that is more like a base camp, skeletally appointed with books, desk, laptop, bed.

"Wait, are you smoking?" my mother says.

"No, I stopped ages ago."

"Oh, it sounded like you—see! People do change!"

Maybe so. But if she is, or was, only a dilettante—"I didn't like who I became," she tells me, when I press her on the question of her writing again—what am I? A draft of my novel is almost finished, but what am I doing working in the executive end of the movie business, a job that might require more dispassion than I can manage, that asks me to pretend garbage is gold and vice versa?

"I'm glad you called, Mom."

"I'm glad I did, too, honey."

"I'll try you again soon," she says. "Sleep well."

I didn't like who I became. The phrase lingers in my head. The movies have offered my father a vital set of illusions, the illusion of being who he is, even if this illusion is largely generated by his client roster, the list of names that accrue around his own. My mother has walked away from the same set of illusions ("writer") in the interest of becoming who she really is instead. But take away luck, take away timing, take away historical circumstance from either. Who, really, is left?

★ ★ ★

LINDSAY LOOKS OVER as we lie together on the couch.

"What are you reading?"

"A book my mother sent me."

"How is it?"

"Dunno," I say. "I just started."

Little Compton, Rhode Island, is the name of the town we visit sometimes on weekends. Lindsay's mother has a house there, about a mile from Sakonnet Point. I lie stretched out, gazing for a moment through the window at the cobalt horizon line of the Narragansett Bay.

"Let me know," she says. "I've wondered about that book."

Lindsay is twenty-six and works in advertising. She loves literature as much as I do, which is why Jane had thought to set us up. It is why my father believes the two of us will remain together forever. ("Both of you always with your nose in a novel. She's perfect for you.")

"What about you?" I say. Like me, she writes fiction in her off hours.

"*To the Lighthouse.*"

"Which part are you in?"

"'Time Passes.'"

"Right," I turn my attention back to the book in my hands. "That it does."

In the next room, a radio is tuned to the news, postmortem on Diana Spencer's death. Yesterday, we had attended a lawn party where people were playing croquet, drinking Pimm's Cups, when we heard. This place is so foreign to me. Even as someone who has lived in New England before, it is fantastically WASPy. ("You've never had a Pimm's Cup?" "Of course not. My people drink red wine, like Italians.") It is shockingly beautiful, however. Outside the creaky, clapboard house we're in, one that has been in Lindsay's family for two hundred years, there is a soft green lawn, a cemetery, then a pasture dotted with baled hay and Jersey cattle.

"What's funny?"

"Little Compton," I say. "Really?"

"I still don't get it."

"That's because you haven't been to LA yet."

When she does, in the fall, she will find it as foreign as the surface of the moon. But my father is right, I think. Lindsay and I are made for one another. She sits on the opposite side of the couch in a lime green dress—the one she wore the night we met, stepping out of the rain into a restaurant on Bond Street glowing like a hallucination—with her head bent over her book while I stretch my legs into her lap. She stares down, attentive, somber, until she looks up and her eyes are damp at the corners.

"It's so good," she says. "This book is so good."

"I know."

She smiles. A smile like a Cheshire Cat's, explosive and bright. "Are you jealous?"

"Dunno," I say. I've made some headway now, am about eighty pages in. "This book's pretty good."

"Is it?"

It is. My mother's instincts remain sharp in this regard, as the novel she's sent me, *The Transit of Venus*, turns out to be excellent.

"What's it about?" Lindsay says.

"It's a love story."

"Oh yeah?"

Not what I was expecting. I spend most of my working days reading crappy thrillers, humdrum commercial fiction, literary novels of varying scope and quality. I hadn't imagined a love story, let alone one as unabashedly sprawling and romantic—romantic, yet ruthless, unsentimental—as this one. A story of two sisters, played out over decades on a global, almost a galactic, scale, with portions set in Stockholm, Central America, Australia, London, and New York.

"It's wonderful," I say.

"No kidding?"

Would Fox make a movie out of this now? Would anyone? Can I muscle it through? Figures I would find a novel I might like to pursue at exactly a moment when I'm not really looking, on a weekend when I am reading, as I rarely have time to do these days, strictly for pleasure. Halfway through, I put the book down on the coffee table.

"You don't want to finish?"

"No," I say, stretching. "Let's go to the beach."

"You don't need to find out how it ends?"

"I know how it ends. How does anything end? Let's go to the beach."

The sun is out in full now, splashing across the cemetery next door, brightening the stones carved with names so ancient the engraving is barely legible. I think of Lindsay's grandfather, who comes up here with us sometimes. He's creeping up on ninety, so deaf and distant I sometimes wonder if he notices us at all.

"Let's go." I stand up, feeling the sand on the white pine floors beneath my bare feet, the faint warp of the boards. "C'mon."

How does it end? How does everything end? I stretch my arms, stretch my legs, staring out toward the cemetery with its chipped and crooked stones overgrown with moss, staggered like rotten teeth.

"Let's go," I say, and Lindsay sets her book down next to mine, where both will remain until we realize—too late—we've forgotten them, after we have returned to the city. Soon, the house will be shuttered up for the season. Our novels will remain where we have left them, while the room brightens and darkens, brightens and darkens; while the air smells of late August grass, and then autumn ozone; while the pages start to dampen and curl, the freezing rain turns to February snow, and the stones outside disappear beneath the unshoveled drifts until it's like they were never there at all.

★ ★ ★

"DO YOU LOVE it?"

"I do," I say. I'm back in the office, on the phone with my boss. "I really do."

"Well, what about it?" Laura says. "What do you love?"

It's autumn. The street below is dotted with umbrellas, the asphalt washed black. Pushed to quantify—not just "quantify," but justify—my attachment, I find myself thrown back on my heels.

"It's like *The English Patient*," I say.

"Is it?"

"Yes." It isn't at all, but *The English Patient* made money. "It's exactly like that."

"Put it in the overnight pouch," she says. "I'll read it."

Why do you love it? It is, in some sense, always a ridiculous question—one's expressible reasons for loving are never the true ones, not really—but it is especially so here, where what's being requested is not a reason, but an alibi.

"What did she say?"

I turn. Jane is standing in the doorway.

"She'll read it."

"Did you tell her it's like *The English Patient*?"

I stare down at the street, at the people slaloming among the carts and vendors, moving between the buildings' dark, mirroring faces. "Yep."

Studio executives need their comparables. One thing is like another thing, until the commutative property takes hold, and, in their minds, one thing *is* the other thing. *The English Patient* is a love story. Anthony Minghella's film adaptation of it made hundreds of millions of dollars last year, then cleaned up at the Oscars. *The Transit of Venus* is also a love story. If the resemblance ends there, if the two stories are no more alike than an ax handle and an apricot, it hardly matters. The argument overwhelms the material.

"Tell her O.J. will be mad if she doesn't buy it for us."

She cackles. When I had been to see *The English Patient* in Los Angeles, some months ago, I'd settled into my seat at the Avco Theater, a matinee showing with the theater almost empty, only to be distracted when O.J. Simpson ducked into the film five minutes after it began and sat down next to me, muttering an apology like he was my friend.

"I think I might have to find a more attractive pitch."

"Fair. But the book is adaptable."

"You think?"

She nods. I've had everyone in the office—Jane, our assistants, our interns and hired readers—read it, and all agree. Even so, I'm out on a limb.

"Yep."

I'm out on a limb, because how do you know when what you love is truly lovable? Is it when the corporation plows millions of dollars into it? Or is it unclear even then? I turn back around and direct my attention again to the street. The red crawl of the News Corp Building's ticker, the LED-sign that broadcasts headlines atop the first floor, reflects back from the buildings opposite, but I cannot decipher what is says. So, too, for the motion picture business. All prognostications fail.

★ ★ ★

PROGNOSTICATIONS FAIL, UNTIL they do not. Until a prophet arrives to lead you out of the wilderness. My prophet's name is Bill Mechanic, the COO and chairman of Fox Studios. He stands at a podium inside a ballroom in the Tower Beverly Hills Hotel, where we have convened for a corporate retreat, there to deliver the good news.

"No. More. Middle. Class. Movies!" He punches each word to drive it home, spreading his arms like a TV evangelist. He sounds like *Network*'s Howard Beale. "That's finished. No more."

I like Mechanic. With his black mustache and his raffish smile, he looks like a professional poker player, but in person he is warm and genial. More importantly, he likes movies. No cold apparatchik, he. Without him, there will be no *Fight Club*, and when Terence Malick comes knocking to make *The Thin Red Line*, an expensive and risky proposition after the director's long period of inactivity, he will make it happen. But as I stand in the ballroom's windowless chill, breathing its recirculated air, my ears prick up.

"We can make tentpoles," he says. "We can spend $110 million to make *Titanic*. And we can make things on an ultra-low budget. *The Full Monty* cost three-and-a-half, and it's made almost seventy times that. But what we can't do anymore is make anything in-between."

I sip my tepid coffee. I stare down at the waxy parquet floor. I nudge Jane, who is with me on this trip to Los Angeles—the retreat is for the executives of Twentieth Century Fox's three film divisions—and who I know draws the same conclusions I do.

"What was the budget of *One Fine Day*?" I tick through Fox 2000's releases in my head.

"About $35 million."

"What about *Courage Under Fire*?"

"About forty-five."

"Right." We stand side by side, our gazes fixed on the stage as we talk under our breath. "You think we'll make it back to New York? Maybe they'll fire us today."

Jane nods, her poker face as inscrutable as Mechanic's. She knows I am kidding, but it's easy to see where this argument leads. *Titanic* is a product of Fox's main division, which is equipped for such blockbusters. *The Full Monty* was financed by Fox Searchlight, expressly designed to create such pictures: low-budget movies, little-engines-that-can. But under the rubric just defined, almost every movie Fox 2000 has in its pipeline is "middle class."

"Hey, wait! Wait!" I flag Laura Ziskin down in the parking lot, later. It is the end of the day, and we are heading home. "You haven't read *The Transit of Venus* yet, have you?"

"Not yet." She turns, keys in her hand. "Other things keep getting in the way."

We stand in the cool twilight, in the parking lot behind the hotel. Traffic races along Pico, the swish-and-drone of Los Angeles at any hour.

"Sell me on it a little more," she says. "I need to be convinced."

"OK. *The English Patient* made seventy-eight million domestic, and about twice that much again overseas. It was nominated for a dozen—"

"OK," she laughs. "Fine. But—you really think this is that?"

"Yes. But even if I didn't, I think there's an audience. How often do I bug you like this about a book?"

"Not often enough."

"Exactly," I say. "So what does that tell you?"

"It tells me that you're too particular."

"Really?"

"Yes, really," she says. "You blew it on *Fight Club*. We wouldn't have had that if you'd been working here when Raymond was."

"You wouldn't have had it either," I say. "Raymond had to pester you for months just to get you to read it."

"Touché." She smiles. "I'll read it soon, I promise."

She ducks into her car. I know she is conflicted, that being a studio head means being inundated with such decisions, paralyzed by expensive choices. I know a twenty-year-old novel with an unknown rights situation—she's used its age against me, too: If it's so good, why hasn't anyone made it already?—isn't at the top of her list. But she's a producer at heart, and before she came to Fox 2000 had overseen *Pretty Woman, What About Bob?*, and *To Die For*, strong movies all. She should know private passion counts for something.

"Soon, soon."

She drives off, speeding away in the encroaching dark. *You're too particular.* Maybe she's right, and I am. But love is particular, and movies are particular. Once upon a time, at least, they were.

★ ★ ★

"I NEED TO make a decision."

"Oh?"

Now Laura is in my office. She has come to New York for a visit. It's just before Christmas, and Rockefeller Center is ablaze. We have gone to lunch and now we are back on the News Corp Building's sixteenth floor, idling a moment in the holiday lull.

"My contract is up," she says.

"What does that mean?"

"It means I have to decide whether to stay at the studio or not." She sits on my couch, knees up, a little agitated. She's a fidgeter. "Truthfully, I hate this job."

"Do you?" This is what I like about her. Because she has a restless mind and speaks it straightforwardly. Because she is not a cog, but a person. "Most people would kill to be in your position."

"Maybe. But they don't really know what the position is."

Everyone else in the office has gone home, so it is just the two of us. Outside, the canyons of shadow along the Avenue of the Americas are deep at three in the afternoon. Pedestrians push through the cement-colored gloom carrying heavy bags of holiday gifts.

"Would you wanna do it?"

"What, run a studio?" I say. "God, no."

"Why not?"

"Because I hate making decisions."

She laughs. "You wouldn't do it because you're an artist. That's why."

She pauses, and I realize why she has come. She's not here to talk about her own plans. She's here to talk about mine.

"What do you want to do?" she says. "If I stay, I want you to stay with me. But you'll have to come to LA. I don't want a New York office anymore. I don't need one."

It's true, she doesn't. The company had overbought in the early going, during Raymond's tenure and shortly after I came over. Its development slate is now overcrowded, and so my job is, all of a sudden, unnecessary.

"I don't think so," I say, after a moment. "But thank you."

"No?"

"No." It's the end of the line for me. "If I were going to keep working as an executive for anyone, I would want it to be for you. But I can't do this anymore."

Her face is strangely classical: the Roman nose in profile, the warm brown eyes. Bright blond hair falls below her shoulders. When I see her next, in a few years, she will be riding a high off the success of *Spider Man*, which she will have produced for Sony, and the hair will be gone, lost to chemo.

"What are you going to do?" I say. That will be the last time I see her. She will die in 2011. "You really hate this job?"

"I do. I have too many ideas for a studio head."

"So why do it?"

"You don't have to like it to want it. I don't know. It's a lot of money. You sure you don't want to come to LA?"

I shake my head. I do have to like it to want it, I suppose. The great misfortune of an artist's temperament.

Later, I walk out into frigid darkness. The red ticker scrolls on behind me, bringing news of the Oklahoma City bombing trial, of South Korea's economy in free fall. Love might not stand much of a chance here, in a world in which I have been so elegantly maneuvered into firing myself. I ride the subway downtown, feeling anxious and free, feeling sure I've made the right decision even if I don't quite know what this decision will amount to. Because you live but once. You are a human being, caught within the pendular movement—you are a businessperson, you are an artist; you are a novelist, you are a filmmaker; you are in love, you are heartbroken; you are elated, you are distraught—of these conflicting desires, but you are never sure if that movement is like that of a clock, regular and orderly, or if it is something else: the blow of an axe, the ticking of a bomb, the swift, sharp drop of a guillotine.

★ ★ ★

A LETTER ARRIVES, before Lindsay and I even move in.

"What's that?"

We stand on the stairs of our new apartment on Hicks Street in Brooklyn, sifting through mail—circulars, a notice of utility transfer, things addressed to the previous tenant—when an envelope stops me in my tracks.

"No idea," I say. (Blue, onionskin, with an illegible return address and PAR AVION stenciled on the front.) "I guess we live here now, though."

We make our way up to the attic floor, having rented the top of a Brownstone from an older couple who live below. In the summer this place will collect warmth like a convection oven, and we will stagger around half-dressed, feral and dripping in its unbearable heat, but for now it's pure potential. The cavernous living room's built-in bookshelves were the ultimate selling point.

"You wanna take this room as an office?" Lindsay calls. "We'll use the other as a bedroom."

"Sure."

Our footsteps clop on the bare, slightly uneven floors. The living room windows gaze down on a geometry of rectangular yards, the denuded branches and slush-covered brick of January.

"Who's the letter from?"

"Oh, right." It's not a great time for us to be moving in, I suppose, having just lost my job, without an immediate sense of where my next revenue will come from. But I've stacked a nest egg and plan to finish revising my novel. I unseal the envelope, as Lindsay comes out to the living room to join me.

> *Dear Mr. Specktor. Thank you very much for your generous and feeling letter about my work . . . I happily accept comparison with Middlemarch and War and Peace, fantastical as such analogy is . . .*

"Holy shit."

I finger the pages—there are two of them, blue five-by-seven sheets—that have been typed on a manual machine, then hand-corrected in tiny, in places barely decipherable, scrawl. They have the rough texture of braille. Shirley Hazzard has just returned from Italy, where she lives half the year, and is responding to an inquiry I'd sent months ago regarding *The Transit of Venus*'s film rights.

"How'd she find us?"

Hazzard and I have the same literary agent. "I assume Lynn gave her the new address."

While I was still at Fox, I'd looked her up in the Manhattan telephone directory and sent her a letter. It's been long enough ago now that I'd almost forgotten. The film situation, as she outlines it, is complicated. A few follow-up phone calls will further explain the details: the novel's rights had been purchased outright by an Australian company, UAA, in the early 1980s, and after that project fell apart—David Williamson, who wrote *Gallipoli*, had adapted, with Gillian Armstrong intending to direct—the rights were swallowed by Polygram, a corporation that has since been absorbed into Universal. Even if I still had a studio at my back, this would be a business affairs nightmare, the project now a line on a ledger enclosed within a series of other ledgers: it would be like diving for a shipwreck entombed within a bigger ship. I put the letter on the windowsill.

"What are you gonna do about it?" Lindsay says.

"Nothing."

"Nothing? What do you mean? It's your passion project."

"It's *a* passion project. It's also a total nightmare."

"Whose nightmare?"

"Not mine. Come on, let's go downstairs and unload stuff from the truck."

It's true. Not mine. I'm out of the motion picture business for the moment. The envelope remains propped on its little corner of the windowsill—a charm of sorts, a way of announcing to myself that I am home—for months, as we fill the shelves with our books, the refrigerator with groceries, the apartment with ourselves. Lindsay is working as a literary scout now, in downtown Manhattan, and I am home all day procrastinating, taking long walks along Montague, with its faded ice cream shops and baffling profusion of optometrists, before coming back to grapple with my novel.

"How would you deal with the end?"

"What?"

"*The Transit of Venus*," Lindsay says. "If you were making the movie, how would you deal with the end?"

It's summer, late summer, and we are lying in the dark in our bedroom, windows open, covers off. The janky little air-conditioner we've plugged into one of our windows drones uselessly.

"What makes you think of that?"

In my desk drawer, in the other room, is an engagement ring, although I haven't yet popped the question.

"It's a hundred and ten degrees in here and this is what you're thinking about?"

"I dunno," she says. (No wonder I love her.) "It's a hard ending."

"All endings are hard."

It's true. Ask the novel I am struggling to finish, the novel I will never be able to finish to anyone's satisfaction.

"No, but"—Lindsay tosses on the mattress next to me—"that one's harder than most."

"Maybe."

"Definitely. It's a gut punch."

"Yes. Well."

"But it's not just a gut punch, is it?"

"Not at all."

"So how do you get all that in there?"

"I don't know. I'm not adapting it."

"Yes, but you should."

It's late. A car rumbles along Hicks Street and then—we are alone inside the night's dense quiet.

"I guess— Hey, are you awake?"

In the dark, I can hear her breathing. I can hear, as if from infinitely far away, the oceanic rumble of the BQE. The ceiling glows overhead, painted with streetlamp and shadow. It's possible I have never been this happy, not even as a young child.

"Are you awake?"

Movies end. They set up sequels. They resolve, and everyone lives happily—or miserably—thereafter. They resolve and then the shark or the monster comes hurtling out of the water, to indicate that nothing has ended, that everything begins all over again. But lives, conversations, relationships just . . . stop. Here I am in the middle of all three, only I have no idea what comes next. I don't see a way forward at all.

★ ★ ★

"CAN'T YOU FEEL it going faster?"

"What?"

Then it is fall, then it is winter, then it is summer again, another August of another year. Lindsay squeezes my hand as we walk across the fractured pavement of a parking lot in Fall River, Massachusetts.

"Everything," I say. "Next summer will be here before we know it."

"I guess so. You'd better hurry up and find the right band."

"Why? Are you sure you really want to see your grandfather dancing?"

Twilight, and still the heat is unbearable, as we approach the scarred face of a faded shopping mall.

"Maybe we should just do it here," I say. "Reverend DenUyl won't mind marrying us in a parking lot, will he?"

"How is it we've wound up with an officiant with such a ridiculous name?"

This place seems derelict. Its K-Mart, its Bradlees, its Radio Shack are empty, practically abandoned, with only the dim fluorescence of their interiors letting us know they remain open for business. A group of teenagers, dressed inexplicably for the weather—one wears a heavy sweatshirt, another a wool hat—huddle in front of a Payless, kick-flipping their skateboards in languid slow motion. Behind us a sign rises over the vacant expanse of the parking lot. Its gappy black letters spell out the titles of a half-dozen films.

"It really does feel like time is going faster," Lindsay says. "Didn't we just get here? Wasn't it just June?"

We're here to get out of the heat, to spare ourselves the fury of Little Compton's evening mosquitos, the humid cruelty of its cocktail hour. This, the nearest movie theater, is forty minutes away.

"Slim pickings." I gaze up at the sign advertising *The Phant m M nac*; *The Ru awa Br d e*, *Austen P wers: The Spy Wh Shag ed Me*. It's still blockbuster season.

Beyond the lot, there is Fall River's main drag, a long, curving boulevard of gas stations and grassy plazas. Even by the standards of New England's end-of-the-twentieth-century blight, this town is decrepit, its history as grim as its present. Lizzie Borden lived here. Twenty years ago, there'd been a series of murders connected to Satanic panic. Now it's just another crumbling factory town, big box outlets surrounded by shuttered textile mills and wobbling regional banks.

"Kubrick," Lindsay says. "There at the bottom. *Eyes Wide Shut*."

"Good catch."

We brush past those kids on our way inside, their Metallica tees, the metronomic clacking of their boards and hissing wheels all conspiring to send me straight back to California.

"What do you know about this one?" We approach the ticket taker, weaving through the lobby's array of arcade games and quarter vending machines. "Other than Tom and Nicole."

"Not much," I say, "I haven't read the book, so—"

The theater is empty. Lindsay and I settle into our seats, two in the middle—what does America make now, besides movies and trade agreements?—before the lights go down and we succumb to the film's trance-inducing rhythms. A married couple, played by Kidman and Cruise, get dressed for a black-tie event. They are wealthy Manhattanites. The woman, Alice, fiddles with her glasses in front of a mirror. The man, Bill, can't find his wallet. The setting is cold, golden, and expensive. The soundtrack is Shostakovich. They are on their way to a Christmas party . . .

"Are you into it?" Lindsay whispers, ten minutes in.

"Yeah. Are you?"

"Yep."

No more middle-class movies. Well, this one is middle class, being neither a tentpole nor an indie, but it is about plutocracy, the manners, and the moral rot, of the rich. Nineteen ninety-nine will be remembered as a great year for American cinema, on par with 1939 or 1967, and most of the movies that mark it as such— *Magnolia, Fight Club, The Talented Mr. Ripley*—will be "middle class" in this sense, also. But this is the one that gets under my skin, perhaps because it represents a pending dilemma: Lindsay and I are not married yet, and the movie is about the vagaries of marriage, about how the erotic dream life of one partner remains forever hidden from the other. There is the threat posed by infidelity, but there is also the threat of the dreaming itself. Bill, the husband, is almost seduced by a couple of models. Alice flirts with an older man. Eventually Bill is pulled away by a crisis—a prostitute has OD'd in an upstairs bathroom—and is cast off on a nightmarish voyage of his own . . .

Lindsay and I barely know each other. We barely know ourselves, being young, and so, as the movie unfurls in the dark—it strikes me as I watch that the story is just *Ulysses* in code: the tale of a wayward sailor's long voyage home—we are thrown into our individual loneliness, which is precisely what it is about: the solitude you can't escape, the self that is legible only when you close your eyes. By the time it is over, we are stunned, speechless—it is about these things, and it is about money: how money erodes the borders of who you are, renders every encounter transactional— standing up inside the empty theater and walking into the mall that is now entirely silent. In the darkness of the parking lot, Lindsay's mother's Mercedes sits alone under the glowing yellow sign, dark as a hearse.

"Did you like it?" It feels like a stupid question, as the movie itself doesn't care who likes it, but I am as cloudy as if I have just woken up.

"Mostly, yeah. You?"

"Yeah."

"Mostly" is imprecise. But language itself is imprecise, and the movie we have just watched, so tactically artificial, so full of inscrutable meaning, is closer to our lived experience than anything we can say to describe it.

"Was that long?" Lindsay says, as we climb into the car and pull out onto Stafford Road. "It feels like we were in there forever."

"A little long. Yeah."

I know what she means. Movies are a parachute with holes and a broken rip cord. They're what we have to slow the acceleration of time, and to represent the distortions we encounter in our experience of it.

We drive in silence. We are still at the beginning of our story. And yet we are also already closing, somehow, on that story's end. Nick Nightingale. Alice Harford. The character names, so druggy and romantic, linger like a question between us. The headlights slice through the rural dark, a cloud of insects, little winged creatures fluttering in their beams, thickening our path, and the mood of the movie dissipates at last.

"Man," Lindsay says. We are at the beginning. We are at the very end. Our tires crunch gravel as we pull into the driveway of the house, which looms darkly in front of us, an inscrutable hive of dreamers. Crickets shrill from the pasture opposite. "The more I think about that movie, the better it seems."

"You liked it?"

"Not liked," she says, stepping out of the car, slamming its heavy door shut behind her. "Loved it. Loved."

200 EAST 66ᵀᴴ STREET
NEW YORK, N.Y. 10021

Dear Mr. Specktor --

Thank you very much for such a generous and feeling letter
about my work. I am so sorry that this response is delayed. I returned from Italy only in time to be engulfed by Christmas and by
waiting towers of paperwork. I happily accept comparison with Middle-
March and War and Peace, fantastical as such analogy is; since those
are works to which I feel very close, from which scenes and passages
are vivid to me -- one feels that they are one's own, as Burckhardt
would say, "by right of admiration".

Yes, I am working on a novel, and -- after January -- intend to
spend the remainder of this year completing it. It has been long in
preparation, a few chapters of it have been published in quite separate pieces. But recent years have been largely a hiatus. And now
I find that my work helps me greatly, since my husband's death; and
various short undertakings have been completed. So I'm now feeling
strongly about completing my novel.

As to film rights, of The Transit of Venus. An early, and
serious, attempt to make a film evaporated -- in the habitual way of
such things. But the rights remained with the purchaser. Several
approaches have been made, and I think the issue at least for a time
has turned on buying out the present holder. I haven't kept up to
date with all that; but the knowledgeable person is Ms. Evva Pryor
at McIntosh and Otis, 310 Madison Avenue, NYC 10017, Tel. (212) 687-
7400. M & O were my agents for many years. I have recently made a
change to Lynn Nesbit of Janklow and Nesbit, and the disposition of
foregoing work has yet to be determined. But Evva Pryor is the present
authority on film rights for my T of V. There has also been a long-
standing intention of making The Evening of the Holiday into a film,
and an option is currently held for that book. However, I don't know
whether there has been recent movement there either.

Thank you again for such a warm letter and for taking pleasure
in my books. With all friendly good wishes for this new year, and
best regards --

Yours sincerely,

Shirley Hazzard.

11. TERRIBLE BIRD

1999–2001

A MAN WALKS INTO a movie theater in Hamburg, Germany, having never been to the movies before, not once in his life. He is twenty-five, a student at the nearby Technical University. Some say he is tender, sensitive—later, by some, he will be described this way—but he is, also, awkward and withdrawn. His roommate, who is not really a friend, has invited him, hoping the experience will loosen him up. It's Saturday afternoon, a matinee, and they are planning to get a bite afterward—maybe, because one thing the roommate has noticed is that the man doesn't seem to take much pleasure in eating either—and when they come in to hunt for their seats, the theater is packed. Do you remember your first movie? His is *The Jungle Book*, which is, let's face it, a strange choice, being an animated movie for children, almost three decades out of date.

Still, this is the power of Hollywood storytelling: thirty years after the fact, a Walt Disney film can travel overseas and hold rapt a roomful of adults. People crowd the aisles, perch on the edge of their seats talking with their friends as they wait for the picture to start, munching their bags of sweet popcorn and their *Eiskonfekt*, licking the melted chocolate off their fingers. It's no wild scene, just a regular Saturday afternoon at the movies, only—

"Amir?"

The young man is paralyzed. He's never encountered a situation like this: so many people milling around in the name of pleasure, auditing not information or instruction—he's been in a lecture hall, of course: at the college he studies urban planning—but illusion.

"Amir? What's wrong?"

He slumps down in his seat. The hubbub of voices, the champagne-colored light raining down from the ceiling, the bordello-red curtains and seating, all conspire to rattle his nerves.

"Chaos," he mutters. He has never felt so far from home. "Chaos, chaos, chaos . . ."

★ ★ ★

MY FATHER LOOKS up from his *LA Times*. "Didn't you work on this picture?"

Together we are in his kitchen, squinting at the morning paper. He holds his Calendar section, folded open to an article, across to me.

"Huh? Oh, no." The article is about *Fight Club*, reporting on a controversy around whether the film is too violent. "This is my friend Raymond's movie. I blew it on this one."

"That's life in the movies, kid. Everybody blows it on something."

"I guess so," I say. I study him a moment. "You doing OK?"

He watches me back. "Yep."

He looks armored, fully braced against the day in his suspenders and shirtsleeves, a modified Wall Street look—quieter patterns, a narrower collar—for the end of the century. I'm in a T-shirt and running shorts, flushed, chasing mineral water with an espresso. Lindsay is upstairs sleeping in what was, until recently, my stepmother's den.

"I'm OK," he says, smiling gently. Lately there have been a few changes around here. "Thank you for asking, son."

Lindsay and I have arrived just in time. It's October 1999, and his marriage is over. The house looks like a museum that has been sacked: the kitchen's plates and pottery are missing, there are spaces on the walls where paintings have been removed. In the living room a lonely Eames chair floats like a canoe, angled toward the flatscreen.

"You wanna go see that movie later?"

"Hmm—yeah, maybe. I'll ask Linds, when she's up."

Pamela is gone. My sister has recently moved to Cleveland, having gotten engaged to a man who is regional director of the Jewish Defense League. And so Lindsay and I have arrived just in time, relocating to LA at precisely the moment my father, suddenly a bachelor, could use a little company.

"Sounds good. We can hit Toscana for dinner before, if you like." He sets his espresso cup down on the saucer with a soft clank, swipes up his keys. "Be of good cheer, son."

I watch him go. He puts on a brave face, but I can see him slowing down even physically, his walk heavy like a sloth's as he walks across the courtyard. He is sixty-six. I can't help but feel he is slipping, that, having crossed what used to be the American Century's mandatory retirement age, he is ready for his gold watch, his farewell handshake. Hadn't Lew Wasserman told him long ago that Hollywood is a young person's game? His wife is gone, a couple of his key clients, like Danny DeVito—Danny who is also his dear friend, which gives it the sting of private betrayal—have dropped him now, also. Perhaps he is turning his face toward the grave.

"Morning!" Lindsay comes shuffling down the kitchen's steps in her pajamas. "Did your dad go to work?"

His health is good, at least. But Lindsay and I can't help but worry even so. The circumstances surrounding his divorce are cloudy—if there was infidelity, it wasn't on his side—but I can imagine being married to my father was no picnic. It must have been like being married to an entire industry instead of just a man.

"Lemme see that Business section, willya?" Lindsay slips into the breakfast nook and nods over at the paper. "D'you mind?"

"Not at all." I hand it over. "Be of good cheer."

Lindsay and my father adore each other, which makes our staying here for a moment easier. But together we wonder: What will become of him? A recent piece in *New York* magazine notes the thinning ranks among the upper echelons of the talent agency business, how the rising costs of production at the studios ("No. More. Middle. Class. Movies!") means fewer films and fewer jobs, and thus narrower margins for the agencies. "Rick Nicita and Fred Specktor . . . have . . . been around for twenty-plus years, and they'll probably only leave their offices feet first," the article notes comfortingly, but how consoling is it really to think of my dad as a dinosaur inside a dying industry, whose fatal coronary will arrive just as Hollywood suffers its own last seizure?

"You wanna go see *Fight Club* with the old man tonight?"

Not for the first time, I wonder if he regrets being passed over when Ovitz and the Young Turks were piecing together their succession plans. Does he feel resentment? He's never expressed any, but I can't help but wonder.

"Sure."

What will become of him? And what will become of his industry? I don't know, having stepped outside it for a moment. I'm working as a consultant for a start-up in Silicon Valley, a company that has devised a mechanism for encrypted delivery of manuscripts over the internet, and that will sharply curtail its business before it even gets all the way off the ground. Lindsay, too, is working for a start-up, thinking about applying to business school. We've come here a moment to regroup.

I stare back down at the article my father handed over—"Controversy Could KO or Punch Up Fight Club," reads the headline—wondering, also, why the industry's "controversies" feel so flimsy, so ersatz and manufactured? *Fight Club*, it turns out, has kicked up a bit of a ruckus. The movie's reviews are mixed, and in a few weeks, Laura will depart from the studio in the wake of its commercial failure ("I'm interested in what it has to say about men and society at large," she is quoted as saying in the article, "and why we have all these [material] things and still feel numb and can't sleep at night."), but right now it is all over the news. It's not that the movie isn't good—when I see it, I'll enjoy it, and when its reputation is rehabilitated, a few years later, I'll be glad—but how transgressive is it, really, when News Corp spends $63 million on a movie it pretends is a scathing indictment of late capitalist rot?

"What is it?"

"Don't you think it's boring?" I toss the paper aside. "What's all this for?"

"What do you mean?"

"I mean what's all this handwringing about? *Fight Club* is too violent? Who are these people getting worked up about this stuff anyway?"

Lindsay shrugs. Maybe she doesn't care, as this isn't a problem for her—not if she's going to business school especially—the way it is for me and for my father, whose life is the industry. But to whom do the movies, and their attendant "controversies," now speak? My dad likes to pretend Hollywood is cyclical. What goes around, comes around. Maybe he's right, and the movies will get better again—more organic, wilder, less neutered by a corporate ownership that dresses up its marketing campaigns as transgressive examples of creative freedom—but right now it seems dire.

"People outside Hollywood," Lindsay says, evenly. "They don't see things like you do."

"Right. But how do they see them, exactly?"

She shrugs. She doesn't know, and I don't either. Nobody here does, it seems to me, the people who make the movies least of all.

* * *

TO WHOM DO the movies speak? To people around the world they do, to people who love America as well as to those whose feelings are more ambivalent, but still not to all people. They do not speak to people like our student, whether they are anti-capitalist critiques, like *Fight Club*, or colonialist fables like *The Jungle Book*. In fact, Amir will never go to a movie again. But this doesn't mean he isn't affected by them, as Hollywood reaches even those who refuse it, finds its way to shape even those who would deny its inexorable grasp. He walks home that night shaken, moving along Knoopstraße with his hands in his pockets ("chaos, chaos, chaos"), past the bars and billiard halls, not saying a word to his roommates. When they get home, he just goes to his bedroom and shuts the door. It's OK. The movies aren't for everyone. For Amir, who's interested in architecture and city planning, the cheap, cheesy lines of a Disney cartoon are inelegant, and the sound of Louis Prima singing "I Wanna Be Like You" (what is it about this song? Is it about animal imitation—monkey see, monkey do—or is it about the blithe and racist assumption that a colonized people should wish to resemble their colonizer?) means nothing to him. His English is solid, better than his German, but the movie is not for him, and he does not like crowds. His roommates think he is funny—he has never been to America, but one day he will—and his bad habits, his unwillingness to do the dishes, his tendency to make these disgusting plates of boiled potatoes he mashes up and stores in the fridge until they go bad, get on their nerves. Haven't you ever had a bad roommate? Nobody likes him, not the two men with whom he shares a university-subsidized apartment, not the friends they invite over, not their girlfriends. It's nobody's fault, they just don't like him: the sight of his leather jacket draped over a chair in the kitchen, his flip-flops parked outside the shower are bad news, unhappy indicators that, alas, he is at home. One day, a girlfriend—the one who goes with the other roommate, the one who always knew Amir was a drip—hangs a poster of Miss Piggy in the kitchen. It's no big deal, just Miss Piggy in a negligee, *sexy*, but she'd like to get a rise out of him, or even just make him laugh. She'd settle for that. But he doesn't say a word, doesn't even acknowledge the poster exists. So, it just hangs there for months, peeling off the fridge, ignored until it disintegrates altogether.

★ ★ ★

MARLON BRANDO CALLS, when nobody is home. He leaves a message that is more like a manifesto, pouring out his woes onto my father's answering machine.

"Miss Piggy is my nightmare, Fred. He has no idea what he's doing, and the kid, the executive they sent up to fix things, is worse. He's like Mickey Rooney telling Judy Garland to paint the barn and put on a show for Judge Stone! I gotta get off this picture—"

Lindsay and I arrive and play it back. We've just returned from scouting an apartment, are hoping the landlord called, and hit play to discover America's greatest actor speaking in a bizarre code. "Miss Piggy," we realize, must be Frank Oz, who is directing Brando right now in a movie called *The Score*, and who also happens to be famous for voicing the Muppets character, which he has done for years. Brando is in his twilight, and obviously miserable on the set of what will prove to be the last movie he ever does.

"—I'm peckin' at tranquilizers like a goose at corn. I don't care who you have to sleep with to get me out of this, but I want you to do it. And—give me a call! It'd be good to talk to you, about anything, really."

He sounds like Demosthenes, with a mouthful of stones. He sounds like himself, barely intelligible, but thrilling. Lindsay and I play the message over and over. It's like finding a diamond in a laundry hamper, a birthday greeting from the Queen of England. We study it from every angle, this three-minute monologue, spontaneous tragicomic improvisation—it goes on until the tape cuts off—from an artist of genius. I fetch a bottle of vodka from the freezer, some limes, and Lindsay and I face off, leaning over the marble island to see if we can nail it ourselves.

"I'm peckin' at tranquiliz—wait, wait." I clear my throat, bite down on a lime wedge. Brando's death scene, the moment in the tomato garden in *The Godfather*. Let's see if I can channel that. "I'll try again."

"Pecking," she says. "He says pecking."

"Are you sure?" I clear my throat. "'Look how they massacred my boy.' Play it back one more time."

My father walks in. We are drunk, riotous, eight listens and almost as many vodkas deep.

"Listen," Lindsay wipes tears from her eyes. "Fred, you gotta hear this."

"I'll have one of those." He sets his satchel down, pours himself a short glass. "What's up?"

We play him the message. He listens, poker-faced. He doesn't even crack a smile.

"Dad," I say. Finally, I get my impression right. "'Someday, and that day may never come, I may call upon you to do me a service,' and that service is—Give me a call! It'd be good to talk to you—about anything, really.' What part of this is not funny?"

He lifts his index finger. *Wait.* He drains his vodka, then picks up the receiver and dials, holding the receiver out so Lindsay and I can listen to the actor deliver the same rambling monologue in precisely the same words, with the same exotic metaphors and odd inflections, with even the pauses identical, onto his answering service at work.

"What on earth?" I say. "That's sociopath behavior!" The other message was left an hour and a half earlier. "Did he rehearse that? He memorized his lines for an answering machine?"

My father shrugs. His client is a method actor. The whole point is the illusion of life. He steps into the next room and returns, moments later, with a bottle of wine and some cold chicken from the fridge.

"Is he trying to get fired?" I say. "This is the picture he's doing with De Niro, right?"

Again, he shrugs. It isn't that he doesn't know. He doesn't care, not about this, preposterous and transient, crisis. He has gone from being a person who, long ago, might have had a heart attack over Gregory Peck's misdelivered package to being one who knows Marlon Brando's problems can wait, at least until the morning. He has pierced the veil of illusion.

"You guys want some chicken?" He sits. "There's plenty."

He has pierced the veil, but what lies beyond? Only more illusion. The movies are—or at least they were once—America's dream of itself, a dream that was incomplete, like all dreams, but which showed people of my father's generation how to live. Now that he has awakened from it, it is like he sees that John Wayne was never real after all and the dream was always a lie.

"There's some salad in the fridge," he says. "Bring a couple glasses over here."

A lie that was also the truth, because some dreams are like that. But the movies, which persist in repeating themselves ad infinitum—*The Score* won't turn out to be very good, a heist movie like a million others—now seem to neither live nor die. They exist in a kind of undead space, to show us who we almost were but also who we never will be again.

"Sit," my father says, untroubled, it seems, by any of this. He holds his bottle—it's a nice one, with a faded-cream label that indicates an Italian wine at least twenty years old—toward Lindsay and me as we approach. "This is the good stuff. There, there. Cheers." He lifts his glass. "Hooray for Hollywood, huh?"

★ ★ ★

NOW WE ARE married, now the New Year has come and gone, and we are moving into a house on Arizona Avenue, a California Craftsman that is like a dollhouse, maybe seven hundred square feet in all. We stand in the living room, organizing our books.

"Is this yours or mine?" I say.

"We're not still shelving separately, are we?"

"No, no. I have a sentimental attachment to this one is all. I'll take it out to my office."

I want it for inspiration, as I am employed now as a screenwriter, having recently been hired to adapt *The Transit of Venus*. I turn to carry the copy of *Underworld* out to a glass-walled shed that sits across a yard little bigger than a Ping-Pong table.

"You think these helicopters are ever going to go away?"

As I step out of the kitchen I gaze up at the whirlybirds—two of them now, one news chopper and one police—that have been circling over our house for days.

"Only when you-know-who dies or goes home," Lindsay says. "They're in it for the duration."

Across the street from our new home is St. John's Hospital. Ronald Reagan is there having his hip replaced. Secret Servicemen camp on our lawn, drinking coffee. They loiter outside their vehicles up and down the block. It's been almost a week.

"I know what I'm rooting for." I stare up at the helicopters, which circle at a respectful distance, allowed only so close, then down at *Underworld*, a slipcovered first edition hardback with the famous André Kertész photograph on the cover. *New York, 1972.* I study the old Manhattan skyline, then go on to the shed, my steps crunching the brown grass as I walk. I enter the shed to confront a nightmare.

"How did you do this?" After a few hours of fruitless struggle, I call my mother. "How on earth did you figure out how to do this?"

"Shouldn't you of all people know?" She laughs. "Mr. Studio Executive finally finds out how hard it is to write a script."

"What about how hard it is to be a studio executive?"

"What about it?" She blows smoke. "A script can still get written without an executive. What can an executive do without a writer?"

Jane Long, my friend and former lieutenant at Fox 2000, had ridden to my rescue. When the start-up I'd been working for let me go, she arrived just a few weeks later with a proposition. How would I like to adapt *The Transit of Venus*? The company she now works for, @radicalmedia, is a commercial production house branching out now into features. They're willing to roll the dice on an unproven screenwriter, and willing to help retrieve the novel's rights—I've finally met someone, a former Polygram employee, who knows where those rights are buried—so I can take a crack at it. They're able to pay WGA scale, as signatories, which will usher me into the Guild.

"Just close your eyes and think of the health insurance," my mother says.

"I shouldn't even be talking to you. Scab!"

"Yes, well." She sighs. "Here you are."

What comes around goes around, I suppose. But where screenwriter was natural for my mother, I find it strangely impossible. Whether or not I will improve at it, at first it is like writing with two left hands, like being forced to monologue in a dream language I read but cannot speak.

"How did you do it?"

"I have no idea. I just did it."

"You weren't a professional."

"Nobody asked me to be a professional," she says. "I just goofed around in my office until it seemed right."

I try to take this advice to heart. Scab or no (was she really just "goofing around"? Now and for the rest of my life, I will never know what was really in my mother's heart at that time), I am comforted by my mother's experience, and so I spend my days trapped in that shed like a lizard in a jam jar, pecking out scenes and then deleting them, my anxiety and panic increasing as my deadline approaches. At the end of each day, I come back inside to air out my misery with Lindsay.

"Maybe you shouldn't be so hard on yourself." She pours a glass of wine and hands it to me. "It's a difficult adaptation."

"They're all difficult adaptations."

"Not like this."

"I'm still not getting anywhere." I stand at the window, staring skyward at a lattice of telephone wires and antennae. "I need to turn something in to get paid."

Rumors abound about other writers who've tried to adapt *The Transit of Venus* over the years. Besides David Williamson, it's said that David Hare, the English playwright, and Tom Stoppard both took a crack at it. The project is an Everest, a summit that has defeated climber after climber.

"If Tom Stoppard couldn't do it—"

"That's just gossip. It's not confirmed."

"Whatever," she says. "It's your first script. It's not gonna come easy."

"I didn't think it would."

"Didn't you?" She takes a sip of wine. "I think you thought it might."

She has a point. But the difficulty is the perfect analogue for the story itself anyway: *The Transit of Venus* is about an astronomer, Ted Tice, who falls in love with an Australian orphan. An anecdote he tells her when they meet, about Venus's intermittent passage across the face of the sun, an event that happens only once or twice per century at most, becomes a metaphor for their relationship: its rarity; its impossibility; its miraculous, if temporary, success. As an adaptation, it's a nightmare: there are too many characters and too many locations, a time span of more than three decades. Hence, I cut, chopping the cast down to only its primary characters, compressing events until the action unfolds over a more manageable dozen years instead of thirty, clarifying the narrative.

"I'm still not getting anywhere." By spring, I've worn a coarse brown divot in the backyard's August lawn with my incessant tramping back and forth into the house for coffee and procrastinatory snacks. "I feel like I'm going in fucking circles."

"Just keep on," Lindsay says. "You'll get there."

Round and round, I think. Like that song my mother used to play me as a child, "The Circle Game." But it's only a love story, one that feels, some days, curiously old-fashioned. Who will finance a movie like this now? Miramax? Sony Classics? None of the majors, I expect, will touch a movie like this today, because it is too expensive for their indie divisions—it is too arty for Fox Searchlight—and not expensive enough for their main arms. It is not *Mission Impossible II* or *The Fast and the Furious*, not *Rush Hour 2* or *Pearl Harbor*.

"Who's gonna see it even if we can get it made?"

"Your mom."

"OK, besides my mom," I say. "I'd like to fill a theater."

"Grandy."

"Grandy? OK, sure. Your grandfather's ninety-three, he probably won't be able to see the screen, but he gets a pass. Who else?"

"Who else? You and me, that's four. Plus your dad."

"My dad. We'll get to six if he brings Marlon Brando as his date."

"Damn straight. It'll be good to talk to him. About anything."

Maybe a movie only needs one viewer, just as it sometimes only needs one studio refusenik to justify living or dying. The industry, like America itself, was this way in the beginning, after all: an idea so crazy it just might work. I top up my wineglass, and Lindsay's, and we toast one another in the thickening dusk.

"Right," I say. "Let's drink to my father, and to the town. As the old man said himself—Hooray for Hollywood!"

★ ★ ★

HOORAY FOR HOLLYWOOD! When Amir comes to Hollywood, as everyone eventually must, he comes to the wrong one: the one in Florida, rather than in California. Still, he might be forgiven for thinking they are practically the same place. America is big, yes, but it is also uniform, with everywhere the same advertisements, the same Best Buy, Target, and Taco Bell. The Hollywood of California—he's been to California now, to San Diego—has oranges and sunshine. The Hollywood of Florida, also, contains oranges and sunshine. Like the one in California, it sits by the sea. So what's the difference? But he knows America by now. He's been to New Jersey, Nevada, Oklahoma, Virginia. He's visited more places than most Americans have in their own country. Does he feel awe or wonder? Not really. When he writes to his father, he tells him that his studies are going well, and that, like his sisters— one is a medical doctor, the other a zoologist—he will soon earn his PhD. When he meets strangers, sometimes he tells them he is a middle manager at a computer company, because that is what he looks like in his khaki pants and short-sleeved shirts, and because it is easier for someone who still doesn't like to talk. ("Urban planning? Neat! So what does that mean, exactly?") He goes to the gym. He shops at Walmart. With his roommates, new ones, he eats Pizza Hut and American fast food. If he has a feeling about the country, really, it is the same one he felt that night at the movies: that it is chaos, disorder, disaster. There are people at home, in Cairo, who still dream of coming here, who would like to see Hollywood, or Disneyland, and who wouldn't care which end of the country they visited first. He is here on a student visa, which will last five years, and the name on that visa is not "el-Amir," but it's OK. This is more than enough time for what he still must learn, and his own name is not the one he has come to America to exalt.

★ ★ ★

"WHAT'S WRONG?"

I come into the kitchen one night to find Lindsay in tears, her elbows propped on the table's salmon-colored surface, palms covering her eyes.

"Grandy," she says, looking up at me.

"Shit." I cross over to her, loop my arms around her neck and shoulders. "Baby, I'm so sorry."

She sniffles. "It's OK. I was hoping he'd make it."

"Me too."

Ninety-three years is a long time to be alive. Imagine being almost as old as the century, as old as the first Model T, and older than the movies as an ordinary fact of life. For the little that I've known him he's been a locked box—mostly deaf, adrift like an astronaut in a private cosmos—but I know in Lindsay's memory he's vibrant and robust, a life-loving Swede.

"Did you talk to your mom?"

"I can't reach her," she says. "She's still in Scotland, so she doesn't even know."

"I thought she was coming home yesterday."

"Tomorrow."

"God, what day is it?" I bend down to kiss her head. "I'm sorry."

"It's OK. How was it out there?"

"Fine. I'm finally getting it, I think. I won't be embarrassed when it comes time to hand it in."

It's late in Scotland. We try the hotel again and then give up—it'll have to wait until morning—and so have wine. We talk about her job, at another internet start-up, and about her b-school applications; about the script, and about our future, whether we should get a dog. Finally, I stand up and go to the window, looking at the night sky.

"What are you looking at? The transit of Venus?"

"Not unless I want to stand here another seventeen years."

"Sixteen. Next one's in 2017."

"Are you sure?"

"Yeah." She comes over and stands next to me. She laces her fingers with mine. "We can wait if you want to. I don't have anywhere else to be."

"I don't either," I say. "Not if I don't even know what day it is. What year."

"It's Monday."

"No, I mean—"

"Shh," she says, kissing me to shut me up. "Who cares?"

★ ★ ★

"JOY KILLS THE heart."

He said that once, to a friend who'd asked him why he never laughed. Laughter, too, is disorder ("What am I looking at? I'm looking at—those birds," I say, slipping into a note-perfect impression of her other grandfather, the curmudgeon, always happy to affix his grouchiness to anything that crosses his field of vision. "Look at that pigeon!" I give my voice a Nixonian quiver. "It's terrible! Terrible bird!"). Laughter is what he saw that night at the movies. But as he walks through the airport this morning ("No, seriously, what day is it? This draft is due at the end of the month!"), he feels neither happy nor sad, neither fear nor hope. He feels clarity, readiness ("It's the tenth," she says. "September tenth.") as he passes through security at Logan International Airport in Boston. He'd come to the other Hollywood not so that he might become famous, but so he might live invisibly, dissolving into the American mass. As he does, also, this morning, moving unencumbered, with a suitcase that will never make it onto the plane already checked through. His box cutter, his utility knives, his chemical spray are on his person, as is his passport, which reads not "el-Amir" but "el-Atta." That name, of course, will be famous. But it is not for fame he has come.

★ ★ ★

"WAKE UP!" LINDSAY shakes me. "Matthew, wake up!"

I roll over. Our bedroom is tiny—it barely fits the bed—but even through the drawn blinds I can see the day's cool and cloudless blue, the Venetian slats glowing and defined. The television set jammed over in the corner is turned on. Lindsay is sitting up, hunched over, shaking me, staring.

"What is it?" I sit up. I fumble for my glasses. I lean forward, squinting, while my fogged mind clears and the image on the TV resolves.

"History is a nightmare from which I am trying to awake." So it was for Stephen Dedalus in my mother's favorite novel, and so it is right now. History is a nightmare. History is a dream. History is two towers collapsing in showers of glass, asbestos, steel, and dust. History runs through Hollywood, which is everywhere you stand. History is *chaos, chaos, chaos*.

UNIVERSAL

12. PROMETHEUS UNBOUND

2005–2007

FASTER AND FASTER, THE world seems to turn, the pace of the business when you are making a movie—it's all happening, every minute! The film seems to weave itself before your very eyes.

"So, Kate's a go?" I say. "She's firm?"

But also slower and slower: it's all happening, but nothing seems to change, the green light keeps flashing but deliverance remains around the corner.

"She's firm."

"And what about Guy?" I say. No wonder people like my father have devoted their entire lives to this. It's like being at the casino at four a.m., the intoxicated heart lurching with every spin of the wheel. "Have we made an offer yet?"

I am on the phone with my producers, Jane Long and Jack Lechner, and with a man named Mark Gill, the head of Warner Independent Pictures. Rain drums furiously on the eaves of a house in West Hollywood, a proper deluge hammering my living room's pitched, barn-like roof.

"Offer's out," Mark says. "We're waiting for a response."

"So, if he's our lead, what else do we need? Can we finally look at a start date?"

Tap tap bang! The rain splats against the windows and the ceiling, against the French doors leading onto a deck and a yard shaded with banana palms. On the floor of this house's second bedroom—for indeed, now we are three—are picture books listing the names of all the animals, one by one, and two by two.

"Unfortunately, no," Mark says. "Because now we're going to need a director."

"What—again?" I cup my hand over the phone. Even with the rain, I might have just awakened the baby. "What happened to Alejandro?"

"Alejandro's out," Mark says. "We're back to the drawing board there."

"Jesus." I stare out at my office, the sodden little shed that already requires five figures worth of repair thanks to the season's rains. Lindsay is making OK money, having just started at Goldman-Sachs as a junior associate, but it's not enough to float the three of us. The future depends on a green light. "Anyone with ideas?"

This is the view from the trenches, what it is like to make a movie, or try to, in 2005. Two years ago, I'd sold my *Transit of Venus* script to the newly created classics arm of Warner Brothers, and now here we are, with a rotating cast of actors, filmmakers, people who keep jumping on and off the project like children mobbing a playground carousel.

"Patricia Rozema?" Jack Lechner says. "Matthew, have you seen *Mansfield Park*?"

Together, my producers and I had sold the script. Eventually, I'd pared the story back far enough that it began to make sense, and Jack, @radicalmedia's resident genius, had slipped the script to Mark, who was just coming aboard to run Warner Independent. Warner Brothers had optioned it, and together we began the process of putting the movie together. Actors came running. Directors have come and gone. Our most recent, Alejandro Agresti, is now leaving to do a movie called *The Lake House* at Warner's main arm for his American debut, opting for a bigger budget, and for Keanu Reeves and Sandra Bullock. Hence, we are back where we began. After I hang up, I close my eyes and wonder why anyone bothers, thinking of all the people who've attached themselves, however briefly, or even just contemplated the project, already: Guy Pearce and Kate Hudson; Rose Byrne and Adrien Brody; Ethan Hawke, Matthew Macfadyen, and Paul Bettany; Peter O'Toole, Rachel Griffiths, Helen Mirren. Why make a movie, when all the possible ones may be more enticing than any you might finish?

"You OK?"

Lindsay finds me like this, still staring out at the afternoon's gray soup. She's home early, as ever. Her job is pinned to New York market hours, which means she's out the door each morning at four-thirty.

"Meh," I say. "She's up, though." I nod to the baby monitor in front of me. "I'll go get her."

The life of an artist turns out to be abject, but perhaps no more so than any other. You only get one, so why am I electing to spend mine chasing phantoms? Watching movies—and not even real movies, but prospective ones, hypotheticals—coalesce, and then fall apart. I bend to pick up Virginia, our daughter, from her crib. She is as heavy, now, as a sack of grapefruits; a few weeks ago, it was more like a bag of tangerines. Shouldn't this be enough, I wonder? The real, with its incremental, yet still miraculous, changes?

"What are you making?" Lindsay is standing by the stove when I come back in. (It is enough. And yet . . .)

"Cream of wheat. I want to see if she'll eat it."

"Ah. Solid food time."

It *is* enough. Virginia, now seven months old—"Vivi," we call her—is navigating her own encounters with the real, every day another piece of it for the first time. What fantasies we spin for her are ambient, bedtime stories she's too young yet to understand. No movies for her yet. No need for them either.

"You like that?" Lindsay says. "You do! She likes it!"

Now we sit at our long, farm-style table, the three of us all at one end. Our marriage won't last much longer—Lindsay and I will be split inside a year and a half—but right now we are united in pleasure, watching Vivi's eyes, cornflower-blue circles, luminous apertures, signal her delight.

"She likes it!"

I like it, too. But it's all flashing in front of us: our marriage, our child's infancy, our lives. Lindsay had made the practical choice, going back to school, putting her creative ambitions, if they still existed, on hold. She's making good money, of course, but not enough of it to carry us both, not that I would want her to, and so—an inequality has entered our relationship.

"It fell apart," I say, after bath time, after playtime, after we have had dinner and then wrestled Vivi back to bed and are lying in the dark ourselves. "*Transit* fell apart."

"Oh," she says. We are flat on our backs, too tired to move, gazing up at the small skylight in our bedroom's ceiling, rain still battering its cloudy surface like that of an unblinking eye. "Shit."

Too tired for sex, or affection. Because we want different things. She deals in practicalities: the robustness of the markets; the needs and the trust of her clients, the wealthy people with whom she golfs or dines in her job as a fledgling money manager, helping their wealth to multiply itself. I deal in dreams, ones that seem just now neither lucrative nor persuasive. Mark Gill likes my script and so he has begun to funnel other assignments to me, but low-budget projects mean low-budget pay. Warner Independent exists to capitalize on the huge margins occasionally captured by inexpensive films, but these films are just as difficult to make as blockbusters, and harder still to project. I've gotten paid WGA scale for a handful of rewrites, but this isn't a living. Not when months can pass between assignments, and so between checks.

"What about Harry Price?" she murmurs. Her voice is like a radio broadcast, fading toward incoherence. "That thing about the ghost hunter."

"Nothing," I say. "That's dead, too, I think."

No more middle-class movies. And no more middle-class people either, just riches and poors. When my parents embarked upon their lives in the entertainment business, forty years ago, it was wide open, at least for those who were white and able, and so they were able to tell themselves a story, that the movies were for anyone and everyone, because they felt, they did, like everything was there for the taking. They could do their part to address the inequalities, either concertedly, like my mother, or casually, like my father, but they also knew the movies would go on and on, that they could pan for gold and come up empty, this time or the next time, but that the creek itself would keep on rushing. Maybe this was never fair—obviously, it wasn't—but all things seemed possible, even fairness. Now that studios have quarantined their output into tentpoles and arthouse pictures, and now that they are making fewer movies annually than they used to, winnowing their slates down every year, that promise is evaporating. What's left is the cold, dead mechanics of meta-corporate capitalism, a system that will reward the same few people again and again and again.

"Linds? You awake?"

My screenplays aren't budging. My novels—neither the first one, nor the second, which I wrote while Lindsay was pregnant—

aren't selling, and maybe this is just an ordinary artist's dilemma, a bad luck that deserves no dispensation or sad violins. But the shrinking cultural and economic landscape will suffocate everybody in the end.

"Lindsay?"

I listen to her slow, steady breathing for a moment, then rise and tiptoe off to the living room to read. The sisal flooring is damp and clammy, as if the water that was leaking into my office is seeping up through the floorboards as well. I find a chair, switch on a lamp—in the morning Lindsay will find me here, passed out with my head thrown back—and settle in, as the rain picks up once again, accelerating until it is pounding, relentless, the sound of a pitiless, almost biblical, flood.

★ ★ ★

I LIE ON Vivi's bed, the narrow twin that has recently replaced her crib. There's a book in my hand, the two of us together on our backs. "Which one should we read? This one?"

"This."

I stifle a sigh as her pointing finger lands on my least favorite story in the *Disney Princess Collection*. I don't remember buying this, but it seems to have sprung up on her floor like a mushroom. Perhaps it was always there.

"Again, huh?"

She nods, mouth closing around her thumb, head against my chest. "Mmm-hmm."

Repetition is the soul of childhood, the scourge of adult life: we build our passions around it and collapse them the same way. The myths and fairy tales of my own boyhood were the same, less branded, perhaps, but identical. Hermes, the God of tricks, was my favorite. Some things, it turns out, endure.

"Who do you like best?" I say, playing along. "Lumiere? Mrs. Potts?"

Soon, she will see these movies over and over. She will sit in my lap in the dark at the Arclight and at the Grove and be delighted, not knowing anything has been lost, and I will sit beneath her feeling crushed, despondent over everything, the city and the cinema of my earliest youth, that is gone. But now she lies nestled against me in the evening's long twilight, the day's last sun falling over the hedge and through her window.

"Again," she says when I finish. "Again."

Over and over, she wants to hear them, these stories that are new to everyone once, and which remain, somehow, incorruptible no matter how the Disney Corporation claims them. I can feel her breath beginning to regulate as she sinks into a trance, plummeting toward sleep.

"Again."

I flip back to the beginning. I would like this interminable story, this flat rendition of it, to end. I would like this delicious moment, Vivi's soft cheek against my neck, her blond hair's baby-shampooed sweetness filling my lungs, to last forever. Between these two extremes, the wish to conclude and the wish to go on indefinitely, lies every narrative. I slide out from underneath her, careful not to shift her dreaming head, and set the book back on the floor. I watch her sleep, her small chest rising and falling. In a moment I will go into the kitchen and fix dinner, and then Lindsay and I will continue our conversation about division of assets, mediation, about when exactly I am going to move out. Lindsay will remain here, in a house with a mortgage she can now afford, and I will move into an apartment a few blocks away. My movie, *Transit of Venus*, is dead, having fallen at last into that limbo where most Hollywood hopes eventually come to rest.

"Is she down?"

From the next room, Lindsay's voice is low, taut, impatient. She would like to get down to business. I would like this story to go on forever. Instead, I find myself ejected in its middle, creeping through my own house, my own life, on soft paws like a burglar.

★ ★ ★

MY FATHER CALLS.

"You're home!" he says. "You wanna go to the movies?"

I stand by the window of my apartment off the Sunset Strip, a single room overlooking a courtyard that is like the unit occupied by Humphrey Bogart in *In a Lonely Place*. There is a trickling fountain, the sun-warmed slabs of pink brick surrounding it the color of yesterday's bubblegum. Tall, skinny palms wave in the November breeze above.

"C'mon," he says, "the office is closed for the holiday. I'll pick you up."

Here is my father at seventy-three. Here am I at thirty-nine. I don't remember the last time he and I went to the movies together. It's been years, if not decades. He arrives in yet another new German sedan, his smile wide, his very person seeming to sparkle somehow.

"Nice earring," I say, after I've studied him just long enough to pick up on what's different. "Where did that come from?"

"You like it?" He pulls away from the curb. "It's growing on me."

"So, you won't mind if I put mine back in?"

He smiles. When I was sixteen, I'd pierced my ear and hadn't heard the end of it, but times have changed.

"Pierce whatever you like, kid. Just be sure to sterilize first."

The earring is a trophy. He's been chasing Morgan Freeman for years and, now that he has signed him, has added a small gold hoop in emulation of his client. A chameleonic touch, but it suits him. With his silver hair, his air of wealth, he looks like a successful pirate. A platinum band, already showing its satiny patina, rests on his finger. He has remarried again. My stepmother, Nancy, is a successful clothing designer, presently home at their place in Brentwood. He turns left on Sunset, and we head west through the diminished traffic of a pending holiday. Tomorrow is Thanksgiving.

"Where are we going?" Earlier it had rained. The tires hiss across rainbow-smeared asphalt. "Something you wanted to see?"

"Bond." He upshifts. "James Bond."

Indeed. When I was a boy, he'd taken me to see a bunch of these: *Diamonds Are Forever, On Her Majesty's Secret Service, Live and Let Die*. It figures he would want, now, to see the latest, *Casino Royale*. As we flash down the Strip and into Beverly Hills, I wonder what's on his mind—the older he gets, the more inscrutable he seems, hidden behind the veil of his success—but just then, before I can ask, he speaks.

"You know what I'm thinking about?"

"No idea."

"I'm thinking about the first movie I ever saw."

"What was it?"

He shakes his head, as if the wonder of it has returned to him full force. "*The Wizard of Oz*. I was six."

The holiday is making him sentimental, perhaps. Even now, he is not given to retrospection at the best of times. Memories will only ever escape him unbidden, when I am not prodding for them. But now, there is something on his mind.

"Where did you see it?"

"I don't remember," he says. And then, "Yes, actually, I do. Carthay Circle."

"Is that right?"

The tires hiss. The air conditioner hums. Sunset Boulevard is green, bare, as we cross Doheny and plunge into a landscape largely unchanged since the days of my father's youth. His family's modest home was a mile and a half south of here on a line. Up here, the houses flanking the boulevard are massive, set back from the street, hidden behind iron gates and high hedges. Their long lawns must have seemed the size of baseball fields to a young boy. This was another world to him then, the province of movie stars and wealthy swells, a world he never thought he'd enter, not even in his dreams . . .

★ ★ ★

"COME ON, COME ON."

An impatient man, my father was once an impatient child, standing at a streetlight, urging his family to catch up.

"C'mon!" He bounces from foot to foot. "We'll miss it!"

An impatient boy on a Sunday afternoon, for when else would Reuben Specktor—Sabbath-observant, hardworking, given to wasting neither his money nor his time—take his family to the movies? It is 1939, and there is a war on overseas. In a few years, when he moves his family to Kingman, Arizona, Ruby will host Shabbat dinners for the Jewish American soldiers who serve at the training base on the outskirts of town. He is a patriotic man, as this country had opened itself up to him, and he is a divided one, as some part of him remains in that world he left behind so long ago. It is this part that will be the source of his and my father's trouble. But today, Ruby is in a mild mood. My father races ahead of him, ahead of his mother and sisters, skittering up Pico Boulevard to the crosswalk.

"Come on!"

The city is old, the city is new: oil derricks still sprout beyond the canals in Venice, in Huntington Beach, and by the high school in Beverly Hills. The red and green awnings that jut out over the pavement read GLATT KOSHER and PARVE YASHAN, and so Ruby might almost feel himself at home—the white spire stretching skyward a few blocks ahead looks Moorish, like the ones he would've known from Odessa—but this place remains, too, as foreign to him as the moon.

"Do not cross!" Stella yells. "Freddy, do not cross the street until we catch up."

Perhaps not. He has been here now almost twenty years, and his wife was born in Oakland, but Ruby can never forget he is a Jew, and an Eastern European. Here in the Kosher Belt, the southern edge of Beverly Hills where he lives, almost everyone is, but so much of Los Angeles is high gentile, xenophobic. Barely five years ago, the city's mayor was an active Klansman.

"Freddy!" He cups his hand to his mouth. "Wait!"

What is my father trying to get away from? He looks back—Ruby is in his Sunday suit, open-collared for once; Stella is dressed for an outing, matronly and plump in her cat's-eye glasses—and pogoes in place, vibrating in his hurry: Come on!

"OK." Ruby lays a hand on his shoulder. "Now we can cross together."

What is he trying to get away from? Is it just family, to the outer eye as symmetrical as was then the American ideal? Or is it rather—this is what I have not understood until now—that he is running toward something, a destination he will spend the whole of his life trying to reach? Together the family crosses the street (is this destination "success"? Not quite, although for many years it will present itself that way to him), but my father keeps surging ahead. He can't help himself. He barely knows what a movie is, knows only by rumor and schoolyard reputation—it is a magic trick, one of the wonders of the world—but he doesn't really know. Still, he is eager to leave Pico Boulevard, its kosher market smells and twinned gilt-lettering in Hebrew and English decorating every window, behind.

"Can I have Jujubes?"

From the outside, the Carthay Circle Theater is massive—at night its steeple lights up in blue, and for premieres they sweep the sky around it with searchlights—but inside it feels bigger still,

with eighteen hundred seats. The crowd, even for a Sunday matinee, is overwhelming.

"Don't be greedy."

"Shh." My grandmother opens her handbag and slips my father
a dime. "Get for your sisters, too."

My father in short pants, his two sisters in matching yellow
dresses, although Marcia, ethereal and pale, is already the swan,
and Myrna already the crooked duckling, with her oblong face and
lazy eye. They have entered a world of giants, filled with plash-
ing courtyard fountains, forty-foot murals on the walls, a ceiling
higher than that of any synagogue they've ever been to. They push
into the auditorium, with its Wurlitzer sounds and the floor-to-
ceiling drop curtain stitched with images of the Donner Party. The
theme here is California history, a history into which my family
has been dropped whether they know it or not. The lights dim.
Stella nudges my father.

"Watch. Stop kicking."

Why this movie, I wonder? Nineteen thirty-nine will prove itself to be one of the all-time greatest in cinema history, and so
there are others, perhaps more suited to Ruby's taste, he might
have just as easily chosen. *Stagecoach, Ninotchka, Only Angels
Have Wings*. The girls are too young to understand anyway, and
Freddy might enjoy any of those equally. Somewhere outside in
the city, only a mile or two away, Lew Wasserman is getting his
bearings, learning the coordinates of a place that is brand new to
him, having recently stepped off a plane from Chicago. Few people outside of the radio or the nightclub business have heard of the
Music Corporation of America. The movies are still the province
of Harry Cohn, David O. Selznick, and Louis B. Mayer, whose
company, MGM, produced this one. The room goes dark. And
then we are drifting through the sepia-yellow clouds over Kansas,
watching Judy Garland and her dog race home through a field to
find her family packing up against an advancing tornado.

My father does not experience any grand imaginative awakening. In the end, the movie will frighten him—he will have nightmares about the Wicked Witch and her flying monkeys for weeks—and when *The Wizard of Oz* bursts into Technicolor, it will fill him with delight, but he will not take the medium especially to heart. If somewhere in the crowd there lives a future artist whose response is intoxication, my father's is more ordinary. He is simply part of the collective, the audience ooh-ing and ahh-ing over the film's persuasive sense of spectacle. *The Wizard of Oz* may be dedicated "to the young at heart," but it is not just for children. It is for everybody. There have been movies in color, and ones with Technicolor inserts, for more than a decade, so this one is not as groundbreaking as some will imagine later, but it is enthralling and impressive. Even Ruby, who prefers straight realism—two years ago, he'd sat in this room and watched *The Good Earth*, a drama about Chinese farmers that starred Paul Muni, and that remains his favorite movie, a story of struggle he can relate to—succumbs. Slouching in his seat, tugging on his Chesterfield, he gasps and applauds along with everybody else. He and my father will never resolve their differences, as we know, but sitting in the dark, child and man, they are as close as they will ever get.

"It's OK, Freddy." As he leans over to whisper the consoling words that will ring for a generation, my father can feel the softer weave of his summer suit. "It's just a movie."

But my father knows that, and so does Ruby. Child and man are the same. What aligns them is their exposure to a dream, a dream that is larger than their individual problems and fears. Even Ruby, whose bouts of depression can run deep—one day, when my father is in high school, he will return home in his suit soaking wet, having tried to drown himself in the Pacific before changing his mind at the last minute and struggling his way back to shore—can forget his unhappiness for now. This dream enters them both, but it will affect them in radically different ways. For Ruby, the effect will grow into a resentment. If what my father grows up to do for a living will seem frivolous to him, it is because the movies have shown him something of himself that he'd rather not see, a person who is capable of forgetting, easily amused. But for my father? The movies are an X-ray, an autopsy of power, even if he will not recognize this for many years yet to come. They are proof of what you can do with the strength of illusion. My father is neither a domineering nor an avaricious boy, any more than he will be these things later in life—the money he will earn is an accident, really, of a different kind of drive—but even so he can feel illusion's seductive tug: the Wizard, with his rumbling voice like thunder, his body a column of flame. Talking scarecrows and simpering lions. Nothing is as it seems, but he follows Dorothy in her blue gingham dress, down that road that is paved—as the path to power always is—with stones of glittering gold . . .

A decade and a half later, when he enters the world of motion pictures as an adult, he will pretend the reason is happenstance: he meets a girl, he wants to impress the girl, and then there it is. He begins at the bottom and works his way to the top, because this is the story—one story, although it is true no longer, if ever it was—of capitalism. But behind this story, which I've heard told all my life, lies another: the story of illusion itself, and its almost boundless capability. Every person my father meets on the road to his own summit, every man he works for, will understand the same thing: that power is nothing compared to the idea of power, and the world bends like light passing through a jar when you are the Wizard of Oz. Power? Power is just the crude manipulation of other people to selfish, stupid, or violent ends, but the illusion of power is greater yet, because dream is stronger than reality, and fear, like love, is stronger even than death.

★ ★ ★

"YOU LIKED IT?"

"No. I told you, I had nightmares."

We're parked behind the AMC Avco Cinemas, walking past Pierce Brothers Memorial Park, where Marilyn Monroe is buried.

"Really? Dad, those effects are cheesy."

The infant my parents lost before me is interred here, too, the little girl who would have been my older sister. He never speaks of her either, and now we hurry through a sun shower, a quick spattering of rain.

"Not in 1939. Not when you are six years old."

The Avco was the palace of my own childhood. I saw *Star Wars* here; *Moonraker*, on my first ever date; *Alien*, with my younger sister Johanna. It's changed under new ownership, been renovated so it isn't precisely the same place, but the shape of the experience remains as we head up an escalator to the lobby.

"I guarantee you," my father says. "One day Vivi will see this movie we're about to watch and tell you it looks cheesy."

"Maybe she'll think it's dated in other ways."

"Could be. No matter how you slice it, the movies will look different in fifty years."

"That's assuming they exist."

"What are you talking about?" He looks at me blankly. "Of course they'll exist."

The lights dim, the advertisements wind to their close. I stare at the screen, thinking of this room and my long history inside it. Will there be movies at the end of this century, another twenty-one iterations of the James Bond franchise, the endless extension of however many other cinematic universes? It's too soon to know. My father's blind faith bugs me, somehow. But then the room goes dark, and the screen lights up, and it's too late to fight about it anyway.

★ ★ ★

THERE IS ONE more story my father tells me, after the movie is over and we are sitting in a booth at Kate Mantilini restaurant in Beverly Hills, having done our postmortem and eaten our dinner, lingering, now, over espressos. It is something that has haunted me for years. We are talking about Ovitz, the last days of the old CAA—it is long enough ago that people rarely think of former management anymore: Ovitz has left the business, moved on to the world of venture capital; Ron Meyer still runs Universal—and I ask if he resents the fact he was passed over, that Ovitz never offered him a role in the succession.

"Does it bother me?"

"Yeah."

"Not really."

"Come on."

He looks at me. "You really wanna know?"

I do. More than anything, somehow, I do.

★ ★ ★

"WHAT IS IT exactly that you want?"

"Mike, you know what I want. This isn't right."

My father and Ovitz are in the latter's office. It is the summer of 1995, and Ovitz is still the Wizard, he's just changing shape. Leverage is on his side, as he prepares to go over to Disney.

"I understand you have to look out for yourself," my father says. "I understand what you have to do for Richard and them, but it isn't fucking right."

My father's conversations with Ovitz are never heated, and this one is likewise restrained. Most of the agency is going to the Young Turks, who've been nipping at Ovitz's heels for a few years now—it's their time—but the rest, equity shares of substantial value, will wind up in the hands of four of my father's peers, who are not senior to him.

"You're angry," Ovitz says. "You don't want to work for a bunch of people who are thirty years younger."

"Not at all. You know how I feel about Richard. You know how I feel about all of them."

This is true. My father loves Richard Lovett as he does few people on earth, and he begrudges nobody at the company their success. If anything, he will thrive under the Young Turks far more than he has under Ovitz. But there is a principle involved here.

"You think it's unfair?" Ovitz stands behind his desk, as impassive as the travertine wall behind him. His Rolex Daytona gleams in the late-day sun that slants through the blinds. "You know I can't just carve this place up like a wedding cake. Not everybody gets to buy in."

"Maybe. But I'm a fucking earner. I've been here a long time."

"You are. And you have."

"So? I deserve consideration."

What are they arguing about really? Is it just—what everyone thinks—money, the way these dark moguls always do? Or is there something underneath? There are tens of millions of dollars on the table, so let's not pretend the money isn't important, even if neither man truly needs any more than they have. But there is something else. Always, there is something else.

"You'll be able to make a deal," Ovitz says. "Richard will take care of you. All those guys will."

"That isn't the point."

"Maybe. But they will. You'll be able to make a very nice deal."

What are they arguing about? Because money is just paper. It represents a dream of stability, a stability that never arrives. This room, with its stone walls the color of white honey, its decapitated gardenias floating in a glass bowl on the coffee table, represents the same thing: stasis, the promise of empire that will stand until Los Angeles sinks into the sea.

"Fuck you, Mike. This isn't right."

"Maybe. But it's how it is."

This dream, this promise, is always a lie. Always. But as my father turns and walks out the door, what he really wants is recognition, which is the thing he's been running toward his entire life. It's what everybody wants, in some way: to be seen, to be thanked, to be valued. Money is an imperfect gauge of this, but it's what exists in the world of business.

And Ovitz? As he watches my father go, I would imagine he feels many things. Fred Specktor is a good soldier, and Ovitz—when my father was sick a few years ago with pneumonia, Ovitz was there at the hospital by his bedside—has taken good care of him, also. He'll get over it, Ovitz knows, and he will. The two of them will not speak for many years, and by the time they do many things will have transpired. Ovitz will have been pushed out at Disney—his tenure there will be brief as he will encounter a businessman even colder and more ruthless than he is, Michael Eisner; he will discover that he is temperamentally unsuited to be anybody's second-in-command—and the false mythology of his failure will have proliferated. But he will walk away from Disney with hundreds of millions of dollars. He will go on to do other things, to found a talent management company, then to philanthropic endeavors and the world of venture capital, some of which will work out and some of which won't, but what will remain is this company, this rock which he, indeed, has founded.

This rock. I will leave him at precisely the moment he has unchained himself from it, a moment in which he must feel, like Prometheus, unbound, released from an experience that has been his torment as well as his joy. He wants to be an artist. He is tired of being a salesman. He wants to create, and to build again because even for someone like Michael Steven Ovitz, art represents, still, an opportunity for deliverance. When he stands alone at night before the Jasper Johns that hangs in his living room, he feels not just avarice, or a sense of money well-invested, but ecstasy, wonder, surrender. It is the one thing that all art has in common, every novel, every painting, every film, and every tall tale, too. *Surrender*, it whispers. *Surrender, surrender, surrender.* You can believe what it tells you, or not. But the only alternative to surrender is death: to live in a way that prefigures your own oblivion, all surface and no depth, empty days and empty nights, before you are gone, not just for now, but for always.

★ ★ ★

"YOU REALLY SAID that?"

"Said what?"

"You told Mike Ovitz to go fuck himself?"

"Not exactly." He laughs. Trying to get a straight answer out of him about things like this, about such deciding moments of his life, is impossible. He wriggles and deflects. In this, only, he is like his first boss. "Close enough."

"Close enough?"

He shrugs. "He said I'd be able to make a deal. I may have told him off a little. I don't remember."

We sit in our window booth at Kate Mantilini, alone with our dregs of espresso and dessert. In this room, this very booth perhaps, my father's client, Robert De Niro, shot an iconic scene for the movie *Heat*, that very same year Ovitz left, but now it is just a dwindling shell of itself, mostly empty and with jacked-up prices. Still, its cool, mid-century feel, its glass walls and concrete pillars remain strangely comforting.

"Say more."

"I already told you—"

"You didn't tell me shit. You gave me the broad strokes."

"Yeah, well." He reaches for his billfold. "That's the type of guy I am."

Sure, I think. And this is the type I am: preoccupied with the smallest details, the ephemeral things no one quite remembers anyway, and which no two people ever seem to recall the same. He's the businessman. I'm the artist. Nothing will ever align our perspectives all the way.

"Private equity," I say, staring out through the glass wall at the street, at the intersection's tangle of office towers and bank buildings, their bottom floors strung with FOR LEASE signs. "Fucking private equity."

"What's wrong with it?"

"Everything," I say. "It doesn't know where to stop."

"I see why you got divorced."

"You're goddamn right," I say. "That's exactly why."

The movies, for him, will go on forever. He will never retire, for how could he? There will always be someone wanting to make a picture, at least in his lifetime, and there will always be someone needing him to close a deal. It is only for me, and for people like me, that the movies are broken, and Hollywood is gone.

"You don't think it's over?" I say.

"No, I don't think it's over." (If he has a sense of limit, of knowing how much is enough, it is this that is his saving grace. It's what's kept him in the game this long, and also what keeps him real.) "It's not what it used to be—"

"That's what I mean."

"—but so what?" he says, standing up, laying his money on the table. "Nothing is what it used to be. And that movie we saw tonight was pretty good."

"That's true."

But when Ovitz started CAA—and when Wasserman grew MCA; when Robert Benton went to the movies; when Bert Schneider and Bob Rafelson decided to rebel against Bert's father's studio—there was always the one thing that guided them, the first stubborn principle that guides everything in the movies, and in art.

"Non serviam," I mutter.

"What?"

"It means—"

"I know what it means," my father says. "But what are you talking about?"

Together we walk toward the door.

"It means the movies have run out of real estate," I say. "It means there's nothing left for their parent corporations to conquer."

Maybe so. The movies have always been about land, after all; about those deals the moguls made to transfer each patch of acreage from one set of hands to another, as if it wasn't enough to own the light and the air and the space behind your eyeballs: they needed to have the earth, California, as well.

We stand on the corner of Wilshire and Doheny Boulevards, waiting for a valet to pull his car around. (It's what I've been trying to tell you all along: that these dreams, these fevered entertainments for the young and not-so-young at heart alike, are as real as the earth you walk upon, are the drivers of the late American story, a story that may be winding toward its unfortunate conclusion.) The car arrives and we climb inside. Behind us the restaurant blazes yellow, its interior lit with the cozy, half-obsolescent glow of a phone booth. The air is cool, with a distant smell of woodsmoke; the pavement is still damp. But the street itself is deserted, the intersection free of traffic, the stoplights signaling to no one, as if we are standing somewhere on a studio lot after hours, on a replica of a city block that goes on and on in darkness, extending itself into a world without end.

★ ★ ★

MY MOTHER WALKS out of the fellowship hall. There is a book under her arm, there is a purse over her shoulder, there is the same old circumspection, almost a furtive quality to her body language, as she steps onto the street, stooping in the watery sunshine like a stork.

"Kay!"

"Hmm?"

She remains tall and graceful, but even in her age she carries that quality of self-erasure, as if every gesture contains an apology for itself. She swivels in the pearly light—overhead it is neither cloudy nor clear, the sky as shifting as an opal—to see her friend coming out of the hall behind her.

"Got a smoke?"

My mother smiles, that curious grin—teeth flashing, eyes narrowing—that is almost more like a wince. "Of course."

She digs in her purse. It is summer 2006, the day humid but cool, and she roots in her bag to find the slim pack of More cigarettes, offering one to her friend. She is only seventy, but she seems, somehow, older: her hair is the drab gray of iron filings; her complexion is ruddy with sun, and her cheeks are veiny, still, with broken capillaries. She wears canvas sneakers and threadbare sweats, not like a glamorous person who doesn't care what the world thinks, but like someone who has largely abandoned the world of appearances altogether.

"I almost screwed up last night," her friend says. "I stopped for a scratcher and while I was standing there in line at the counter the bottles all looked so inviting. Y'know?"

My mother nods. She does know, but she hasn't fallen off the wagon now for many years. She has abandoned almost everything except the one thing that matters: her sobriety. Together they stand beneath the eave of the hall, the modest Puyallup, Washington, storefront flanked by a tavern and an electrical supply shop. They huddle in that instinctual way that smokers do, bound together by a habit that feels faintly forbidden even here outside the metropolitan belt.

"How do you do it, Kay?" The woman drags on her cigarette. She is younger, in her thirties. "What do you do when you feel tempted?"

"One day at a time," my mother says. She likes it here, in a world that is less bedazzled and, therefore, she feels, more genuine. "I hate to say it, but it really is true."

The woman nods. My mother, in fact, is her sponsor. "I read that book you suggested. *The Recovery Book*. It was helpful."

I haven't seen much of her in these years. She'd come to my wedding; after Vivi was born, she flew down to LA to meet her grandchild. But most of our relationship is conducted over the phone, where, somehow, my mother's discomfort and shame seem to recede enough for her to open up some and be present.

"What have you got there?" The woman stares at the book under my mother's arm. "Is that something I should look at, too?"

"Not for sobriety." My mother hands it over. "It's the kind of book that could drive a person to drink."

The woman stares down at the brick-red hardcover, a Viking Press edition with no dust jacket that has been sitting on my mother's shelves for almost half a century.

"*Finnegans Wake*? Kay, are you nuts?"

My mother smiles again, that sheepish baring of her teeth. *Who, me?*

"If not now, when? I've had that thing since I took a college class on *Ulysses*. I figured I'd better read it while still I can."

"How is it?"

"Ask again later." She laughs. "I just started."

It is June 17, which makes another reason she has thought to pull *Finnegans Wake* off her shelf. Yesterday was Bloomsday. But I remember the book, also, from when I was growing up, remember her talking about its difficulty, the novel that is written in a dialect so punning and involuted it is hard for some people to get through. She's always planned to read it, this book about Humphrey Chimpden Earwicker and Anna Livia Plurabelle, which ends in the middle of one sentence ("a way a lone a lost a last a long the") and begins in the middle of the same ("riverrun, past

Eve and Adam's), so it forms a circuit, an open loop like a film reel.

"What's the matter?"

"Huh?" My mother looks up.

"You're rubbing your forearm."

"Oh, I tweaked it playing golf. It's been bothering me now for a few months."

"My brother's an orthopedist. He'll be happy to have a look at it for you."

Small talk, the kind we make every day in the world with the people we know and the ones we don't. How is the weather? Is that sandwich good? We never listen to the answers, even though we should.

"I should go." My mother tucks the paper with the brother's name and phone number into her purse. "Tom and I have a two o'clock tee time."

"Call him. He's great with things like that."

"I will. You know you can call me too, anytime, day or night."

Their voices float down the quiet corridor of the street, before my mother turns and walks to her car, moving now through a landscape she loves. It is so far from Los Angeles, the afflu-ent world into which she was born and lived for so many years, that world of illusion and pretension—my father's world, and my own—she had sloughed off when she moved here in 1989. Mount Rainier looms in the distance, framing the little township with its broad and quiet streets, its low structures of brick and brown ply, its sleepy rail station across the way, with a rugged grandeur. A few drops of precipitation, not-quite rain, peck her cheeks as she pushes through the breeze toward her husband's car—she's driving the pickup, as hers is in the shop—which sits up the block at an expired meter.

She has done it. She has escaped the movies altogether, which is hard to do once you have been enmeshed with them, been drawn to their beauty as the moth is to the light. She has walked away to become a regular person. She golfs. She plays piano. She is retired, with a husband who loves her and two chaotic dogs, a person who does crossword puzzles and gardens and watches the ducks that glide over the pond in her backyard. She sits in her car, kneading her forearm. She thinks it is tendonitis, but she is wrong, because it shoots up sometimes to the other side of her elbow, and after she visits this doctor, and then another, she will discover that it is a symptom of a cancer that began in her lungs but has already spread to other organs.

She turns the key in the ignition, and just for a moment it seems the car won't start, that there is something wrong with the electrical. She rests her hand on the wheel and lowers her eyes, modest to the end.

"Shoot!" But then the engine turns over and the truck sputters to life.

* * *

WHAT IS HER dream? In these last untroubled moments of her life before she enters her descent—the illness that will kill her in just under three years—what does she want? Unlike my father, she is legible to me. I know her fear, her hesitance, her despondency, and her grief. I can reconstruct moments, and even days of her life, like this one, from her journals. But I will never know her history, not in full. She was an aspiring actress, and then a wife, and then a secretary, and then a wife again; she was a mother, she was a housing activist, she was a teacher, and then a screenwriter. She passed through these roles as if none of them really suited her, which is true, and soon, she will be just another person confronting her mortality, which is the role that suits everybody whether we want it to or not. But as she drives home on this given day, rubbing her arm absently, anticipating her golf game, glancing over at the book that rests on the passenger seat—it ends in mid-sentence just like life, but it goes right back to its beginning, the same story unspooling itself over and over from one generation to the next—she is a stranger to me, just like a newborn is to her parent. Who is this person? Where has she been? What does she dream of? I don't know, it turns out. I still don't know.

She drives down Meridian Avenue E., past the Dairy Queen, the Walgreen's, the veterinary hospital, the drive-through coffee stand that is her favorite, because nothing is better than a latte and a cigarette, that one habit that is more lethal than the one she gave up, and which she will not relinquish, alas, until it is too late. Sunlight pushes through the clouds. Finally, the day is clearing. The stereo plays a CD I have burned for her of favorites old and new: Alison Krauss, Brad Mehldau, Emmylou Harris, Tom Rush. She turns left on 152nd Street, then onto the cul-de-sac where she lives, the single block of ranch-style houses with the ducks and the water tucked behind it.

What does she dream of, as she pulls up in front of the one with a blue garage and a red door, whose inside smells of stale ash and round-the-clock coffee, and of the ineradicable leavings of her incontinent retriever? I know what I do, as she arrives at this place where she has found more happiness than she has ever discovered anywhere else. I want her happiness to go on longer than it does. I want it to go on for at least another decade, and I want her to have the life she should have had from the beginning: one of determination and purpose, in which she hadn't needed to accede to the egotistical needs and demands of every man she'd ever met, and in which her own mother had been really able to love her. I can't give her that, of course, but I would if I could. I would.

She idles for a moment in the driveway. The sun is out. Her hands rest lightly upon the wheel and the CD plays a sequence of songs I know by heart: "Oh, Atlanta"; "Wrecking Ball"; "The Circle Game"; "Dear Prudence." She sits in the sun, letting it warm her knuckles and her face—the garage door is open, and the air smells of cut grass and gasoline—while she closes her eyes and listens, waiting for whichever song it is to play through. Before she steps off the carousel of time forever, before her nightmare, the one from which she has struggled all her life to awake, reaches its end, and her happiness, which comes and goes just like anybody else's, disappears as well, let her have this moment in which she rides on the tide of a fiddle or a piano, in which she feels the light on her face and hums under her breath and the car shudders like a painted pony until the song stops and she is all alone in the quiet.

13. ALWAYS NOW

2008–∞

"Hey, ho, pencils down! Hollywood is a union town!"

I walk around in a circle—around and around and around—on Pico Boulevard, part of a line of people blocking the gates of Twentieth Century Fox. Our picket signs are slung over our shoulders, our voices hoarse from chanting all morning.

"Network bosses rich and rude! We don't like your attitude!"

My feet ache. My throat is raw. Truthfully, my heart is only halfway in it. These slogans feel dopey to me. If screenwriters are exploited labor in Hollywood—this strike, like its predecessors, is mostly about residual payments, this time from streaming services—this action still feels cosseted, a revolution that is also catered by the enemy.

"Who sent those pizzas over there?" someone says. Writing is labor, like any creative act, but who sends food to the Amazon delivery drivers who rumble by in their trucks? "Leno?"

"The donuts are from Leno. The pizzas are from CAA."

The sun is high, but the day is mild. It's January 2008, and across the street is a golf course attached to a park—green, rolling, light-dappled—where my mother used to take my sister and me to swim as children.

"Hey, ho, pencils down—"

The chants continue. I suppose it is simply that I feel like a hypocrite. I used to work for this studio, after all. My mother was a scab. If I crane my neck in any direction—a few blocks east of here is the building where I used to work in CAA's mailroom—I can see the places where I stood on the other side of the line, and the ruins of the world in which I grew up, places that leave me indiscriminately tender. I may as well walk up to the pale plaster walls of the studio that rise above Pico, the central hub of the enemy, and kiss them.

"Hey, Chernin! How much you earnin'?"

I put my sign down. I know exactly how much, after all, and my shift is over. I walk down Pico back to my car, which is parked near the hotel where Bill Mechanic made his speech about middle-class movies almost a decade ago. Depressingly, this strike will only collapse that middle class even further. Over the next three months, the studios will lose hundreds of millions in revenue, and they will use this as an excuse to trigger force majeure clauses. Writers will suffer, as these places trim their overhead and shrink the pie even further, leaving most of us to fight for crumbs. I climb into my car and drive home, looping around up Avenue of the Stars so I can drive past CAA's new office, the building people call the Death Star in Century City. The Young Turks, now as middle-aged as I am, eventually grew tired of paying Michael Ovitz rent. How small it all seems to me now. How small, really, is this cosmos in which I grew up.

"Hi, Mom. How are you feeling today?"

The MCA building that once seemed so grand to my father is home to just another private equity firm now, too nondescript to notice when you pass it on the street. The I.M. Pei building will soon be converted into a WeWork. And as I'm cutting up Santa Monica Boulevard, two blocks from my childhood home on Warnall Avenue, my mother calls. It's like she can read my mind.

"Not so bad, honey." Even the screens are small, these days, like the one I now hold in my hand. "Were you out on the line today?"

"I was."

"Good for you." Her laugh is a wan, throaty rumble. "That's what I should have done before I did anything else."

How small the story of Hollywood is, really. When I was a teenager working on Century Park East—there is the building flashing by, half a block to my right—CAA pretended to have offices in Zurich, London, and Rome, but these were just switchboards, another of Ovitz's wizardly illusions, created to make the agency seem international. Now, they have fully staffed offices everywhere: in Nashville, New York, and Beijing, soon, also, in Stockholm, Shanghai, Memphis, Munich. The American motion picture industry still papers the globe, but do people still care about its product? Do *Alvin and the Chipmunks* and *Alien vs. Predator: Requiem* whisper to people in their dreams, or do the one thing required for an art form to live on, which is to inspire people to emulate them?

"You think it would have been different for you, Mom, if you had?"

"I don't know." She sighs. "Maybe . . ."

Surely, they do. Forms don't die. Only people, and civilizations, are mortal. Films, novels, paintings, poems. These things will never defeat capitalism, but they will surely outlast it, and all around the world there are those for whom these forms are new, and who go now to encounter them, as my Vivi has, for the first time.

"You remember the first movie I ever saw?"

"Of course," my mother says. "*Let It Be.*"

"Where did we see it?"

"We saw it at the Crest Theater in Westwood. My God, do you remember that?"

I do. I remember stumbling, dazed, into the blinding summer light of Westwood Boulevard on a hot afternoon in 1970, following my mother to her car. That moment is etched into my memory with perfect clarity: the red Volvo sedan at the curb, the theater's yellow-edged marquee, the street itself, with its locksmiths and

Persian restaurants. Only much later, when I look it up, poring through archived copies of the *Los Angeles Times*, looking through the movie advertisements day by day by day for confirmation, will I discover *Let It Be* never played at the Crest, but only at the Vogue in Hollywood, where my parents saw *Bonnie and Clyde*.

"It changed my life," I say.

That it did, only—that life keeps changing, and will continue to do so until I die. Memory is not reliable. Writing is imprecise. Only the image remains, however easily falsified or manipulated, to show us how it was: how it looked, how it felt, what was there.

"How's *Finnegans Wake*?" I say. These days, when my mother and I talk—she's always tired from being blasted with radiation and chemotherapy—I keep her on the phone just like this, drifting from topic to topic. Her voice is consoling to me, and I hope mine might be to her also.

"Still going."

"Really?"

"Yes. It's slow—I get so tired, creeping along. But it's wonderful. The language is so funny and alive."

She will never finish. When she dies, in just a few months, I will find the bookmark parked not so far from the beginning, the book itself still resting on her nightstand.

"You should try it sometime."

"Maybe I will." Vivi and I visited her just a few weeks ago, and for the rest of my life I will remain glad we did. "Or I could just keep rereading *Ulysses*."

"You could," she says, "but why not try something ne—"

Before she can finish her thought, she cuts off. Cell service is patchy here in Beverly Hills, but that's life, too. It ends mid-sentence, the one story that never comes to a full stop. I drive on into West Hollywood, to the apartment off Sunset where I am still living. I'll call her back when I get there. I roll down Hayworth Avenue and park, stopping on my way inside to pick up a card from my sister—she still lives in Cleveland, with her husband and three kids—and a copy of the *New York Times* from my stoop. I still subscribe to the print edition, and I'm interested in how they're covering the strike. Today's article reports "signs of internal discontent over tactics" within the Writers Guild, but this is largely misinformation seeded by the Alliance of Motion Picture and Television Producers to gain leverage. Even so, this particular strike is confounding. The streaming market won't flower for a few years yet, and so both sides are squabbling over a DVD trade they don't know is about to collapse. With film and television production stalled around town, NBC has just shifted its reality show, *The Celebrity Apprentice*—one they were an eyelash away from canceling—into a primetime slot to fill the void. It's a move not unlike the one undertaken by the same network half a century ago, when Lew Wasserman booked his client, Ronald Reagan, as the host of *General Electric Theater*, thereby elevating a washed-up actor into a national celebrity. It's the same old story, I think, as I toss my newspaper aside and walk over to my desk, which holds a laptop and the pages not of a script—I will not write another feature film for a long time—but of a novel, one I will complete during this strike and then sell.

It is the same story, it is a different one, not because history runs in circles, but because it cannot help but almost rhyme, stuttering over and over against the same problems. Because it is old, and because it is new, because it is a nightmare from which we struggle to awake but also, always, a dream, a dream that encloses all the other dreams America has ever had about itself. And no dream, as Stanley Kubrick and Arthur Schnitzler both told us, is ever just a dream.

★ ★ ★

I SUPPOSE I should tell you how the story ends, and how my own little nightmare, such as it is, finally comes home to rest. I am signing books at the Bel Air Hotel one morning in 2013 when a woman comes out of the crowd and studies me.

"Have we met?"

"I don't think so." I look back as I reach for my pen. She looks familiar to me, too, but I'm confident I would have remembered. "No."

We talk for a moment. I ask where she lives ("Shanghai"), where she grew up ("Here, in Hollywood"), and what her name is, so I can inscribe the book.

"Samantha Culp."

"Like the actor? Robert Culp?"

"Yep. He was my dad."

We don't say much—the event is crowded, a benefit for PEN America—and when she melts back into the throng, I assume I'll never see her again. After all, my mind is on other things: the novel I have just published; a recent, unusually difficult, breakup; a television pitch I have just sold to a cable network. She walks off, her blond hair flashing almost white against the June gloom, the blue jacarandas popping in the hotel courtyard, framing her fair and lovely face as she looks back and waves. Of course, I will never see her again. She is like her father—like all of us, outside the amphitheater of our own skulls—not a star but an extra, a player who does her part, holds the screen for a moment, and then disappears . . .

Years pass. Years and years. Until I am visiting my father on a Saturday afternoon, shortly before a pandemic arrives, one that will wipe out much of the moviegoing experience for a long while, knocking it into a tailspin.

"You want another espresso?" he says. We sit by his swimming pool, the afternoon shadow creeping across its turquoise surface as we face each other across a low stone table.

"Yes—actually, no," I say. "I should get going. I have a date."

"A date, huh? With who?"

My father is creeping up on ninety. He shows no sign of slowing down or stopping, still goes to work each day at the Death Star in Century City, where he is the oldest person standing.

"Some girl I met on an app," I say. "I dunno, we'll see."

"An app!" He tugs on a cigarette. He has started smoking again, having resumed the habit on his eightieth birthday. "I should get on one of those."

In a couple hours, my life will change. I will meet, for the second time, the woman who will become my wife, although I will not remember our moment at the Bel Air Hotel until afterward, once I have gone home and she texts me a photograph of the book I had inscribed.

"I don't think Nancy would like that," I say.

"I suppose not." He smiles. In his black jeans and Converse sneakers, with his gold earring glowing, he looks like a teenager: a teenager with thinning white hair and a close-cropped beard the same color. "I do like to stay current."

That he does, I think: this man who is at once all surface and all depth, whose hidden interiors I will never know, whose history I have quarried meticulously until I can almost understand him but fall short. Perhaps I always will.

"I'll see you, Pops."

He stubs out his cigarette. He is like a teenager, a rebellious teenager, still locked inside his eternal present, still greeting each day with the freshness it deserves.

"Be of good cheer, son. Come by the office this week and we'll have lunch."

We are closer, at least, than he and Ruby ever were. My time with him is pleasurable, not dutiful, but this is because we share a history; because the culture in which he lives and the one in which I have are the same.

"Will do."

I walk back inside, stopping to kiss my stepmother goodbye, then step out onto the lawn. My father lives on a hill now, in a mid-century modern house with glass walls that suits him perfectly, being at once transparent and well-hidden, tucked back from the street behind a wide wooden gate. The grass is dry, crunching beneath my feet. California is rationing water. If I were to follow this hill all the way to the top, I would find the charred skeletons of several houses, a black scar running into the canyon that drops off behind them. Not long ago, a fire had ripped through the area, forcing the street's residents to evacuate. My father and step-mother were lucky this time, but the season gets longer, and this tinderbox of a city seems more likely to ignite—next time, there is always the fire next time—every year.

I walk out to my car. As the gate swings shut, I look back to see my father framed inside the doorway of his house. He is just like Ethan Edwards of *The Searchers*, in a way, now that he is in and I am out and he is alone with all the American bounty he has captured, the bloody and terrible spoils of the motion picture industry, which is over. The gate swings slowly shut—it is just like *The Searchers*, only in reverse—and he lifts a hand to wave goodbye before I am alone on the street beneath its desiccated palms, a world that has started to curl and burn, and I know that I am lucky all the same, because my dad is still here and I have cap-tured some of that bounty in the form of experience, which is the only currency I've ever really known how to spend, and because the child, too, is father of—

ACKNOWLEDGMENTS

This book owes a debt to numerous works of Hollywood history, social history, biography, and criticism, among them Dennis MacDougal's *The Last Mogul*, Connie Bruck's *When Hollywood Had a King*, Neil Gabler's *An Empire of Their Own*, Mark Harris's *Pictures at a Revolution*, Mike Davis and Jon Weiner's *Set the Night on Fire: LA. in the Sixties*, Huey Newton's *Revolutionary Suicide*, Elaine Brown's *A Taste of Power*, Frank Rose's *The Agency*, David Leeming's *James Baldwin*, James Baldwin's *The Devil Finds Work*, James Andrew Miller's *Powerhouse: The Untold Story of Hollywood's Creative Artists Agency*, Michael Ovitz's *Who Is Michael Ovitz?*, Nancy Griffin and Kim Masters's *Hit and Run*, and Terry McDermott's *Perfect Soldiers: The 9/11 Hijackers: Who They Were, Why They Did It*. Also to Jarett Kobek's excellent novel *Atta*, which, like all of Kobek's books, deserves your enthusiastic attention.

Additional thanks to:

Christine Sneed, Emily Segal, Lili Anolik, Malerie Willens, Tony Perez, and David Thomson.

Fred Specktor, Marcia Margolis, Pamela Robinson, Deborah McGaffey, Marjorie Meyer, Johanna Ratner, Bob Shapiro, Fred Roos, Bruce Dern, Beau Bridges, Maura Lynch, and Elisa Petrini for information regarding the historical record.

Sam Sweet, Sterling HolyWhiteMountain, John Hilgart, Sean Howe, Jonathan Lethem, John Jeremiah Sullivan, Deborah Shapiro, Tom Bissell, Renata Adler, Dana Spiotta, Griffin Dunne, Toby

Rafelson, Michael Ondaatje, Ayad Akhtar, and Lorraine Berry
messages, memes, and miscellaneous encouragements.

Sarah Murphy, Rachel Sargent, Denise Oswald, Norma Bark
dale, and everyone else at Ecco, past, present, and future. Also, t
Aileen Boyle and Brian Ulicky at Audere Media.

Allison Devereux, my friend, agent, and indispensable advisor.

Samantha Culp and Vivi Specktor, first, last, and always.